BRIGHT
DAYS

DARK
NIGHTS

By Elizabeth Ruth Skoglund

Amma
Burning Out for God
More Than Coping
A Divine Blessing
It's O.K. to Be a Woman Again
Life on the Line
Loneliness
A Quiet Courage: Per Anger, Wallenberg's Co-Liberator
    of Hungarian Jews
Safety Zones
Wounded Heroes
Making Bad Times Good
The Welcoming Hearth
Beyond Loneliness

ELIZABETH RUTH SKOGLUND

BRIGHT DAYS

DARK NIGHTS

With
CHARLES SPURGEON
IN TRIUMPH OVER EMOTIONAL PAIN

**Foreword by
Dr. Ken Connolly**

Baker Books

A Division of Baker Book House Co
Grand Rapids, Michigan 49516

Published by Baker Books
a division of Baker Book House Company
P.O. Box 6287, Grand Rapids, MI 49516-6287

Printed in the United States of America

Library of Congress Cataloging-in-Publication Data

Skoglund, Elizabeth.
    Bright days, dark nights : with Charles Spurgeon in triumph over emotional pain / Elizabeth Ruth Skoglund.
        p.   cm.
    Includes bibliographical references (p.).
    ISBN 0-8010-6192-X (paper)
    1. Suffering—Religious aspects—Christianity. 2. Spurgeon, C. H. (Charles Haddon), 1834–1892. I. Title.
    BV4909.S545   2000
    248.8'6—dc21   99-055498

For current information about all releases from Baker Book House, visit our web site:
http://www.bakerbooks.com

To Alfred Benson, my grandfather, and Alfred J. Crick, who are now together in heaven and, with Spurgeon, are a part of the "witnesses" of Hebrews 12:1.

To Pamela Reeve and John and Beverly West, who influenced me early in life.

To Betty Mayling Hu, always a loving support.

To Rayne, Lance, and Elizabeth Hannah, with love.

Were you ever in a new trouble, one which was so strange that you felt that a similar trial had never happened to you, and, moreover, you dreamt that such a temptation had never assailed anybody else? I should not wonder if that was the thought of your troubled heart. And did you ever walk out upon that lonely desert island upon which you were wrecked, and say, "I am alone,—*alone*,—ALONE,—nobody was ever here before me"? And did you suddenly pull up short as you noticed, in the sand, the footprints of a man? I remember right well passing through that experience; and when I looked, lo! it was not merely the footprints of a man that I saw, but I thought I knew whose feet had left those imprints; they were the marks of One who had been crucified, for there was the print of the nails. So I thought to myself, "If he has been here, it is a desert island no longer. As his blessed feet once trod this wilderness-way, it blossoms now like the rose, and it becomes to my troubled spirit as a very garden of the Lord."[1]

CONTENTS

Foreword   9
Preface   11
Acknowledgments   13

1 Body, Mind, and Spirit   15
2 Confidence   41
3 Depression   63
4 Anxiety   89
5 Loneliness   129
6 Change   161
7 Transition   181

Notes   215

FOREWORD

It was in 1964 when I accepted the pastorate of a thriving city church. My father, concerned for my best interests, donated a sixty-three-volume set of the original Passmore and Alabaster publication of *The Metropolitan Tabernacle Pulpit* to me. These were the sermons of C. H. Spurgeon, published weekly, and then compiled into separate volumes at the end of each year.

His admonition to me was succinct. He said, "Make him your model." What I already knew about Spurgeon, and what I realized about the value of my dad's sacrifice, encouraged me to become a student of this prince of preachers.

Years later, although I already knew Elizabeth Skoglund personally and as an author, it was not until I was required to know her professionally that I realized her reputation as a skilled Christian counselor, especially with teens, had not been exaggerated. God used her to turn one of my teens 180 degrees spiritually, almost overnight. Such teaching and counseling have been her profession and vocation for the past thirty years.

I know at least two types of people who will be fascinated with *Bright Days, Dark Nights*, Elizabeth's book depicting Spurgeon's viewpoint on human emotions. First, there will be the students of Spurgeon. The value of this book, to a market already cluttered, is that the author's objectives are significantly unique. Elizabeth analyzes the impact of various emotions, such as depression and loneliness, on this nineteenth-century pulpiteer.

As is commonly known, Spurgeon suffered immeasurably from emotional pain. His depressions were severe, enhancing the depth and compassion that always surrounded his ministry.

In a day when many still feel that good Christians are not supposed to have emotional problems, Spurgeon is both relevant and current. Indeed, his experience with emotional pain brought him to another dimension. Elizabeth accurately analyzes and represents Mr. Spurgeon's thought patterns on this important subject.

The other persons whom I would encourage to read *Bright Days, Dark Nights* are those who are already victims of such emotions as depression, anxiety, and loneliness. Then there are others who deal with these traumas professionally, as does Elizabeth Skoglund herself. Finally, there are those who become involved because they are in a role of spiritual leadership, or because they have strong shoulders, soft hearts, and find it easy to "weep with those who weep."

Bright Days, Dark Nights should be available in every believer's home.

Dr. Ken Connolly

PREFACE

Years ago in my student days I read an article in Inter-Varsity's *His* magazine on Spurgeon and depression. At the time I was in college emotional problems were considered "sinful" by most evangelical believers, and it was striking to me to read that this famous icon of spiritual teaching, Charles Haddon Spurgeon, not only believed that good Christians could have emotional problems and still be good Christians but actually suffered from depression himself. Perhaps the article struck me with such force because I had just lived through the suicide of a fellow student after she had reached out to more than one Christian who disregarded her pain by implying that depression was either not to be taken seriously or that it was out-and-out sin.

After that time Spurgeon represented more to me than sermon illustrations and theological debates. But not until much later did I undertake to read him seriously. Once I approached the study of his unedited sermons, I realized the full impact of what Spurgeon had to say regarding emotions. What he once said about the Scriptures, I would apply to his own writing as well: "It is a gold mine; there are nuggets upon the surface, but there is richer gold for the man who can dig deep."[1] The wealth of insight that Spurgeon portrays regarding emotions and emotional problems is what I discovered as I dug deep into his works. What I found is the essence of this book, which I hope will bring great comfort and deliverance to those who read it.

ACKNOWLEDGMENTS

If Churchill was correct in feeling that in writing a book one acquires a companion whose loss is felt upon the completion of that endeavor, then I am comforted by the fact that in writing about Charles Spurgeon there have been faithful companions and supports who will remain.

From the point of view of actual emotional and prayer support as well as time, talent, and temporal backing, none are higher on my list of those to thank than Rayne and Lance Wilcox, Carolyn and Ken Connolly, and Rachel and Andrew Chu.

Bob Ross of Pilgrim Publications in Pasadena, Texas, and his son Mike were of inestimable help regarding available material on Spurgeon. To Gene Albert I owe the privilege of using unpublished writing from Spurgeon along with the personal pleasure of reading from Spurgeon's own one-hundred-plus-years-old handwriting. Many thanks to George Thomson and Esther Copeland for their encouragement and the books they generously provided. To all those who prayed and encouraged—Marsha Means, Bruce and Martha Kober, John and Beverly West, Pamela Reeve, Gordon Bear, Karl Weiskopf, Matthew and Lucie Pearl Conolly, Richard Baltzell, who has always been there, and so many others—I am deeply indebted. My thanks also to my agent Lois Curley for her encouragement and hard work, to Pam McQuade and Mary Wenger, who edited this book, and to Paul Engle for his time and support.

Many others have encouraged along the rather long journey of reading volumes of sermons and trying to put it all together in a form that would bless many and show what perfect balance there can be between biblical teaching and sound psychological thinking. My gratitude extends to those unnamed people.

1

BODY, MIND, AND SPIRIT

The old man sitting in the damp prison cell is truly alone. Winter is coming on and he is without a coat. He is a prominent Christian; still, no throngs stand at the prison gate demanding his release. He is a leader of leaders, but no witnesses come to his trial to vouch for his innocence. He is a scholar, yet he has no books.

His name has once been popular, his needs met. He has known the comfort of a wife who has been gone for a long time now.[2] He has enjoyed the closeness of friendship. Yet now he is alone, imprisoned for his faith.

Nearby there is a group of believers, a group to whom he has often preached. Surely someone there has a coat and books. Surely someone will at least visit him and even defend him. But only one person comes, an old friend who has remained loyal.

The old man writes a letter to a younger man whom he has mentored. "Can you bring me my coat," he implores, "and my books? And can you come quickly, for winter is coming soon." The letter, carried on the back of an animal, starts on its 600-mile journey. It will not be delivered soon. In a few short months the old man will be dead, killed as a martyr for his faith while those of his own faith a few miles away do nothing. Will his young friend come in time?

"What is wrong with this man's faith?" you may ask. "Can he not trust God enough to be delivered? Furthermore, what is cold weather and a lonely cell to one who walks with God? More than that, surely he must have failed if even those who believe as he does do not come to his aid. Surely a mature Christian would not have gotten himself into such a mess. Perhaps he should repent so that God could rescue him and the church support him once again."

But rather than repent, he cries out triumphantly, "I have fought a good fight . . . I have kept the faith." For the old man is none other than Paul the apostle, the leader of the first-century church.

Charles Haddon Spurgeon is considered by many to be the greatest preacher of nineteenth-century England. During a period when there were other popular evangelical preachers like F. B. Meyer and G. Campbell Morgan, Spurgeon preached without a microphone to several thousand people at a time. He wrote prolifically as well. His appeal reached to the monarchy as well as the ordinary day laborer.

Charles Spurgeon was married to Susannah, who shared his commitment and supported him. In addition to raising his own family, he started orphanages as well as a school for divinity students. He not only comprehended the past and related well to the apostle Paul and other ancient divines, but he had an ability to transcend time itself and become contemporary in a timeless fashion.

In his description of that first-century prison cell we understand more fully what Paul must have been experiencing. "It is almost too dark to see him—we will find him out in that frightful den. The horrid dungeon—the filth lies upon the floor till it looks like a road which is seldom [cleaned]—the [draft] blows through the only little slit which they call a window. The poor old man, without his cloak, wraps his ragged garment about him. Sometimes you see him kneeling down to pray, and then he dips his pen into the ink, and writes to his dear son Timothy."[3] For Paul there is "no companion, except Luke, who occasionally comes in for a short time. Now, how shall we find the old man?"

Answers Spurgeon: "We find him full of confidence in the religion which has cost him so much. . . . We hear him say: '. . . I am not ashamed: for I know whom I have believed, and am persuaded that he is able to keep that which I have committed unto him against that day.' No doubt, often the tempter said to him, 'Paul, why you have lost everything for your religion! . . . The very men you have converted have forsaken you. Give it up, give it up, it cannot be worth all this. Why, they will not even bring you a cloak to wrap around you; you are left here to shiver, and very soon your head will be struck from your body. . . . Retire,' they advise. 'No,' answers Paul. 'I know whom I have believed.'"[4]

Continues Spurgeon: "He is confined to prison. . . . He is as obscure as if he had never had a name. . . . The Philippian Church, ten years before, had made a collection for him when he was in prison. . . . Now he is old, and no Church remembers him. He is brought to trial . . ." and by his own admission, "'no man stood with me.' . . . He served his God, and worked himself down to poverty for the Church's sake, yet the Church has forsaken him! Oh! how great must have been the anguish of the loving heart of Paul at such ingratitude."[5]

His success has been greater than that of most religious leaders throughout recorded history. Yet the depths of his rejection, the level of his poverty, and the ultimate torture and denigration of his death have defied the very definition of success as we view it. In the words of Spurgeon, "Why did not the few who were in Rome, if they had been never so poor, make a contribution for him? Could not those who were of Caesar's household, have found a cloak for the apostle? No; he is so utterly left, that although he is ready to die [from the cold] in the dungeon, not a soul will lend or give him a cloak. What patience does this teach to those similarly situated? Has it fallen to thy lot, my brother, to be forsaken of friends? Were there other times when your name was the symbol of popularity, when many lived in your favour like insects in your sunbeam—and has it come to this now, that you are forgotten as a dead man . . . ? In your greatest trials do you find your fewest friends? Have those who once loved and respected you, fallen asleep in Jesus? And have others turned out to be hypocritical and untrue?

"What are you to do now? You are to remember this case of the apostle; it is put here for your comfort. He had to pass through as deep waters as any that you are called to [cross], and yet remember, he says, 'Notwithstanding the Lord stood with me, and strengthened me.' So now, when man deserts you, God will be your friend."[6] And to be the friend of God is the real test of success. For without that our whole basis for success lies in the temporary acclaim of the world only rather than in the permanent glory of eternity. "This God is our God *for ever and ever*—not in sunshiny weather only, but for ever and ever. This God is our God in dark nights as well as in bright days.

"Go to him, spread your complaint before him. Murmur not. If Paul had to suffer desertion, you must not expect better usage. . . . David has his Ahithophel, Christ his Judas, Paul his Demas, and can you expect to fare better than they? As you look at that old cloak, as it speaks of human ingratitude, be of good courage, and wait on the Lord, for he shall strengthen thy heart. 'Wait, I say, on the Lord.'"[7]

Twenty centuries later the message is still the same. A striking picture of a youth appeared on the front page of the *Los Angeles Times* during the week following the death of Mother Teresa of Calcutta. It portrayed a young Indian boy, dressed in worn garments, clasping in his two hands a simple bunch of flowers. The photograph was entitled "Humble Homage."[8] Mother Teresa worked with the "poorest of the poor" and reportedly died with two garments and one pair of sandals in her possession. Rich? Never! Successful? Very! She was often criticized for operating on her one-on-one approach rather than building a greater mass of organizational machinery. But she could not forget that one homeless person, that one abandoned baby, that one naked person who needed help now, and, above all, who needed love and dignity.

So she died. A leader of the twentieth century, yet poor in this world's goods and only very tentatively accepting of the accolades of men. When she was awarded the Nobel Prize she even turned down the dinner so that the money so saved could go to the poor.

It has become acceptable even in Christian circles to judge success by money, power, and even the miracles of those who play the "name it and claim it" game where God becomes a kind of giant Santa Claus, fulfilling our every whim and desire and eliminating all opposition and conflict. However, those who have been great in God throughout recorded history have not gauged their success by material prosperity. Furthermore, they have seemed to suffer at times even more greatly than others. "Is it not a curious thing that, whenever God means to make a man great, he always breaks him in pieces first?"[9] Furthermore, "great hearts can only be made great by great troubles."[10] Yet regardless of outward evidences of success the works of great persons have lived on.

Explains Spurgeon, "You cannot kill a good man's work, nor a good woman's work either, though it be only the teaching of a few children in the Sunday-school. You do not know to whom you may be teaching Christ, but assuredly you are sowing seed which will blossom and flower in the far off ages. When Mrs. Wesley taught her sons, little did she think what they would become. You do not know who may be in your class, my young friend. You may have there a young Whitefield, and if the Lord enable you to lead him to Jesus, he will bring thousands to decision. Aye, at your breast, good woman, there may be . . . one whom God will make a burning and shining light; and if you train that little one for Jesus your work will never be lost. No holy tear is forgotten, it is in God's bottle. No desire for another's good is wasted, God has heard it. A word spoken for Jesus, a mite cast into Christ's treasury, a gracious line written to a friend—all these are things which shall last when yonder sun has blackened into a coal, and the moon has curdled into a clot of blood. Deeds done in the power of the Spirit are eternal."[11] Such is the nature of success. And, while our attention is so often focused on the fruits of success, we forget that there is also a price to be paid, a test to be endured.

With enormous spiritual insight Spurgeon once preached: "You will find the bravest of God's servants have their times when it is hard to hold their own; when they would be glad to creep into a mouse-hole, if they could there find themselves a shelter."[12]

During these times of conflict our very faith may be attacked. "At such seasons it will happen that our graces will refuse to act. Like some flowers that shut up their cups when the sun is gone, so will our love and our faith shut themselves up. They are reflectors, when there is no light without they cannot reflect any within. I have known what it is to search my heart through and through without being able to discover any spark of love to Jesus Christ in it, aye, and to bring my soul to the closest investigation, with diligent enquiry asking, 'Is this faith, or is it presumption? Is it really trusting in Christ, or is it all a fond persuasion of my own, an unwarranted confidence, a false security?' At such times you may rest assured that the devil will cast in suggestions to torment us."[13]

"Perhaps at this moment we turn to the word of God: and it seems all a blank. The very promises that used to cheer us refuse to speak to us. We go where the saints of God go to hear the gospel, but we find no comfort there. The word appears to condemn rather than console us. Peradventure, at that very minute we are assailed with some temporal trouble, and when spiritual trouble and temporal trouble come together and two seas meet—ah, it is hard for the poor bark to keep above the water at all.

"Yet have we known it so. There has been a perplexity about money, or an anxiety about a sick child, or sore disquietude concerning a dear sick wife, or a dire apprehension that the health of our body, or the stability of our circumstances is menaced. A strange fever, a wild deliriousness has seized us. At the same time there has been this horrible thought, 'After all may I not have been deluded?' and Satan howls out, 'Why, of course you were! You are no child of God!' and the flesh prevails awhile over the spirit, and conscience itself becomes a tormentor, upbraids and accuses us; then alas! for our poor vessel—it seems as if all hope that we should be saved were utterly taken away."[14]

Contrary to what most people think, "A Christian man is seldom long at ease. Our life, like April weather, is made up of sunshine and showers."[15] Why? Spurgeon explains it this way: "The great Owner of heaven's jewels thinks it worth his while to use a more elaborate and sharp cutting machine upon the most valuable stones: a diamond of the first water is sure to undergo more cutting than an inferior one, because the King desires that it may have many facets, which may throughout eternity, with greater splendour, reflect the light of the glory of his name."[16] In view of this it makes sense that when God decides to make a person successful he will also subject him to the most rigorous preparation and training: to be so chosen is the truest success.

Spurgeon has a unique illustration for the use God makes of trials that seem to slow divine progress, whereas in actuality the progress is enabled by the trial. Says Spurgeon: "A gentleman once asked a friend, concerning a beautiful horse of his, feeding about in the pasture with a clog on its foot, 'Why do you clog such a noble animal?' 'Sir,' said he, 'I would a great deal sooner clog him than lose him: he is given to leap hedges.' That is why God clogs his people. He would rather clog them than lose them; for if he did not clog them, they would leap the hedges and be gone. They want a tether to prevent their straying; and their God binds them with afflictions, to keep them near to him, to preserve them, and to have them in his presence."[17] That weight, that clog, which seems to slow us down or even seems to prevent us from doing "Christian service," may actually be the very thing which keeps us from "good" activities so that we can do that which is God's best for our lives. If we go far with God on this earth we will usually find that we each have our own "clog" that God uses to slow us down to do His will.

"[Perhaps], dear brethren, we have thought that Jesus did not care for us because he has not wrought a miracle for our deliverance, and has not interposed in any remarkable way to help us. You are at this time in such sore distress that you would fain cry, 'O that he would rend the heavens and descend for my deliverance!' but he has not rent the heavens. You have read in biographies of holy men the details of very extraordinary providences, but no extraordinary providence has come to your rescue. You are getting gradually poorer and poorer, or you are becoming more and more afflicted in body, and you had hoped that God would have taken some extraordinary method with you, but he has done nothing of the sort."[18]

"If we hear Paul speak of his visions, let us recollect his thorn in the flesh; if we meet with a brother who rejoices abundantly, and whom God owns and blesses, let us not conclude that his pathway is all smooth. His roses have their thorns, his bees their stings."[19]

We cannot evaluate spirituality by the level of suffering, nor can we judge spiritual success by the size of bank accounts or the extent of influence. In speaking of our uniqueness Spurgeon says: "I was particularly pleased to find that Rosenmüller thought it [Paul's thorn in the flesh] to be the gout; but then other critics think it to be weak eyesight, stammering, or a hypochondriacal tendency. Richard Baxter, who suffered from a very painful disorder . . . thought that the apostle was his fellow-sufferer. One divine is of opinion that Paul endured the earache; and I generally find that each expositor has selected that particular thorn which had pierced his own bosom." And many of these "thorns" have been used as "weights" or "clogs" to keep the life centered on the will of God. Continues Spurgeon: "Now, I believe that the apostle did not tell us what his peculiar affliction was, that we may every one feel that he had sympathy with us—that we may every one believe that ours is no new grief."[20]

"But who is Charles Spurgeon?" some may ask. For those it is well to answer that question further before going on. Charles Spurgeon was born in 1834 in Kelvedon, England, and died in 1892 in Mentone, France. His life covered a large part of the Victorian period of English history. As a preacher to tens of thousands at a time he also influenced the history of the nineteenth century.

For the first years of his life Charles Spurgeon lived with his grandfather, who was a man of deep faith. Those years were happy ones and, while his removal to his parents' home when he was seven had advantages, parting with his grandfather was traumatic. To ease the transition his grandfather reminded Charles that when they looked up at the moon each night, they would be looking at the same moon. That thought united them for years and shows his grandfather's sensitivity to a small child.

In 1844, when Charles returned to spend summer vacation with his grandfather, an incident occurred that deeply influenced Spurgeon's life. Says Spurgeon of that time: "'I was staying at my grandfather's, where I had aforetime spent my earliest days, and as the manner was, I read the scriptures at family prayer. . . . On one of these occasions, Mr. Knill, then of Chester, now of "New Jerusalem," whose name is a household word, and whose memory is precious to thousands at home and abroad, stayed at the minister's house, on Friday, in readiness to preach at Stambourne for the London Missionary Society, on the following Sunday. He never looked into a young face without yearning to impart some spiritual gift. He was all love, kindness, earnestness, and warmth, and coveted the souls of men as misers desire the gold their hearts pine for. He heard the boy read, and commended him. A little judicious praise is the sure way to win a young heart. An agreement was made with the lad that on the next morning, Saturday, he would show Mr. Knill over the garden, and take him for a walk before breakfast; a task so flattering to juvenile self-importance was sure to be entered upon. There was a tap at the door, and the child was soon out of bed and in the garden with his new friend, who won his heart at once by pleasing stories and kind words, and by giving him a chance

to communicate in return. The talk was all about Jesus, and the pleas-
antness of loving him. Nor was it mere talk; there was pleading too.
Into the great yew tree arbour, cut into the shape of a sugar-loaf, both
went, and the soul-winner knelt down, and with his arms around the
youthful neck, he poured out vehement intercession for the salvation
of the lad. The next morning witnessed the same instruction and supplication, and the next also; while all day long the pair were never far
apart, and never out of each other's thoughts. The mission sermons
were preached in the old Puritan meeting-house, and the man of God
was called to go to the next halting-place in his tour as deputation for
the Society, but he did not leave till he had uttered a most remarkable
prophecy. After even more earnest prayer with his little *protégé*, he
appeared to have a burden on his mind, and he could not go till he had
eased himself of it. In after years he was heard to say that he felt a singular interest in me, and an earnest expectation for which he could
not account. Calling the family together, he took me on his knee, and
I distinctly remember his saying:—"I do not know how it is, but I feel
a solemn presentiment that this child will preach the gospel to thousands, and God will bless him to many souls. So sure am I of this, that
when my little man preaches in Rowland Hill's chapel, as he will do
one day, I should like him to promise me that he will give out the hymn
commencing,—

> 'God moves in a mysterious way
> His wonders to perform.'"

'This promise was of course made, and was followed by another,
namely, that at his express desire I would learn the hymn in question,
and think of what he had said.

'The prophetic declaration was fulfilled. When I had the pleasure of
preaching the Word of life in Surrey Chapel, and also when I preached
in Mr. Hill's first pulpit at Wotton-under-Edge, the hymn was sung on
both occasions."[21]

Yet not until he was fifteen did Charles Spurgeon come to know Christ
in a personal way. Again in Spurgeon's own words: "'One snowy day—
it snowed so much I could not go to the place I had determined to go to,
and I was obliged to stop on the road, and it was a blessed stop to me—
I found rather an obscure street, and turned down a court, and there was

a little chapel. I wanted to go somewhere, but I did not know this place. It was the Primitive Methodist Chapel. I had heard of these people from many, and how they sang so loudly that they made people's heads ache; but that did not matter. I wanted to know how I might be saved, and if they made my head ache ever so much, I did not care. So, sitting down, the service went on, but no minister came; at last, a very thin-looking man came into the pulpit, and opened his Bible, and read these words: "Look unto Me, and be ye saved, all the ends of the earth." Just setting his eyes upon me, as if he knew all my heart, he said, "Young man, you are in trouble." Well, I was, sure enough. Says he, "You will never get out of it unless you look to Christ." And then, lifting up his hands, he cried out, as only a Primitive Methodist could do, "Look, look, look!" "It is only look," said he. I saw at once the way of salvation. Oh, how I did leap for joy at that moment! I know not what else he said. I did not take much notice of it—I was so possessed with that one thought.'"[22]

"Several years after his conversion, on 11th October, 1864, Mr. Spurgeon preached in the Primitive Methodist Chapel, at Colchester, and took for his text the ever-memorable words (Isa. xlv. 22), 'Look unto Me, and be ye saved,' &c. 'That was the text,' said he, 'that I heard preached from in this chapel, when the Lord converted me.' And pointing to a seat on the left hand, under the gallery, he said, 'I was sitting in that pew when I was converted.' This grateful reference to the place and work done by the Lord there, made a profound impression on the congregation, the hearts of many being thrilled with joy, and drawn out in love to the young preacher."[23]

While his decision to preach, and even his becoming a pastor, seemed almost immediate, his decision to forego college was different. At the outset Spurgeon went in the direction of college. Then that decision was reversed. In his own words: "That afternoon having to preach at a village station, I walked in a meditating frame of mind over Midsummer Common, to the little wooden bridge which leads to Chesterton, and in the midst of the Common, I was startled by what seemed to be a loud voice, but which may have been a singular illusion; whatever it was, the impression it made on my mind was most vivid; I seemed very distinctly to hear the words, 'Seekest thou great things for thyself, seek them not.' This led me to look at my position from a different point of view, and to challenge my motives and intentions. I remembered my poor but loving people to whom I had ministered, and the souls which had been given me in my humble charge; and although at that time I anticipated obscurity and poverty as the result of the resolve, yet I did there and then renounce the offer of collegiate instruction, determining to abide, for a season, at least, with my people, and to remain preaching the word so long as I had strength to do it. Had it not been for those words, I had not been where I am now."[24] The greatest preacher of nineteenth-century England and perhaps of all time, the founder of a college that trains for the ministry even to this day, himself never received a college degree and consistently refused ordination.

As a man Spurgeon was utterly committed to serving his Lord. Yet there was a very human side to him. He set up orphanages for homeless children, and when he encountered any children he always had enough candy in his pockets to go around. In his free moments he would often shop for something special, like a clock, for his wife, Susannah, whom he married in 1856. Susannah, along with Spurgeon, had many health problems throughout the years. Yet their relationship was deep and mutually supportive, and Spurgeon enjoyed affirming Susannah, who was in her own right intelligent and involved in various worthwhile projects.

Gardening was another form of relaxation for Spurgeon, as was walking. He especially enjoyed being outside with Dick, his cat, and Punch and Gyp, his dogs.

Spurgeon's keen sense of humor probably helped him handle some of the criticism that plagues any public figure. An illustration of his attitude toward smoking shows his lack of stuffiness and his sense of humor as well as any. Spurgeon smoked cigars during a time when there was no knowledge of its ill effect on health. Yet he was sometimes criticized for this habit. "An American preacher, Dr. G. F. Pentecost, preached at the Tabernacle on one occasion, dividing the sermon with Spurgeon. All unwittingly, Dr. Pentecost mentioned his struggles in renouncing his cigar, and Spurgeon, when his turn came to speak, most unfortunately declared that he hoped that very evening to smoke a cigar to the glory of God. The Press seized joyfully on this incident, and the statement was widely discussed. Could one really smoke to the glory of God? Spurgeon's photograph even appeared on tobacco packets. He wrote a letter to *The Daily Telegraph* in which he acknowledged his smoking habits, but maintained that it was no sin. He claimed liberty so to indulge. He said that smoking relieved his pain, soothed his brain, and helped him to sleep. It was not a very satisfactory letter, and it did not mend matters. No doubt had Spurgeon lived in our own day when medical science has established a connection between smoking and lung cancer, Spurgeon would have thought and acted differently."[25]

In his recreation, his sermons to crowds of several thousand at a time, his relationships with people and his charities, Spurgeon's life was seamless, with balance and yet intensity, moderation but always conviction. A friend wrote: "I told him of one of whom I had recently heard spending three hours on his knees. 'I could not do it,' he replied, 'if my eternity depended on it! Besides, if I go to the bank with a cheque, what do I want loafing about the premises for, when I have got my money? I go to God with a promise, which is in reality a cheque issued by God Himself on the bank of heaven; He cashes it for me, and then I go and use what He has given me, to His glory. This I take to be the true way of praying. The fact is, long prayers are often the result of unbelief. Yet it is possible, without the formal act of kneeling, for the heart to be praying always. I think I can say that seldom many minutes elapse without my heart speaking to God in either prayer or praise.' And every one who knew him intimately must have felt it was really and indeed so; for in all his humorous moments he was reverent; and, strange to say, in his most solemn moments he was often humorous. He had not two lives, one religious and the other secular; his whole life was one of uniform and irrevocable consecration to God."[26]

Yet as always Spurgeon was balanced, and when it came to a man or woman's private wrestling before God, he had a different viewpoint of prayer than when that prayer was public. "I like to think of Welch, who used to cast a Scotch plaid over the bed where he rested at night, and would always rise in the night and cast this plaid about him, and pray for one or two hours; and he says in his biography, 'I cannot understand how a man can sleep through the night without prayer.' That is a point to which few of us have ever thought of coming. David Brainerd, too, speaks of rising one morning by four of the clock, and the sun had not risen at six, and he says that in those two hours of prayer he had so wrestled with God that he was wet with perspiration. Such was the earnestness of his spirit as he pleaded before the Lord. I am afraid we do not practice much of this sacred importunity. We are sad hands at this devout exercise, whereby saints became famous in the days gone by. God restore us to the spirit of prayer, and all other blessings will come as the result."[27]

There was further flexibility in Spurgeon regarding the mode of prayer. "Men may pray acceptably standing, sitting, kneeling, or lying with their faces upon the earth; they may meet with Jesus by the river's side, in the temple porch, in a prison, or in a private house; and they may be one in the same Spirit although the one regardeth a day, and the other regardeth it not."[28]

Consistent with his sense of balance, he was very understanding of human frailty. When a friend asked him whether or not he would ever get over his nervousness before preaching, Spurgeon replied: "'If ever you do, all your power will be gone. . . . I suffer from it, and always have done, as no tongue can tell.'"[29] If one defines legalism as the obligation to play by certain rules only, then Spurgeon could never be called a legalist. He had a tolerance for humanness and a compassion for suffering. He was balanced and yet strong in his stand against out-and-out sin.

When the same friend referred to in the last paragraph once asked him a difficult question, Spurgeon answered with balance and yet with respect for the power of almighty God. "Allusion was made in our conversation one day to the singular application of the text to his mind when he was seeking to go to college, 'Seekest thou great things for thyself? Seek them not,' which seemed to have changed the current of his career. I told him that soon after I came into college I began to suffer from deep depression of spirit, occasioned by the sudden change from an active life in the country to the sedentary life of study in the class-rooms beneath the Tabernacle. The present college was not then built. I was ready to give up all idea of the ministry in sheer despair, when one day in the interval between the classes I went alone into the Tabernacle pulpit, and looked round in admiration and astonishment at the magnificent building. When, as distinctly to me as any voice I ever heard, someone said, 'You will preach here one day,' I turned round to see 'the voice that spake with me,' but no other person was in the building. I felt assured then, and still do, that God did thus speak. I told no one at the time, but I was greatly cheered by the assurance given that I should yet be able to preach with sufficient acceptance to preach there. It was not until I had occupied the Tabernacle pulpit a number of times that I ventured to speak to Mr. Spurgeon of this, to me, real, though singular, experience. He bowed his head and said, 'Yes; I do believe God does thus speak to men sometimes.'"[30]

Charles Spurgeon was a steady, down-to-earth, Baptist preacher, well grounded in biblical truth. But perhaps part of the beauty and unusualness of his life rests in his ability to accept that God is still the Lord of the supernatural and that we cannot limit God to the boundaries of our earthly understanding.

Susannah Spurgeon wrote of a very striking experience that was related to Spurgeon by the famous English writer John Ruskin. Of Mr. Ruskin she relates: "A Christian gentleman, a widower, with several little ones, was in treaty for the occupancy of an old farm-house in the country, for the sake of his children's health. One day, he took them to see their new residence, before finally removing into it. While he talked with the landlord or agent, the young people set off on a tour of inspection, and scampered here, there, and everywhere over the garden and grounds. Then they proceeded to examine the house, and rushed up and down stairs, looking into every room, dancing with delight, full of fun and frolic, and shouting out their joy over every new discovery. Presently, when they seemed to have exhausted the wonders of the old house, one of them suggested that the underground premises had not yet been explored, and must therefore be visited at once. So the merry band went helter-skelter in search of a way below, found a door at the head of some dark stairs, and were rushing down them at great speed, when, midway, they suddenly stopped in startled amazement, for, standing at the bottom of the steps, they saw *their mother*, with outstretched arms and loving gesture, waving them back, and silently forbidding their further passage. With a cry of mingled fear and joy, they turned, and fled in haste to their father, telling him that they had seen 'Mother,' that she had smiled lovingly at them, but had eagerly motioned them to go back. In utter astonishment, the father listened to the children's tale, and at once perceived that something unusual had happened. Search was made, and close at the foot of those narrow, gloomy stairs, they found a deep and open well, entirely unguarded, into which, in their mad rush, every child must inevitably have fallen and perished, had not the Lord in His mercy interposed."

Continued Susannah, "Stories of the supernatural are seldom worthy of credence; but, in this case, both my dear husband and Mr. Ruskin were convinced that God permitted the appearance of their mother to those dear children, in order to save them from a terrible death; and that nothing else, and nothing less than such a vision could have attained this object, and prevented the calamity. . . .

"There have been many other well-authenticated instances of similar appearances permitted by the Lord in seasons of special danger to His children; and the calm and reverent consideration of such a subject, by devout minds, might have the happy effect of bringing the soul very close to the veil which separates the things that are seen, and are temporal, from the things that are not seen, and are eternal."[31]

As a man aware of his times, with relationships that extended as high up in society as the royal family itself, Charles Spurgeon reflected some of the views of his time. In the area of emotional problems, the Victorians had attitudes that were at times more compatible with the 1990s and the twenty-first century than they were with the views that were prevalent during the early part of the twentieth century, following Freud and his influence on psychology. As far back as the eighteenth century, extending into the nineteenth century, the mind and the body were treated together. While Victorian medicine began to separate the two, in actual treatment, mind and body were treated together until almost the end of that period.[32] The result was a lack of stigmatization regarding common emotional problems like depression, anxiety, and nervousness. This thinking seems to explain some of Spurgeon's compassionate attitudes regarding emotions like depression. He understood the interrelatedness of the body, mind, and spirit. He didn't see emotional suffering as incompatible with spirituality.

With the advent of Freud in the early twentieth century, and his emphasis on sexual dysfunction as an underlying factor in emotional problems, psychotherapy changed, and anyone with emotional problems became stigmatized. The understanding of the connection between body and mind—and eventually spirit—was lost for the most part. With that loss the mind was seen as solely responsible for emotional problems and thus the implication was drawn by some that such problems could be controlled by the will alone. In this way the overspiritualization of emotional problems became reinforced.

Convenient as it may be to compartmentalize a human being and say, "This problem is all spiritual or all psychological or all physical," such an attitude is simplistic and can increase a person's difficulties rather than solve them. While people are made up of all these components, each interrelates with the other until they often become blurred and indistinguishable one from the other.

In "The American Scholar" Ralph Waldo Emerson discusses the paradox of the whole having several parts and yet being one. "It is one of those fables which out of an unknown antiquity convey an unlooked-for wisdom, that the gods, in the beginning, divided Man into men, that he might be more helpful to himself; just as the hand was divided into fingers, the better to answer its end.

"The old fable covers a doctrine ever new and sublime; that there is One Man—present to all particular men only partially, or through one faculty; and that you must take the whole society to find the whole man. Man is not a farmer, or a professor, or an engineer, but he is all. Man is priest, and scholar, and statesman, and producer, and soldier."[33]

To take Emerson's idea one step further, any individual is not divided neatly into three parts but is a total of all three. A loaf of bread is made up of several ingredients such as flour and eggs and milk. Each is distinct from the others, but once they are combined into a loaf of bread, they cease to be distinct and separate. Instead of being eggs, flour, and milk, they become bread. Likewise a person is not three equal parts—body, mind, and spirit—but a whole made up of all three. Yet, in spite of this interrelationship, at times one part may stand out from the others, and here the loaf of bread analogy stops.

A sixteen-year-old with a drug problem came to my counseling office. In the course of our sessions she became a Christian. The psychological effect was profound. Instead of floundering around, without friends or purpose, she began to fill her life with meaningful activities and, eventually, healthy relationships. Christianity greatly affected the progress she made in counseling. In her, the spirit had been most neglected.

Suzanne, a Christian in her late forties, had a very low regard for herself and suffered from some psychosomatic problems as well. Counseling consisted partially of convincing her that she did not have to feel "sinful" because she had some emotional problems. Once over that hurdle, she responded more quickly than some in developing greater self-esteem. Her stomach problems disappeared, and it became easier for her to relate to God when the neurotic guilt was gone.

Michael, in contrast to the other two, was an eleven-year-old child who had suffered from a variety of rather serious illnesses all his life. His low self-esteem seemed very much tied in to the fact that he was always sick. His sickness made him feel weak and inadequate. He would say things like, "I'm just a bother to my parents. They have to stay home all the time." Progress in counseling was slow. Just about the time he really began to improve, Michael would get sick, and the cycle would start all over again.

A person's body, mind, and spirit make up a totality in which one or the other may emerge predominantly at any given time. A woman going through menopause may experience periods of depression that should not be labeled as primarily psychological or spiritual. She may derive help from spiritual or psychological sources, but the primary cause is physical. Certain drugs are now being used effectively with some forms of mental illness, further validating the biochemical basis for many emotional problems.

Fatigue can point to an underlying state of depression. It has also been shown that stress actually produces its own set of physical responses. Stress can cause a myriad of metabolic imbalances. A young girl I once knew produced asthma symptoms every time she became emotionally upset. Another developed a rash that would leave immediately after the stressful situation was resolved.

A person's spiritual life too may be directly affected by his or her physical and emotional state. It is often more difficult to feel spiritually strong when you feel physically or psychologically weak. Esau sold his birthright, not when he was physically strong, but when he was exhausted and hungry. Peter denied Christ under the duress of a young girl's mockery.

The idea that we are a composite of body, mind, and spirit is not new by any means. The Bible says, "A cheerful heart does good like medicine" (Prov. 17:22), implying a relationship between the body and the mind. In Proverbs 15:30 we read, "Pleasant sights and good reports give happiness and health." "Hope deferred makes the heart sick" (Prov. 13:12). "Reverence for God gives a man deep strength" (Prov. 14:26).

Since the openness of the 1960s the stigma of emotional problems has been diminishing as we have begun to see the potential for the mind and body to affect each other. Our present emphasis on biochemistry and its influence on the mind is in sharp contrast to blaming everything on the psychological part of a person and thereby implying a deficiency in willpower. Once mind and body are interrelated, it is a relatively small step from that point to appreciate the relationship between body, mind, and *spirit*.

Thus once again people seem more able to get psychological help for emotional problems with the added support of treatment for the body, when that is appropriate, and with the support of the spiritual.

This background of the Victorian view of emotional problems helps us understand Spurgeon's view of depression and other emotional problems. From his own personal experience he was acutely aware of the impact of the body on the mind—such as physical fatigue, gout, and rheumatoid-type illnesses—as well as how the mind connects with the spiritual state of an individual. The result in Spurgeon was a sympathetic, practical approach. With him, biblical principle always came first. He was aware that many problems arise from sinful living. But Spurgeon could also understand that many emotional disturbances like depression or fear might have no relationship to sin in the person's life. Indeed they might reflect more accurately God's refining influence or the oppression so often connected with the struggle to do God's work.

As we enter the early twenty-first century, with its mind-set that emphasizes how physical disturbances affect the mind, once again we can appreciate the writings of Charles Haddon Spurgeon as they relate to these areas.

Rather than relegating all psychological distress to the category of sin, Spurgeon includes emotional discomfort as part of what a godly, successful person may be called to encounter. Says Spurgeon, "Furthermore, remember that even after you are secure in Christ, and accepted before God, and clothed in Jesus's righteousness, you may sometimes get despondent. Christian men are but men, and they may have a bad liver or an attack of bile, or some trial, and then they get depressed if they have ever so much grace. I would defy the apostle Paul himself to help it. But what then? Why then you can get joy and peace through believing. I am the subject of depressions of spirit so fearful that I hope none of you ever get to such extremes of wretchedness as I go to, but I always get back again by this—I know I trust Christ. I have no reliance but in him, and if he falls I shall fall with him, but if he does not, I shall not. Because he lives, I shall live also, and I spring to my legs again and fight with my depressions of spirit and my downcastings, and get the victory through it; and so may you do, and so you *must*, for there is no other way of escaping from it. In your most depressed seasons you are to get joy and peace through believing. . . . Do stick to this, dear friends, 'Though he slay me, yet will I trust in him.'"[34]

Still, though God never wastes our suffering, it is important not to go to extremes in either direction. The suffering Spurgeon refers to is unavoidable suffering. Enough pain comes to us in this world without our seeking it in order to grow or to understand others. Indeed we must be careful not to anticipate trouble that may never materialize, thus torturing ourselves needlessly.

In reference to those who wrack themselves with the erroneous fear that they do not belong to God after all, Spurgeon gives an excellent illustration: "Feelings are a very uncertain and erroneous gauge indeed, and are not to be relied upon; and to build such a terrible inference as that of your being lost upon a few gloomy feelings, or even a great many of them, is absurd to the last degree. Have you never heard the story of the man who, traveling in the dark over a new country, suddenly came to a place where the earth crumbled from under his feet, and he felt sure that he was slipping over an awful precipice. Clutching at the roots of a tree, which grew out of the bank, he maintained his hold in desperation, feeling that if he let go he should be dashed into a thousand pieces. There he hung till his hands were unable to bear the strain any longer, and, giving up all for lost, he fell, but alighted upon a soft couch of green sward which was just an inch or two beneath his feet. So do many dreads frequently arise from nothing at all. Fancy with her magic wand is busy at creating sorrows."[35]

Regardless of the trials, "Oh, the joy of knowing, when you are gone, that the truth you preached is living still! Methinks the apostles since they have been in heaven must often have looked down on the world, and marveled at the work which God helped twelve poor fishermen to do, and they must have felt a growing blessedness as they have seen nations converted by the truth which they preached in feebleness."[36]

Too often we feel that to have faith in Christ is to eradicate doubt and fear and depression. Perhaps that is why in human relationships sometimes trust is shared only by first sharing in troubles. Explains Spurgeon, "Some five years ago I was the subject of fearful depression of spirit. Certain troublous events had happened to me; I was also unwell, and my heart sank within me. Out of the depths I was forced to cry unto the Lord. Just before I went away to Mentone for rest I suffered greatly in body, but far more in soul, for my spirit was overwhelmed. Under this pressure I preached a sermon from the words, 'My God, my God, why hast thou forsaken me?' I was as much qualified to preach from that text as I ever expect to be; indeed, I hope that few of my brethren could have entered so deeply into those heart-breaking words. I felt to the full of my measure the horror of a soul forsaken of God. Now, that was not a desirable experience. I tremble at the bare idea of passing again through that eclipse of soul: I pray that I may never suffer in that fashion again unless the same result should hang upon it. That night, after sermon, there came into the vestry a man who was as nearly insane as he could be to be out of an asylum. His eyes seemed ready to start from his head, and he said that he should utterly have despaired if he had not heard that discourse, which had made him feel that there was one man alive who understood his feelings, and could describe his experience. I talked with him, and tried to encourage him, and asked him to come again on the Monday night, when I should have a little more time to talk with him. I saw the brother again, and I told him that I thought he was a hopeful patient, and I was glad that the word had been so suited to his case. Apparently he put aside the comfort which I presented for his acceptance, and yet I had the consciousness upon me that the precious truth which he had heard was at work upon his mind, and that the storm of his soul would soon subside into a deep calm. Now hear the sequel. Last night, of all the times in the year, when, strange to say, I was preaching from the words, 'The Almighty hath vexed my soul,' after the service in walked this self-same brother who had called on me five years before. This time he looked as different as noonday from midnight, or as life from death. I said to him, I am glad to see you, for I have often thought about you, and wondered whether you were brought into perfect peace. I told you that I went to Mentone, and my patient also went into the country, so that we had not met for five years. To my enquiries this brother replied, 'Yes, you said that I was a hopeful patient, and I am sure you will be glad to know that I have walked in the sunlight from that day till now. Everything is changed and altered with me.' Dear friends, as soon as I saw my poor despairing patient the first time, I blessed God that my fearful experience had prepared me to sympathize with him and guide him, but last night when I saw him perfectly restored, my heart overflowed with gratitude to God for my former sorrowful feelings. I would go into the deeps a hundred times to cheer a downcast spirit: it is good for me to have been afflicted that I might know how to speak a word in season to one that is weary.

"Suppose that by some painful operation you could have your right arm made a little longer, I do not suppose you would care to undergo the operation; but if you foresaw that by undergoing the pain you would be enabled to reach and save drowning men who else would sink before your eyes, I think you would willingly bear the agony, and pay a heavy fee to the surgeon to be thus qualified for the rescue of your fellows. Reckon, then, that to acquire soul-winning power you will have to go through fire and water, through doubt and despair, through mental torment and soul distress. It will not, of course, be the same with you all, nor perhaps with any two of you, but according to the work allotted you will be your preparation. You must go into the fire if you are to pull others out of it, and you will have to dive into the floods if you are to draw others out of the water."[37]

The first time I saw Carlos Sanchez was at a high-school assembly. At that time I was still with the schools, doing group counseling with tenth graders. Our new school building was incomplete, so we had no auditorium. Therefore, 1,800 of us were seated outside on bleachers under what seemed a hundred degrees of hot blazing sun. It was difficult to see against the strong sunlight, and the voices of the various speakers seemed to fade into the expanse of space on the football field.

35

Then Carlos was introduced: young, in his twenties, nervous but sincere. "There are two words you will hear today," he proclaimed in a sharp, loud voice that seemed to penetrate the air: "Jesus Christ and the Bible."

Having thoroughly captured his audience by the force of his voice and by that unexpected statement, he went on to tell of his background in a middle-class, respectable home. Then he described his first experiments with drugs at age twelve until he had finally run the gamut of available drugs and ended up a heroin addict.

Three years earlier he had gone to visit his sister to ask for money with which he meant to buy a fix. She said that if he would first read a book she had about God, she would give him the money he wanted. But after reading the book, Carlos forgot about the money and his fix. Later he committed his life to Christ, and he was profoundly changed.

Now at this school assembly we met and felt a common bond. Carlos was effectively helping teenagers on drugs, some of the same teenagers I was counseling. Yet he had a vast experience which I envied.

We had lunch and talked. Then we pooled our efforts and for months had a direct combined influence on a large number of teenage drug users. He had such a dramatic experience with God that I felt at first a little defensive. After all, my background had been pretty sheltered. I had never smoked a joint or gotten drunk. And I certainly had not seen God perform the kind of dramatic miracles in my life that Carlos had seen in his.

Yet in the back of my mind grew the gnawing, uneasy feeling that all was not right. Carlos had no social life, except with kids who needed him twenty-four hours a day. He began to show signs of fatigue; he mentioned God less and less. And from the beginning he seemed obsessed with proving to the establishment, who had denigrated Carlos the addict, that Carlos the speaker, counselor, and Christian was indeed a man to be respected.

And respected he was by adults and kids alike. Indeed he had an intuitive sense of how to approach teenagers in trouble. They listened to him while those of us who watched learned more from him about counseling than we had learned in many college courses.

Fourteen months later he was dead from an overdose of barbiturates. This driven man had done great things and had shown great potential, but he *was* driven. In spite of his spiritual outlook and the powerful effect that God had on his life, his own low sense of self-esteem, combined with some biochemical factors and just sheer exhaustion, had driven him to a desperate act. I have often wondered if he would have been alive today if psychological and medical help had been combined with his spiritual experiences.

"'And he said, My presence shall go with thee, and I will give thee rest.'"[38]

". . . The most important thing to a Christian worker, as it was to Moses, is to have rest. 'I do not expect any rest,' says one, 'while I am here.' Do you not? Then you will not do much work for the Lord. They who work most must rest most; and if they work with their mind they cannot do it well, indeed they cannot do it at all, unless they have plenty of rest."[39]

"Mark the kind of rest that is here mentioned. 'I will give thee rest.' All the rest that God gives us we may safely take. No man ever rested too long upon the bosom of Jesus. I believe that many Christian workers would be better if they enjoyed more rest. I was speaking to the ministers at the Conference upon this matter, my subject being the Saviour asleep during the storm on the Sea of Galilee. He knew there was a storm coming on, but he felt so happy and restful in his Father's love and care that he went into the hinder part of the ship, the best place for sleeping, deliberately took a pillow, lay down, and went to sleep. It was the very best thing he could do. He had been busy all day, teaching and feeding the multitudes, and he felt that it was his duty to go to sleep that he might be ready for the next day's toil. When *you* get very weary, and perhaps worried as well, the best thing you can do is to go to sleep. Go to bed, brother; and go to sleep. It is astonishing what a difference a night's rest makes with our troubles. I would say this literally to fidgety, worrying people, like myself, 'Go to bed, brother, go to bed.' But I would also say it spiritually to all sorts of people; when you are feeling weak, and disturbed, and you do not know what to do for the best—'Go into the presence of God, and there get rest.' 'My presence shall go with thee, and I will give thee rest.'"[40]

While Spurgeon would always have us place the spiritual as the predominant factor in human dilemmas, he shows his characteristic balance in these words: "What strange creatures we are! I suppose every man is a trinity, certainly every Christian man is,—spirit, soul, and body,—and we may be in three states at once, and we may not know which of the three is our real state. The whole three may be so mixed up that we become a puzzle to ourselves. Though certain mental philosophers would say that I egregiously err in asserting that such a thing can be, yet nevertheless I am quite certain that it is a very common experience of the child of God."[41]

Yet, while Spurgeon never failed to preach about man's sinful nature, even here there was divine balance. For while he did not feel that sin was relative, he did believe that people sometimes sinned unknowingly. "Even the best of men have done this in the past. For instance, John Newton, in his trading for slaves in his early days, never seemed to have felt that there was any wrong in it; and Whitefield in accepting slaves for his orphanage in Georgia, never raised or dreamed of raising the question as to whether slavery was in itself sinful. Perhaps advancing light will shew that many of the habits and customs of our present civilisation are essentially bad, and our grandsons will wonder how we could have acted as we did."[42]

Perhaps Spurgeon would be disappointed in the progress made in the century following his death, a century he put some faith in. He once said: "I am more and more astounded at this nineteenth century; I have heard it praised up for its enlightenment and progress till I am sick to death of the nineteenth century, and am right glad that it is nearing its close, and I hope the twentieth century will be something better."[43]

Maybe the twenty-first century will yet do better. But maybe not. Perhaps our best hope still is "Come quickly, Lord Jesus!" But while we wait, the plea of Spurgeon would be to affirm each other, not to be a source of discouragement to our brethren. He once said: "Advice is usually given gratis, and this is very proper, since in most cases that is its full value. Advice given to persons who become depressed in spirit is usually unwise, and causes pain and aggravation of spirit. I sometimes wish that those who are so ready with their advice had themselves suffered a little, for then, perhaps, they would have the wisdom to hold their tongues. Of what use is it to advise a blind person to see, or to tell one who cannot lift up herself that she ought to be upright, and should not look so much upon the earth? This is a needless increase of misery. Some persons who pretend to be comforters might more fitly be classed with tormenters. A spiritual infirmity is as real as a physical one. When Satan binds a soul it is as truly bound as when a man binds an ox or an ass. It cannot get free, it is of necessity in bondage. . . . I may be speaking to some who have bravely attempted to rally their spirits: they have tried change of scene, they have gone into godly company, they have asked Christian people to comfort them, they have frequented the house of God, and read consoling books; but still they are bound, and there is no disputing it. As one that poureth vinegar upon nitre, so is he that singeth songs to a sad heart: there is an incongruity about the choicest joys when forced upon broken spirits. Some distressed souls are so sick that they abhor all manner of meat, and draw near unto the gates of death. Yet, if any one of my hearers be in this plight he may not despair, for Jesus can lift up those who are most bowed down."[44]

On another occasion he himself comforted troubled souls as he preached: "You all know what it is to be in the dark, and you know that material darkness is not comfortable. I remember being in a third-class railway carriage, with a large number of other people, travelling a long journey at night; and somebody struck a match, and lit a candle. That became the most cheerful part of the carriage, and our eyes could not help turning in that direction, for we did not like the darkness. Nobody does. There is a kind of mental darkness, in which you are disturbed, perplexed, worried, troubled,—not, perhaps, about anything tangible; you could not write down your troubles, it may be that you really have not any, but you feel troubled and dismayed. Other people say that you are nervous, and they blame you, and say, 'You ought not to give way in this manner.' That is what they think; but when a person gets into your present condition, that is the unkindest thing that anyone can possibly say, and the least likely to do any good to the poor troubled soul. I do not mind a trouble which I can see and understand. Manfully would I shoulder it in my Master's strength; but when the spirit itself is in the dark, one imagines a thousand evil things. Even good things themselves seem to be evil, and what should be to your encouragement becomes often a source of discouragement. Have any of you ever been in that condition? If you have, and if Jesus has not come to you then, I am sure that you have felt it very hard, and you have greatly needed his presence.

"There are a great many of you who appear to have a large stock of faith, but it is only because you are in very good health and your business is prospering. If you happened to get a disordered liver, or your business should fail, I should not be surprised if nine parts out of ten of your wonderful faith should evaporate. I have noticed that certain brethren, who talk about being perfect, are generally persons of robust constitution, with a very comfortable income, and not much to do except to go about to conferences and conventions, and talk about themselves; but the tried people of God do not often ride upon those high horses. They have to cry out very frequently, and they have so many anxieties and cares which, although they cast them upon the Lord, make them realize that they are not yet pure spirits, but are still in the body. Let a man have a bad headache for about half an hour, and let him see whether he does not feel himself to be mortal."[45]

And for those who totally despair, Spurgeon's word for all the centuries until Christ returns would be: "His people never can be in a place where he cannot get at them.

"And what is more,—let this comfort you,—*he will come to you, for he did come to his disciples*. He came walking on the water, and so reached them, and he will come for you also."[46]

It is not security, but carnal security which we would kill;
not confidence, but fleshly confidence which we would overthrow;
not peace, but false peace which we would destroy.[1]

It may be possible that you are only barren in your own esteem.
It is possible that God may have blessed you to many, though you
think he has never blessed you to one. . . . though you thought you
did not succeed the other day in your attempt, it is just possible that
you are not a good judge of your own success.[2]

2

CONFIDENCE

"Before I found Christ I hated myself," said an attractive young woman at the end of a class I was teaching. "Then," she continued, "I became a Christian and I felt a confidence I had never known before."

With a look of despair on her face she explained her dilemma. "Since coming to know Christ I've been going to church and listening to sermons that always seem to say how bad I am. Now once again I almost feel as I did when I started, down on myself and depressed." To her the choice seemed to be either to doubt God and his seemingly negative estimate of her or to trust God and hate herself. Either way, it would seem, she would have to continue through life disillusioned and insecure. In essence she would have to go back to feeling the self-doubt she had experienced all her life, up to the time she became a Christian.

As we enter the third millennium, one of the greatest destructive concepts arising out of the increased acceptance of psychotherapy is the sense of me-ism, which relegates God to our errand boy and the needs of our fellow man to insignificance next to our own. Old-fashioned ideals like loyalty and self-sacrifice seem foreign to our way of thinking, and the notion of the absolute sovereignty of God over our lives is repugnant to many. We'd prefer to do it our way.

On the other hand, those who oppose such a view of man often counteract it with an opposite extreme: that confidence is sinful and that self-hate is godly. From this point of view, God, who is the perfect Creator, in an off moment made junk when he created man. This attitude implies that God who is the God of truth wants his creation to deny any good qualities that he gave them. God-given talents are denied with a self-deprecatory "I'm not very good at what I'm doing" attitude. Achievements, when commended, are brushed aside with "Oh, it wasn't that important" or some similar statement indicating that what was done was either an unusual happening or really wasn't that great a job after all. In the process humility becomes a smarmy self-hate rather than the simple freedom from self-occupation that accompanies a good self-image.

When Spurgeon talks about self-esteem he can appear contradictory at times. While approving of self-confidence in one place he seems to disapprove in another. The key to understanding his position lies in paying close attention to the context in which the words are used. When he is speaking of the self of the old nature of Romans 6, he calls it sin. Therefore when he is emphasizing our judicial standing before God apart from Christ, he is clear in his belief that before God our righteousness is as filthy rags. On the other hand, he is very affirming about having confidence in our God-given abilities to do a task and to feel positive about a task well done.

Spurgeon achieves perfect balance in understanding the sinfulness of man; at the same time he fully appreciates that we are made in the very image of God. A similar pattern of balanced biblical thinking is also exhibited in his dealing with emotions like anxiety, depression, and loneliness. He does not automatically relegate these feelings to sinfulness, but at the same time he never forgets that sin does at times play a part.

Spurgeon illustrates biblical balance when he discusses the Old Testament example of Jacob's dealing with Laban. Remember that Laban had dealt dishonestly with Jacob—making a business deal of seven years' labor for the marriage of Laban's daughter Rachel and then after seven years adding seven more. In a sermon on humility and prayer Spurgeon says of Jacob: "I do not think that Jacob could have prayed unless he had stripped off the robes of self-justification which he wore in his controversy with Laban, and had stood disrobed before the infinite majesty of the Most High.

"Observe that he here speaks *not as before man, but as before God;* and he cries, 'I am not worthy of the least of all thy mercies.'" Before God he was not worthy. But before man, before Laban in particular, Spurgeon explained, Jacob was talking to a man "who had made a slave of him, who had used him in the most mercenary manner, and who had now pursued him in fierce anger because he had quitted his service with his wives and children that he might go back to his native country. To Laban he does not say, 'I am not worthy of what I possess,' for, as far as churlish Laban was concerned, he was worthy of a great deal more than had ever been rendered to him in the form of wage. To Laban he uses many truthful sentences of self-vindication and justification. Laban's substance had greatly increased under Jacob's unceasing care. He cared for Laban's flocks with constant diligence, and he says, 'In the day the drought consumed me, and the frost by night; and my sleep departed from mine eyes.' He declares that he had never taken a ram of the flock wherewith to feed his own family; that he had, in fact, for many years worked with no wages except the daughters who became his wives; and he goes the length of saying, 'Except the God of my father, the God of Abraham, and the fear of Isaac, had been with me, surely thou hadst sent me away now empty.' The same man who speaks in that fashion to Laban turns round and confesses to his God, 'I am not worthy of the least of all thy mercies.' This is perfectly consistent and truthful. Humility is not telling falsehoods against yourself; humility is forming a right estimate of yourself. As towards Laban it was a correct estimate for a man who had worked so hard for so little to claim that he had a right to what God had given him; and yet as before God it was perfectly honest and sincere of Jacob to say, 'I am not worthy of the least of all thy mercies, and of all the truth, which thou hast showed unto thy servant.'"[3]

In speaking of the centurion in Matthew 8:8, Spurgeon comments: "This centurion was a worthy man from the human point of view; but he called himself unworthy when he turned towards our Lord. He was so excellent a man that the elders of the Jews, who were by no means partial to Roman soldiers, pleaded with Jesus that he was worthy. Had he been personally there, he would have repudiated their plea; and he did so by the second party of friends whom he sent to our Lord. As one set of friends had said, 'He is worthy,' another set of friends was bidden to say, in his name, 'Lord, I am not worthy.' The worthiest men in the world do not think themselves worthy; while the most unworthy people are generally those who boast of their own worthiness, and, possibly, of their own perfection. We should not have wondered had this man been proud; for he was one of the conquering race, and the representative of a tyrannical power. If he was not a very great officer, but only the captain of a hundred men, yet it is not unusual for petty officers to be more haughty than their superiors. If a man is placed in a very high and responsible position, he is frequently sobered by his responsibilities; but a mere jack-in-office is usually greater than the emperor himself. However, this centurion was a man of gentle mould, and said of himself, 'I am not worthy.'"[4]

Low self-esteem may well be one of the greatest hindrances to spiritual growth. If I hate myself, I am more likely to imagine disapproval from others when it doesn't even exist. I am also more likely to lose my temper over trivia because so many things threaten me deeply. I will be also less likely to apologize to my brother because I will need to be perceived as always right, even to myself. Or I may apologize endlessly for anything I am accused of because I'm so sure that I must be wrong. In this context low self-esteem is the devil's tool. It gives him an opportunity or vehicle through which to perform his havoc, for he is the prince of lies and deception.

Adolf Eichmann, the killer of the Jews of Budapest among others, had succeeded at nothing until he became *somebody* in the Nazi Party during World War II. Killing Jews was the only thing he ever did well. Adolf Hitler wanted to be a great artist, but nobody in Germany's art galleries perceived any talent in him. So he went on failing until he found success as a political leader who masterminded the killing of 6 million Jews, 3 million non-Jews, and the casualties of a world war. Other major factors enter in. But one cannot help but wonder what the course of that period of history would have been if Hitler and Eichmann had both succeeded early in their lives. Maybe then their insecurity would not have been so great that it combined with other spiritual and political factors that in truth made them lash out at the world as mass killers. Low self-esteem does not always evoke evil. Nor does evil need human self-deprecation in order to succeed. But it helps, and Satan often uses the fragility of the human ego as a vehicle for evil.

True balance demands that we acknowledge and use those talents that God has given us. "No man ought to court publicity for his virtue, or notoriety for his zeal, but, at the same time, it is a sin to be always seeking to hide that which God has bestowed upon us for the good of others. A Christian is not to be a city in a valley—he is to be 'a city set upon a hill;' he is not to be a candle put under a bushel, but a candle in a candlestick, giving light to all. Retirement may be lovely in the eyes of some, and the hiding of oneself is doubtless a blessed thing, but the hiding of *Christ in* us can never be justified, and the keeping back of truth which is precious to ourselves, is a sin against our kind, and an offence against God. Those of you who are of a nervous temperament and of retired habits of life must take care that you do not too much indulge your natural propensity, lest you should be useless to the Church. Seek in the name of him who was not ashamed of you to do some little violence to your feelings, and tell to others what Christ has told to you. Keep not the secret—it is too precious—it too much concerns the vital interests of man. Speak! if thou canst not with trumpet tongue, yet speak with still small voice. If the pulpit must not be thy tribune, if the press may not carry on its wings thy words, yet say, as Peter and John did, 'Silver and gold have I none, but such as I have give I unto thee.' And speak, too, as thou canst—gently to ones, if not loudly to twenties; quietly to twos, if not publicly to scores. By Sychar's well talk to the Samaritan woman, if thou canst not on the mountain preach the sermon; in the house, if not in the temple; in the field, if not upon the exchange; in the midst of thine own household, if thou canst not in the midst of the great family of man. At any rate, hide not thy talent; wrap it not up."[5]

Balance in the area of self-worth seems consistent with the biblical teaching that God is a God of truth. "There is no humility in such self-depreciation as would lead you to deny what God has wrought in you, or wrought by you: that might be willful falsehood, and certainly would be grievous error. Falsehood is not a constituent element of anything that is gracious; we are not required to call five talents one in order to be humble. If we make a fair and just estimate of ourselves we shall certainly discover nothing therein to boast about, and we shall not then be likely to borrow from the lips of others words and confessions which do not accurately represent our character, or state our feelings; and ought not, therefore, to be employed by us."[6]

A radio preacher of some depth in teaching sprinkles self-deprecating remarks throughout his sermons. "I'm not that well read but. . . . I'm no authority on theology but. . . . I'm no example but. . . ." He usually goes on to preach in a way that proves he *is* indeed well read or authoritative or a good example. Some people interpret his behavior as modest. In actuality the behavior indicates a rather extensive lack of self-confidence.

In his private life his behavior reflects his low self-esteem even more clearly. His wife dominates him, and even his children rule. Yet with someone under him, like a clerk in a store or a teenager mowing his lawn, he can be overly sensitive. For example, he once misunderstood totally when a perfect stranger admitted that he didn't always listen to his broadcast. To the preacher it meant that the stranger didn't like his broadcast, and the preacher treated the stranger abruptly as a result. In general because of his low self-esteem he fawns over people of importance, cannot accept criticism even when it is warranted, feels wrong in areas of his life where he is actually right, and in ultimate frustration takes his anger out at anyone who will take it.

Aptly Spurgeon continues, "The mimicry of humility is a very common piece of masquerading. You shall find persons speaking in very lowly terms of themselves, but they do not expect you to believe them. A brother who has called himself worldly in prayer, if you should tell him in private conversation that you were glad to hear his truthful description of himself, would not take it all kindly, but would ask who and what are you that you should judge him; he is as spiritual as you are, and perhaps more so. A monk, we remember, confessed that he was so great a sinner that he had broken all the commandments, and when afterwards one of his friends began to charge him with breaking first one commandment and then another, the hypocrite averred that he had not broken any one of them. Men are so little humble that when they smite on their breasts they may be still boasting in their hearts. Mock humility creeps around us, cringing and fawning, but every honest man loathes it, and we may be sure that God loathes it too."[7]

A Bible teacher I once knew made the comment that low self-esteem helps people trust God more. There is a certain aspect of truth to that statement in that desperation can drive people to God. However, it can also drive people away from God in bitterness and hopelessness. What often happens is that when people begin to develop self-confidence they become free enough to make real choices. They are no longer paralyzed by fear and self-doubt. A man who is afraid to confront his superiors for a deserved pay raise, for example, and then gains in self-confidence is presented with the choice of when and how to make his request. When his self-confidence is low he will either ignore the subject or he will ask poorly by becoming overly demanding or by losing his temper. "You owe me more money," he may scream. "You've never been fair to me." But with more confidence he may say in a calm tone of voice: "I would appreciate your consideration of a raise in pay. I've been here two years and my responsibilities have gradually increased. Perhaps we can talk when it's convenient."

In speaking of the apostle Paul, Spurgeon explains: "Now, if the apostle had said that he was not an apostle at all, that he had never suffered anything for Christ, or done anything to spread the gospel, he would have been speaking, as some say, 'humbly'; but this is a mistake—he would have been telling lies. He therefore does nothing of the kind. He says that he is not a whit behind the very chief of the apostles, speaks of his sufferings and his toils, and of the manifestations of divine grace to his soul; and yet for all that he finishes his detail of experience by saying, 'Though I be nothing.' Brethren, do not deny what God has done for you, or by you. Look at all of it and value it, and bless the Lord for it;

but still when all is said and done you must—nay, I trust you cheerfully will—come back to this, 'Though I be nothing.'"[8]

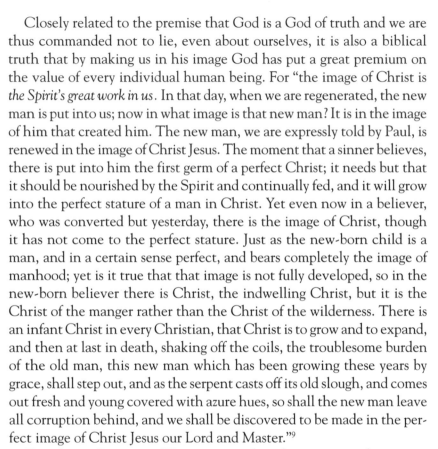

Closely related to the premise that God is a God of truth and we are thus commanded not to lie, even about ourselves, it is also a biblical truth that by making us in his image God has put a great premium on the value of every individual human being. For "the image of Christ is *the Spirit's great work in us*. In that day, when we are regenerated, the new man is put into us; now in what image is that new man? It is in the image of him that created him. The new man, we are expressly told by Paul, is renewed in the image of Christ Jesus. The moment that a sinner believes, there is put into him the first germ of a perfect Christ; it needs but that it should be nourished by the Spirit and continually fed, and it will grow into the perfect stature of a man in Christ. Yet even now in a believer, who was converted but yesterday, there is the image of Christ, though it has not come to the perfect stature. Just as the new-born child is a man, and in a certain sense perfect, and bears completely the image of manhood; yet is it true that that image is not fully developed, so in the new-born believer there is Christ, the indwelling Christ, but it is the Christ of the manger rather than the Christ of the wilderness. There is an infant Christ in every Christian, that Christ is to grow and to expand, and then at last in death, shaking off the coils, the troublesome burden of the old man, this new man which has been growing these years by grace, shall step out, and as the serpent casts off its old slough, and comes out fresh and young covered with azure hues, so shall the new man leave all corruption behind, and we shall be discovered to be made in the perfect image of Christ Jesus our Lord and Master."[9]

For, claims Spurgeon, "Know ye not that the saints are the *masterpieces of his workmanship?* God has shown his wisdom in balancing the clouds, and guiding the stars in their orbits; infinite wisdom is discoverable in every flower and in every living thing; but the wisdom and the skill of God are far more clearly to be seen in the believer, than in any other work of the divine hand. Man, born the first time, was fearfully and wonderfully made, but new-created, and regenerated, he is far more full of marvels than he was before. Well therefore, because of the divine skill which has been shown in our re-creation, may we be the objects of divine care.

"When Bernard Palissy had, after long struggles, invented that valuable ware which still remains unmatched, we can suppose that, if a person had entered his room and broken those invaluable dishes, which were worth their weight in gold, he would have said, 'I had sooner that you had burnt my house, or that you had maimed my person, than break these things which have cost me so much thought, so many trials in the furnace, and so much daily watching, and nightly care.' When the poor man had pulled up the very floor of his room, to heat the furnace for the last time, before he saw the precious stuff come from the crucible, his work must have been dear to him; and when we think that God, our God, hath made his people the objects of his eternal thoughts, the trophies of his noblest skill, vessels of honour fit even for the Master's use, it is but little wonder that he should guard them with a jealous care, even as men do the apple of their eye.

"Moreover, all the people of God are the object of *the dearest purchase* that was ever known, since they were redeemed not with corruptible things, as with silver and gold, but with the precious blood of Christ. Stand ye at the foot of Calvary, and let the groans of Christ pierce your heart; behold his head crowned with thorns; see ye his hands and his feet streaming like fountains of blood; think for a moment of the awful anguish which his spirit suffered, of the unknown pangs he bore, when he redeemed our souls unto God; and you will readily conclude that love so amazing, which could pay a price so stupendous, would not easily loose its hold of that which it has thus purchased unto itself. We think little of ourselves, when we value ourselves at any thing less than the price which Jesus paid; we dishonour the Lord which bought us, if we think ourselves only fit to live unto the flesh, and to this poor temporary world; when, indeed, we are fitted for a heavenly world, and for divinest purposes, seeing that Christ the Son of the Highest shed his very heart's blood to redeem us from our sins. Well, I say, may he value highly, those whom he has so dearly bought!

"Yet, again, no doubt there is a special reason why God is thus jealous over his people, since he who touches them, does to a certain degree, touch *the person of Christ*—the Father's firstborn. Are they not members of his body, of his flesh, and of his bones?"[10]

Furthermore, in reference to God's word to the apostle Paul, when he was yet "Saul" and was persecuting Christians, Spurgeon says: "The cry of Christ from heaven, 'Saul, Saul, why persecutest thou me?' clearly shows that Christ looks upon the persecution of humble men and women as an insult to himself. Should any wound your hand and then say, 'I have not injured *you*;' you would reply, 'But it is *my* hand and it is so much a part of myself that I cannot separate myself from the injury.' So is it with Christ, the poorest, meanest, most illiterate Christian, is in the closest union with the glorious head of the body, and it will be at the foeman's eternal hazard if he touch him since he is part of Christ's mystical body. If you hurt his people wilfully, the Son of man will say, 'Inasmuch as ye did it unto one of the least of these my brethren, ye have done it unto me,' and the recompense shall follow."[11]

The church, the body of Christ, has a similar relationship with its various members. As I was finishing a manuscript, I needed some last quiet moments—and a lot of help—in order to complete my work on time. A friend and I went to the beach, where I rented a cabin. I was able to give her a week at the ocean. She cooked and ran errands. Another friend called long distance because he hoped I was doing well as the week drew toward its end. Another friend came down for two days and typed for me. Interrelatedly, we helped each other with the skills and time that we possessed. And each person involved felt a greater sense of worth for what he or she gave and received in the relationship.

On a superficial level, this is what the church is to be doing. On a deeper level, one must consider all the gifts of the Spirit that are listed, like teaching, prophecy, healing, miracles, wisdom, and faith. All these indicate the deep capacity the church has to minister to its members.

But the bottom line in a church that functions in such a way as to truly foster a good self-image among its members is contained in one word—*love*. We read in 1 Corinthians 13:2 that no spiritual gift has value without love. One cannot mitigate the power of that word *nothing*. "If I had the gift of faith so that I could speak to a mountain and make it move, I would still be worth *nothing at all without love*" (italics added). For it is love that spreads to another human being, like water received by dry, parched soil, and revives that person's being, making him or her feel that he or she is truly a person of worth. One little girl summed up the value of love very succinctly when she said, "I don't want to be a Christian like my mother but like my sister. She loves people."

Spurgeon concludes: "I know you read of what some great men have done for Jesus; what they have enjoyed of him; how much they have been like him; how they have been able to endure for his sake; and you say, 'Ah! as for me, I am but a worm; I can never attain to this.' There is nothing which one saint was that you may not be. There is no height of grace, no attainment of spirituality, no position or assurance, no post of duty, which is not open to you, if you have but the power to believe. Get ye up, get ye up from your dunghills; lay aside your sackcloth and your ashes. It is not meet that ye should grovel in the dust, oh children of a king."[12]

It is of interest to me that self-deprecation and self-worship seem to have become more polarized in our time than in Spurgeon's. Another British divine, F. B. Meyer, a contemporary of Spurgeon's, wrote essentially the same message as Spurgeon concerning the relationship of self-confidence and our being made in the image of God. In his commentary on Exodus Meyer states: "The first step toward self-reverence is to see God, to worship Him, to bow down before Him, to know that He is God alone, and then we begin to reverence the nature made in His image, which we are to hold sacred for His sake."[13]

Those who go to the extreme of self-hate are often immersed in a sense of guilt. Guilt that is experienced because of wrongdoing or even because of an accurate assessment of one's sinful nature is godly. If I sin, I should feel guilt. As I am aware of my natural depravity, I will cry out to God for deliverance. But balance is once again the issue. For unreasonable guilt, neurotic guilt, can be destructive to a person's effectiveness for God. Speaking of the danger of depending on the accuracy of mere feelings in this arena, Spurgeon commented: "It often happens that a man has the grace which he seeks for, and does not know he has it, because he makes a mistake as to what he should feel when he has the blessing. He has already got the boon which he asks God to give him. Let me just put it in another shape. If you are sorry because you cannot be sorry enough on account of sin, why you are already sorry. If you grieve because you cannot grieve enough, why you do grieve already. . . .

"My dear hearer, let me assure you for your comfort, that when you go down on your knees and say, 'Lord, I groan before thee, because I cannot groan; I cannot feel; Lord help me to feel;' why, you do feel, and you have got the repentance that you are asking for. At least you have got the first degree of it; you have got the mustard seed of repentance in tiny grain. Let it alone, it will grow; foster it with prayer and it will become a tree. The very grace which you are asking of God is speaking in your very prayer. It is repentance which asks God that I may repent more. It is a broken heart which asks God to break it. That is not a hard heart which says, 'Lord I have a hard heart; soften my heart.' It is a soft heart already. That is not a dead soul which says, 'Lord I am dead; quicken me.' Why, you are quickened. That man is not dumb who says, 'Lord I am dumb; make me speak.' Why, he speaks already; and that man who says, 'Lord I cannot feel,' why, he feels already. He is a sensible sinner already. So that you are just the man that Christ calls to him. . . .

"When we say that Christ came that there might be drink given to the thirsty, you are just the man we mean—you are thirsty. 'No,' you say, 'I don't feel that I am thirsty, I only wish I did.' Why, that wish to feel thirsty is your thirst. You are exactly the man; you are far nearer the character than if you said 'I do thirst, I have the qualification;' then, I should be afraid you had not got it. But, because you think you have it not, it is all the clearer proof that you have the qualification, if indeed there be any qualification. When I say, 'Come unto Christ all ye that labour and are heavy laden;' and you say, 'Oh, I don't feel heavy laden enough,' why, you are the very man the text means. And when I say, 'Whosoever will, let him come,' and you say, 'I wish I were more willing, I will to be willing,' why, you are the man. It is only one of Satan's quibbles—a bit of hell's infernal logic to drive you from Christ. Be a match for Satan now, this once and say 'Thou lying fiend, thou tellest me I do not feel my need of a saviour enough. I know I feel my need; and, *inasmuch as I long to feel it I do feel it*. Christ bids me come to him, and I will come—now, this morning. I will trust my soul, just as it is, in the hands of him whose body hung upon the tree. Sink or swim, here I am resting on him, and clinging to him as the rock of my salvation.'"[14]

And if we are to acknowledge our own strong qualities, we are certainly to affirm others so that they might be encouraged to continue in a right direction. Spurgeon once preached: "I do not think that we should be so slow as we sometimes are in praising one another. There is a general theory abroad that it is quite right and proper to point out to a brother all his imperfections, for it will be a salutary medicine to him, and prevent his being too happy in this vale of tears. Is it supposed that we shall cheer him on to do better by always finding fault with him? If so, some people ought to be very good by this time, for they have had candid friends in plenty. Find fault with a brother and he will be kept from growing too proud; and he will, no doubt, go forward blessing you very much for your kind consideration in promoting his humility. Remember also that it is so much to the increase of brotherly love to have a clear eye to see the imperfections of our friends. Does anyone in his senses think so? I should suppose that after having given a sufficient trial to that manner of procedure, it would be quite as well at times to try another, and to rejoice in everything which we see of grace in our brethren, and sometimes to thank God in their hearing for what we perceive in them that we are sure is the fruit of the Spirit. If they are what they should be, they will not think so much of our little praises as to be unduly exalted thereby; but they will be sometimes so encouraged as to be nerved to higher and nobler things. If a man deserves my commendation, I am only paying a debt when I give it to him, and it is dishonest to withhold it under the pretence that he would not use the payment rightly. Men who deserve praise can bear it, and some of them even need it. I should not wonder that the kindly words of God's people may be but a rehearsal of that 'Well done, good and faithful servant' which will one day sound in their ears; and be a useful rehearsal, too, helping them on their weary way. Good men have many conflicts, let us minister to their comfort. At any rate, the great Head of the church did not think it unwise to say to the church at Philadelphia that he thought well of it because it had kept his word. Let us give honour to whom honour is due, and encourage those who are aiming to do right."[15]

Continuing this thought Spurgeon adds: "For one word may be enough to bring you consolation!"[16]

We humans are both very strong and very fragile. We have a strength that can survive the horror of Dachau and at the same time egos that cannot tolerate a social slight or rejection by one we love.

G. K. Chesterton once wrote, "I felt and feel that life itself is as bright as the diamond but as brittle as the windowpane, and when the heavens were compared to the terrible crystal I can remember a shudder. I was afraid that God would drop the Cosmos with a crash.

"Remember, however, that to be breakable is not the same as to be perishable. Strike a glass, and it will not endure an instant; simply do not strike it, and it will endure a thousand years."[17]

We too are often breakable—but not perishable. We can endure much suffering, but, like the piece of glass windowpane, one sharp blow can almost do us in. How sharp that blow must be and how breakable we are depend largely on the strength of our self-images.

There is a danger in needless self-deprecation going so far at times as to refuse the very grace of God because of one's unworthiness. "There are some whose sense of unworthiness *turns to sullen rebellion*. I will not speak harshly of them; but I do know some few who frequent these courts, of whom I must say that they are their own jailors and tormenters. Like one of old, they must confess, 'My soul refused to be comforted.'"[18]

Spurgeon is very sensitive to the times when a person will be most vulnerable to excuses in either direction relating to self-esteem. Some circumstances tend to drive a person to underevaluate himself, others to overevaluate himself.

For example: "The dark side of much that is called Christian experience is not the work of the Holy Spirit at all. In many, it is occasioned by a natural crabbedness of disposition: some are so hard that God must use iron wedges with them before their hearts will be reached. There are men with such a proud spirit, that they need to be brought down to feed a swine before they will arise and go to their Father. Others are obstinate, and wear a brow of brass; and these must be made faint with labour before they will yield. In many instances, the mental distress which attends the work of the Spirit is produced by sickness of body: it is not repentance, but indigestion or some other evil agency depressing the spirits. A sluggish liver will produce most of those fearsome forebodings which we are so ready to regard as spiritual emotions. There is such a blending of the physical with the mental, that it is hard to name our feelings."[19]

And of a more subtle nature: "High places and God's praise do seldom well agree; a full cup is not easily carried without spilling, and he that stands on a pinnacle needs a clear head and much grace."[20]

Yet Spurgeon has great insight into the value God places on us regardless of our status or level of perfection. In a word of our day, he is *affirming*. "What should you think if Jesus should meet you at the close of the day, and say to you, 'I am pleased with the works of to-day?' I know you would reply, 'Lord, I have done nothing for thee.' You would say like those at the last day, 'Lord, when saw we thee hungry and fed thee? when saw we thee thirsty and gave thee drink?' You would begin to deny that you had done any good thing. He would say, 'Ah, when thou wast under the fig tree I saw thee; when thou wast at thy bedside in prayer I heard thee; I saw thee when the tempter came, and thou saidst, "Get thee hence, Satan;" I saw thee give thine alms to one of my poor sick children; I heard thee speak a good word to the little child and teach him the name of Jesus; I heard thee groan when swearing polluted thine ears; I heard thy sigh when thou sawest the iniquity of this great city; I saw thee when thine hands were busy; I saw that thou wast not an eye-servant or a man-pleaser, but that in singleness of purpose thou didst serve God in doing thy daily business; I saw thee, when the day was ended, give thyself to God again; I have marked thee mourning over the sins thou hast committed, and I tell thee I am pleased with thee.' 'The smell of thy garments is like the smell of Lebanon.'

"And, again, I hear you say, 'But, Lord, I was angry, I was proud;' and he says, 'But I have covered up this, I have cast it into the depths of the sea; I have blotted it all out with my blood. I can see no ill in thee; thou art all fair, my love, there is no spot in thee.' What would you do then? Would you not at once fall down at his feet and say, 'Lord, I never knew love like this: I have heard that love covers a multitude of sins, but I never knew a love so broad as to cover all mine. And then to declare that thou canst see no sin in me at all—ah! that is love?' It may melt our heart, and make us seek to be holy, that we might not grieve Christ, make us labour to be diligent in his service, that we might not dishonour him.

"I dare say some of you think when ministers preach or go about to do their pastoral duty, that of course Christ is very much pleased with them. 'Ah,' says Mary, 'I am only a poor servant girl; I have to get up in the morning and light the fire, lay out the breakfast things, dust the parlour, make the pies and puddings for dinner, and clear away the things again, and wash them up—I have to do everything there is to do in the house—Christ cannot be pleased with this.' Why Mary, you can serve Christ as much in making beds, as I can in making sermons; and you can be as much a true servant of Christ in dusting a room, as I can in administering discipline in a church. Do not think for a single moment that you cannot serve Christ. Our religion is to be an everyday religion—a religion for the kitchen as well as for the parlour, a religion for the rolling pin, and the jack-towel, quite as much as for the pulpit stairs and the Bible—a religion that we can take with us wherever we go. And there is such a thing as glorifying Christ in all the common actions of life."[21]

Many times we fight semantics more than meaning when we talk about self-image. A person is said to have a "big ego" when he boasts, when in actuality he is usually so lacking in confidence that he brags more for his own ears to hear than those of anyone else. A person who has to tell you how great he is usually has little self-confidence. The person who says she is no good and the person who claims to be perfect have the same problem of low self-esteem. They just express it differently. Neither arrogant pride nor groveling self-hate have anything to do with a good self-image. Nor, as has been said, does the word *self* as it is used here have any relationship to the "self" of Romans 6 (KJV), where it relates to the old sin nature for which Christ died.

In an interesting commentary on the words *meek* and *pride* Spurgeon says first of the word *meek*: "It is used in the New Testament in the third beatitude—'Blessed are the meek, for they shall inherit the earth;' and by Peter, when speaking of 'the ornament of a meek and quiet spirit.' Of our Lord also it is said—'Behold thy king cometh for thee, meek, and sitting upon an ass, and a colt the foal of an ass.' The original word has the significations of 'mild, gentle, soft, meek.' Such is the heart of Christ. . . . Our Saviour, who never sought the praise of man, says of himself, 'I am meek,' because he desired to remove the fears of those who trembled to approach him, and would win the allegiance of those who feared to become his followers, lest his service should prove too severe. He, in effect, cried, 'Come to me, ye offending men, ye who feel your unworthiness, ye who think that your transgressions may provoke my anger; come to me, for I am meek.'"[22] In another place Spurgeon says: "Humility is a thing which must be genuine; the imitation of it is the nearest thing in the world to pride."[23] And in another: "It is not humility to underrate yourself."[24]

On the other hand, relating to the word *pride*, Spurgeon continues: "It would be no pride for a man to say, 'I am strong,' if he would thereby induce a drowning person to trust him for the saving of his life; neither would it be wrong for a person to say, as a physician practically does say, 'I am wise in medicine,' in order to lead a dying person to take the medicine which he felt sure would heal him. We may and must assert ourselves, and avow those qualities which are truly ours, if, by so doing, a great benefit can be bestowed upon others, and Jesus therefore saith, 'I am meek,' because this gentle attribute would silence fear, and lead the timid to approach him and learn of him."[25]

While Spurgeon admonishes his reader to give an honest estimate of himself, he is always on guard for the extremes either way and maintains a rather incredible consistency throughout his works. Using the word *self-esteem* as we would use the word *pride* when it implies arrogance rather than satisfaction over a job well done, he warns, "Self-esteem is a moth which frets the garments of virtue. Those flies, those pretty flies of self-praise, must be killed, for if they get into your pot of ointment they will spoil it all. Forget the past; thank God who has made you pray so well; thank God who has made you kind, gentle, or humble; thank God who has made you give liberally; but forget it all and go forward, since there is yet very much land to be possessed!"[26]

In like manner, in a very lovely summation of the essence of true humility, Spurgeon once said: "Where there is the most precious grace, there is always a jewel-case of humility to keep it in."[27]

To further clarify the terms, *self-esteem* or *self-image* is the view that one holds regarding oneself. It is the estimate one makes of one's worth. Sometimes that estimate is accurate; sometimes it is not. At times it is an unconscious attitude, for it is often too painful for people to face what they really think about themselves. The person who drinks excessively in order to "get courage" to fulfill obligations may only rarely admit that he or she does not like him- or herself. Even more rarely would the conceited person who claims to be better at everything than anybody else admit or even realize that conceit is an unrealistic cover for self-hate. Among Christians and non-Christians alike, the terms *low self-esteem, conceit, pride,* and *humility* have become confused and often distorted.

Low self-esteem is a feeling of worthlessness about oneself. Sometimes the feeling is conscious. At other times, it is very unconscious. Excessive drinking or pill taking, high levels of generalized anger, self-pity, excessive shyness, loudness at parties, depression, a martyrlike attitude, and even many physical symptoms may in essence stem from a low self-image.

The advertising business is tuned in to this tendency to doubt ourselves and the temptation to meet the need for greater self-esteem by the use of superficial, easy answers. Prestige cars, clothes that sell more for their labels than for their quality, impressive homes, and the need for important friends who have the right jobs and social status are all feeble, ineffective ways to feel worth. The result of using such things to elevate one's sense of worth is zero. Yet millions are spent every year on such things. In spite of our attempts at easy answers, low self-esteem is a very real problem in our society and is probably the root factor in most people's emotional problems.

It cannot be emphasized enough that frequently a low self-image and a good self-image are confused with the biblical concepts of humility and pride. Humility is not groveling. It does not imply hating oneself or putting oneself down. True humility could best be defined as an absence of occupation with oneself, because people who truly like themselves do not have to keep evaluating their worth. They forget themselves in their tasks or in other people.

A few months ago, I visited a college professor who had done extensive research in a specific area of psychotherapy. I had done considerable reading on the subject but *he* was the expert. Expecting him to expound on his ideas, I was surprised to hear him asking me questions. When I gave answers, he seemed pleased with many of them and asked more. To me, he was the great scholar. Yet he himself acted with humility. He was confident, pleased with his work, anxious to learn more, and eager to teach. He accepted himself so fully that he was free enough from himself to be involved in someone else's thinking.

In contrast, a false humility—when people tell you that they are not good at their jobs at all, though they are actually very proficient—is not humility at all but is just another manifestation of low self-esteem. Yet I have heard Christians say such things as "If you don't think much of yourself, God is more free to help you." To the contrary, I have found that people who truly like themselves are more likely to be free and strong enough to trust God. When we trust ourselves, we find it easier to trust others, including God.

Conceit, too, is often misunderstood, particularly among Christians. The Psalms say that God hates a proud heart above all. In Psalm 131:1, we have a good definition of pride: "Lord, I am not proud and haughty . . . I don't pretend to 'know it all.'" To "know it all" is the essence of conceit. Conceit actually reflects a *low* self-image. The teacher who says to his or her class, "I'm the best teacher you could have," is really saying, "I hope I'm OK." That person is trying to convince him- or herself and the class that he or she is at least adequate as a teacher. Such people brag, hoping above all that they will eventually believe themselves. It is accurate to conclude that if I'm sure I'm OK I don't have to tell you about it. If I'm sure I'm OK, I probably won't ever have to *think* about it. If I'm sure I'm OK, I will have a positive view of myself that will free me from pride and make me truly humble.

In an apparently unpublished, handwritten work by Spurgeon, I found the following insight on self-esteem. Even at the end of life, confidence in what we have been as well as what we have done should comfort us. "When the Lord Jesus came to Paul . . . He said, 'Be of good cheer, Paul:

for thou hath testified of Me in Jerusalem.' This comfort lay in an assurance that his work was accepted of his Master. . . .

"'Thou hast testified of Me in Jerusalem.' It's true that the apostle had done so; but he was too humble to console himself with the fact till his Lord gave him leave to do so by uttering gracious words of praise. . . . It may be that your conscience makes you more familiar with faults than with your services. You rather sigh than sing as you look back, but your loving Lord covers all your failures, and commends you for what His grace enabled you to do in the way of witness bearing. It must be sweet to you to hear Him say, 'I know your work, for thou hast a little strength and hast kept My word and hast not denied My name.' Be faithful to your Lord, dear reader, if you are now in prosperity, for thus you will be laying up a store of cheery memories for years to come. To look back upon a well-spent life need not cause a storm of legal boasting, but it may justly create much holy rejoicing. Paul was able to rejoice that he had not run in vain, neither labored in vain, and happy are we if we can do the same."[28]

In the same manuscript, Spurgeon expands the idea one step further. In speaking of the lepers whom Christ healed, he reminds us that although ten were healed, only one returned to thank. Says Spurgeon: "Were there not ten changed? We sometimes cry, 'Where are the nine? Where are the nine?'" Then in comparison Spurgeon refers to Bartimaeus, whose sight was restored: "But this man immediately [after] he received his sight followed Jesus in the way. . . . he used his sight for the best purpose—to see his God."[29]

Concludes Spurgeon: "If God has given your soul peace and joy and liberty, use your new found liberty in delighting yourself in Him."[30]

After years of working with people in a counseling setting, I have come to realize that when a person develops a good self-image, it does not necessarily follow that he or she will use that newfound confidence for God. There is always the temptation to use it to more effectively earn money for selfish needs or to engage in social endeavors that are contrary to godliness. With added self-confidence anyone can assert his or her rights and use that ability for selfish ends. Me-ism is the result.

This is where the power of choice enters in, for God has made us people who can choose between right and wrong. Once a person's confidence is restored—or depression is gone or anxiety is lifted—there is a moral obligation to choose to use the newfound freedom for God's glory.

The same principle is true in the physical realm. A person who trusted God well under the cloud of illness can use his newfound health to please himself or to serve God more effectively.

Confidence, when it is under the control of God, can be an attractive quality. On the other hand, a lack of self-esteem can be very unattractive. Good friends gathered at a dinner party. The conversation flowed, healthy debate ensued, and the evening seemed to end with a sense of well-being and goodwill. A few days later one of the people received a phone message from another, which in essence said: "You put me down the other night. You don't think I'm bright or have any good ideas." Stunned, the recipient of the phone call shared the message with several others who had been present. No one agreed. No one could relate. What became clear was that the person who felt injured had been extremely oversensitive and had shown his feelings of inadequacy. But as so often happens, he not only suffered as a result of his self-image, but he deeply hurt the innocent object of his attack and put a limitation on further interaction between the whole group of people involved. Feelings of inadequacy damage relationships.

The subject of self-esteem, by whatever words you use to express the issue of confidence, is one that is fundamental to the well-being of any individual, but it is a subject that is often exaggerated, abused, distorted. Describing the idea of balance as the goal in such debates, Spurgeon once defined balance in a graphic manner: "We do not want to see a truth, and therefore we say we cannot see it. On the other hand, there are others who push a truth too far. 'This is good; oh! this is precious!' say they, and then they think it is good for everything; that in fact it is the only truth in the world. You know how often things are injured by over-praise; how a good medicine, which really was a great boon for a certain disease, comes to be despised utterly by the physician, because a certain quack has praised it up as being a universal cure; so puffery in doctrine leads to its dishonour. Truth has thus suffered on all sides; on the one hand brethren would not see all the truth, and on the other hand they magnified out of proportion that which they did see. You have seen those mirrors, those globes that are sometimes hung up in gardens; you walk up to them and you see your head ten times as large as your body, or you walk away and put yourself in another position, and then your feet are monstrous and the rest of your body is small; this is an ingenious toy, but I am sorry to say that many go to work with God's truth upon the model of this toy; they magnify one capital truth, till it becomes monstrous; they minify and speak little of another truth till it becomes altogether forgotten."[31]

On Lord's Day morning November 17, 1867, Spurgeon used Galatians 2:20 (KJV) as his text: "I am crucified with Christ: nevertheless I live; yet not I, but Christ liveth in me: and the life which I now live in the flesh I live by the faith of the Son of God, who loved me, and gave himself for me."[32]

Of that verse he said something that concisely states the biblical view of good self-esteem: "How many personal pronouns of the first person are there in this verse? Are there not as many as eight? It swarms with *I* and *me*. The text deals not with the plural at all; it does not mention some one else, nor a third party far away, but the apostle treats of himself, his own inner life, his own spiritual death, the love of Christ to *him*, and the great sacrifice which Christ made for *him*. 'Who loved *me* and gave himself for *me*.' This is instructive, for it is a distinguishing mark of the Christian religion, that it brings out a man's individuality. It does not make us selfish, on the contrary, it cures us of that evil, but still it does manifest in us a self-hood by which we become conscious of our personal individuality in an eminent degree."[33]

I often feel very grateful to God that I have undergone fearful depression of spirits. I know the borders of despair, and the horrible brink of that gulf of darkness into which my feet have almost gone; but hundreds of times I have been able to give a helpful grip to brethren and sisters who have come into that same condition, which grip I could never have given if I had not known their deep despondency. So I believe that the darkest and most dreadful experience of a child of God will help him to be a fisher of men if he will but follow Christ. Keep close to your Lord and he will make every step a blessing to you.[1]

3

DEPRESSION

"If I ever 'crack up,'" a colleague said to me over an evening meal, "I know I will do it by being depressed. Everyone has a psychological vulnerability," he continued, "and I think that if the pressure ever got too great for me, it is in the area of depression that my symptoms would occur."

I had to admit I had never thought of how I would "crack up," should that time ever come. Yet as he spoke I knew my own vulnerability would not be depression; it would be anxiety. Instantly I had related to what he was saying. Perhaps, therefore, he had a point about each of us having one area of vulnerability where our own unique psychological symptoms would come out.

Others share my colleague's supposed area of weakness. I thought of the five-year-old child who ran in front of cars crying, "Don't stop me, I want to die." I thought of an elderly woman who suffered from depression for years and was refined into fine gold before she was finally released from its pain. She reminded me of those saints in Hebrews 11 who suffered and of whom the Bible says this world is not worthy.

I thought, too, of the "confess-your-depression" type Christians I have met who seemed to have suffered little, but who criticize much. Most of all, I reflected on those people who seek counseling from people like me, people who battle quietly with depression and feel inadequate because of their pain. "If I were a better Christian" or "If I were stronger" are phrases that ring in my ears.

In the midst of my thoughts I tended to feel that if human beings, even Christian human beings, have one major area of vulnerability psychologically, perhaps it *is* depression above all of the other negative emotions.

It is reassuring that Charles Spurgeon, the "prince of preachers," felt the pain of depression without calling that depression sin. Explained Spurgeon: "Fits of depression come over the most of us. Usually cheerful as we may be, we must at intervals be cast down. The strong are not always vigorous, the wise not always ready, the brave not always courageous, and the joyous not always happy. . . . Knowing by most painful experience what deep depression of spirit means, being visited therewith at seasons by no means few or far between, I thought it might be consolatory to some of my brethren if I gave my thoughts thereon, that younger men might not fancy that some strange thing had happened to them when they became for a season possessed by melancholy; and that sadder men might know that one upon whom the sun had shone right joyously did not always walk in the light."[2]

It was the opinion of Spurgeon that most, if not all great men of God, have suffered from some periods of depression. "It is not necessary by quotations from the biographies of eminent ministers to prove that seasons of fearful prostration have fallen to the lot of most, if not all of them. The life of Luther might suffice to give a thousand instances, and he was by no means of the weaker sort. His great spirit was often in the seventh heaven of exultation, and as frequently on the borders of despair. His very death-bed was not free from tempests, and he sobbed himself into his last sleep like a great wearied child."[3]

Continued Spurgeon, "My witness is, that those who are honoured of their Lord in public, have usually to endure a secret chastening, or to carry a peculiar cross, lest by any means they exalt themselves, and fall into the snare of the devil."[4]

Yet Spurgeon could also see the potential destructiveness of depression: "Depression is a leak through which the soul's force wastes itself drop by drop." And again: "He is but half a man who is a downcast man. . . ."[5]

With that peculiar sense of balance that Spurgeon possessed, he explained: "Spiritual darkness of any sort is to be avoided, and not desired; and yet, surprising as it may seem to be, it is a fact that some of the best of God's people frequently walk in darkness; . . . some of them are wrapt in a sevenfold gloom at times, and to them neither sun, nor moon, nor stars appear. As the pastor of a large church, I have to observe a great variety of experiences, and I note that some whom I greatly love and esteem, who are, in my judgment, among the very choicest of God's people, nevertheless, travel most of the way to heaven by night. They do not rejoice in the light of God's countenance, though they trust in the shadow of his wings. They are on the way to eternal light, and yet they walk in darkness. Heirs of a measureless estate of bliss, they are now without the small change and spending money of comfort which would make their present existence delightful. It is idle to attempt to judge a man's real character before God by his present state of feeling. You may be full of mirth, and yet it may be . . . soon over. On the other hand, you may be bowed down with sorrow, and yet it may only be that 'light affliction which is but for a moment,' which worketh out for you 'a far more exceeding and eternal weight of glory.' We should have thought, judging after the manner of men, that the good were always happy, as one of our children's songs so positively declares."[6]

We realize that while Christians have access to that deep, settled joy and contentment that come from the indwelling Christ, "if instead of judging by the sight of our eyes we had turned to the records of the family of God, we should long ago have been disabused of our ideal heaven below. It is written, 'Whom the Lord loveth he chasteneth, and scourgeth every son whom he receiveth.' Between the head of the way and the Celestial City, the road is rough and the nights are long. . . ."[7]

A while back a young man came into my counseling office, devastated over the loss of his home in one of the California fires. "Why me?" he kept saying over the course of several months of counseling. Joe somehow felt that Christians shouldn't suffer—at least not much! Bad things don't happen to good people. In his thinking, if you pray, God always says yes. That one remaining house on the block, which stood while, for some unknown reason, all the rest of the houses burned, should have been his. What a testimony that would have been to God's protection of his own! But in reality his house had burned while half the block did not. Deep down Joe was angry at God.

This God-always-says-yes theology results in either the feeling that God has failed or the fear that every time God says no it means that we are sinning. Discipline from the hand of God is always viewed as punishment for sin rather than an instrument for growth. Thus not only do we suffer the original pain of our situation, but we suffer for our suffering! We add guilt and the reproach of others to our already desperate state. Explains Spurgeon: "Be not, therefore, surprised as though some strange thing had happened unto you, if you find yourself in darkness. . . . We may fear God and carefully obey his servant, and yet we may be out after dark and find the streets of daily life as foggy and obscure for us as for others. . . ."[8]

By way of example: "Darkness is an evil that our soul does not love, and by it all our faculties are tried. If you are in your own house in the dark it does not matter, though children do not like to be put to bed in the dark even in their own little room: but if you are on a journey and you come to a wild moor, or a vast wood, or to terrible mountains, it appalls you to find that the sun is setting, and that you will be abroad in the dark. Darkness has a terrible power of causing fear: its mystery is an influence creating dread. It is not what we see that we dread, so much as that which we do not see, and therefore exaggerate. When darkness lowers down upon the believer's mind it is a great trial to his heart. He cries, 'Where am I? and how came I here? If I be a child of God, why am I thus? Did I really repent and obtain light so as to escape the darkness of sin? If so, why am I conscious of this thick gloom? Did I really joy in Christ and think I had received the atonement? Why then has the sun of my joy gone down so hopelessly? Where are now the lovingkindnesses of the Lord?' The good man begins to question himself as to every point of his profession; for in the dark he cannot even judge his own self. What is worse, he sometimes questions the truth which he has aforetime received, and doubts the very ground on which his foot is resting. Satan will come in with vile insinuations questioning everything, even as he questioned God's Word when he ruined our race in the garden. It is possible at such times even to question the existence of the God we love, though we still cling to him with desperate resolve."[9]

Yet truly, "a dark cloud is no sign that the sun has lost his light; and dark black convictions are no arguments that God has laid aside His mercy."[10]

Why is this? "By all the castings down of his servants God is glorified, for they are led to magnify him when again he sets them on their feet, and even while prostrate in the dust their faith yields him praise. They speak all the more sweetly of his faithfulness, and are the more firmly established in his love. . . . The lesson of wisdom is, *be not dismayed by soul-trouble*."[11] "Soul trouble" is a term for depression, downness, spiritual emptiness, discouragement, such as experienced by many great people of the Bible, which often appears in older writings but still well defines universally what we all experience from time to time. Says Spurgeon of such feelings: "Count it no strange thing, but a part of ordinary . . . experience. Should the power of depression be more than ordinary, think not that all is over with your usefulness. . . . Even if the enemy's foot be on your neck, expect to rise and overthrow him. Cast the burden of the present, along with the sin of the past and the fear of the future, upon the Lord, who forsaketh not his saints."[12]

In a manner that agrees with the authenticity of twenty-first-century medical knowledge, Spurgeon was acutely aware of the connection between body, mind, and spirit in his understanding of emotions and often connected physical maladies with depression. Indeed, "*most of us are in some way or other unsound physically.*"[13] And even physical ailments can have a profound effect on the emotions. "Here and there we meet with an old man who could not remember that ever he was laid aside for a day; but the great mass of us labour under some form or other of infirmity, either in body or mind. Certain bodily maladies . . . are the fruitful fountains of despondency; and let a man strive as he may against their influence, there will be hours and circumstances in which they will for awhile overcome him. As to mental maladies, is any man altogether sane? Are we not all a little off the balance? Some minds appear to have a gloomy tinge essential to their very individuality; of them it may be said, 'Melancholy marked them for her own' . . . fine minds . . . and ruled by noblest principles, but yet most prone to forget the silver lining, and to remember only the cloud. . . . These infirmities may be no detriment to a man's career of special usefulness; they may even have been imposed upon him by divine wisdom as necessary qualifications for his peculiar course of service. Some plants owe their medicinal qualities to the marsh in which they grow; others to the shades in which alone they flourish. There are precious fruits put forth by the moon as well as by the sun. . . . Pain has, probably, in some cases developed genius, hunting out the soul which otherwise might have slept like a lion in its den. Had it not been for the broken wing, some might have lost themselves in the clouds, some even of these choice doves who now bear the olive branch in their mouths and show the way to the ark. But where in body and mind there are predisposing causes to lowness of spirit it is no marvel if in dark moments the heart succumbs to them; the wonder in many cases is— and if inner lives could be written, men would see it so—how some . . . keep at their work at all, and still wear a smile upon their countenances . . . 'Blessed are they that mourn,' said the Man of Sorrows, and let none account themselves otherwise when their tears are salted with grace. We have the treasure of the gospel in earthen vessels, and if there be a flaw in the vessel here and there, let none wonder."[14]

Such suffering does not require confession of sin, but instead should be met with compassion and support. Certainly this was God's view of Job when he said: "The soul of the wounded calleth for help, and God doth not regard it as foolish" (Job 24:12 ROTHERHAM).

"How low the spirits of good and brave men will sometimes sink. Under the influence of certain disorders everything will wear a sombre aspect, and the heart will dive into the profundest days of misery. It is all very well for those who are in robust health and full of spirits to blame those whose lives are [covered over] with melancholy, but the [pain] is as real as a gaping wound, and all the more hard to bear because it lies so much in the region of the soul that to the inexperienced it appears to be a mere matter of fancy and imagination. Reader, never ridicule the nervous and hypochondriacal, their pain is real—it is not imaginary. . . . The mind can descend far lower than the body . . . flesh can bear only a certain number of wounds and no more, but the soul can bleed in ten thousand ways and die over and over again each hour. It is grievous to the good man to see the Lord whom he loves laying him in the sepulchre of desponding . . . yet if faith could but be allowed to speak she would remind the depressed saint that it is better to fall into the hand of the Lord than into the hands of men, and moreover she would tell the despondent heart that God never placed Joseph in a pit without drawing him up again to fill a throne. . . . Alas, when under deep depression the mind forgets all this and is only conscious of its unutterable misery. . . . It is an unspeakable consolation that our Lord Jesus knows this experience, right well, having with the exception of the sin of it, felt it all and more than all in Gethsemane when he was exceedingly sorrowful even unto death."[15]

For, indeed, "the sharpest pangs we feel are not those of the body . . . but those of the mind."[16]

Such pain does not discriminate between the rich and poor, or even the godly and ungodly. "You may be surrounded with all the comforts of life, and yet be in wretchedness more gloomy than death if the spirits be depressed. You may have no outward cause whatever for sorrow, and yet if the mind be dejected, the brightest sunshine will not relieve your gloom. At such a time, you may be vexed with cares, haunted with dreams, and scared with thoughts which distract you. You fear that your sins are not pardoned, that your past transgressions are brought to remembrance, and that punishment is being meted out to you in full measure."[17]

What causes these dark clouds, however? This knowledge can be reassuring to the believer. For Spurgeon himself there were physical factors mixed in with the psychological and spiritual. In the days of his greatest preaching in the tabernacle, Spurgeon was often in despair and even thought of quitting, for he felt that his illnesses kept him too often from the pulpit. Fortunately the leaders of the church felt differently. They preferred Spurgeon with all his frequent absences to any other man, even one who could be in the pulpit every time the church met. So Spurgeon stayed. Yet his swollen hands and tired body made him an old man while he was yet young.

Biographer Richard E. Day writes: "By means of these tragic hours Spurgeon's reliance was kept on God and not on himself. He finally came to the place where he was sure a great blessing was about to break when depression stormed his soul: 'Depression comes over me whenever the Lord is preparing a larger blessing for my ministry. It has now become to me a prophet in rough clothing. A John the Baptist, heralding the nearer coming of my Lord's richer benison.'

"Often enough he found that richer benison to be a deepened confidence in the sufficiency of grace."[18]

In Spurgeon's life an experience early on in his ministry created a depression that never stopped affecting him. According to Day, "on October 19, 1856, crowds gathered in a new meeting place which happened to be London's 'largest, most commodious and most beautiful building, erected for public amusements, carnivals of wild beasts and wilder men.' It accommodated ten to twelve thousand people. The news of this bold scheme ran through London like wildfire.

". . . the crowd began gathering for the opening service; wild disorder, milling for seats; so that at evening service the hall was packed, and ten thousand more were outside. When Spurgeon saw it he was almost overwhelmed.

"The service began, ran a few minutes, when suddenly a cry, 'Fire! The galleries are giving away, the place is falling!'" There was no fire, but "a terrible panic followed; seven were killed, many seriously injured. Spurgeon's grief over this almost unseated his reason. He was immediately hidden from the public; spent hours 'in tears by day, and dreams of terror by night.' A depression complex deepened upon him from which he never fully recovered.

"But the disaster itself increased the crowds. Charles Haddon Spurgeon became a world figure overnight. On Sunday he was a local celebrity of South London; the next week he was a world figure. All London now wanted to hear him."[19]

Preaching his first sermon a fortnight later, Spurgeon admitted: "I almost regret this morning that I have ventured to occupy this pulpit, because I feel utterly unable to preach to you for your profit. I had thought that the quiet and repose of the last fortnight had removed the effects of that terrible catastrophe; but on coming back to the same spot again, and more especially standing here to address you, I feel somewhat of those painful emotions which well-nigh prostrated me before. You will, therefore, excuse me this morning if I make no allusion to that solemn event, or scarcely any."[20]

With insight that is as appropriate to the day in which we live as it was to its own time, Spurgeon spoke with some detail on various causes of depression. "The times most favorable to fits of depression, I have experienced, may be summed up in a brief catalogue. First among them I mention *the hour of great success*. When at last a long-cherished desire is fulfilled, when God has been glorified greatly by our means, a great triumph achieved, then we are apt to faint. . . . Excess of joy or excitement must be paid for by subsequent depressions. While the trial lasts, the strength is equal to the emergency; but when it is over, natural weakness claims the right to show itself. . . .

"*Before any great achievement*, some measure of the same depression is very usual. Surveying the difficulties before us, our hearts sink within us. . . . Such was my experience when I first became a pastor in London. My success appalled me; and the thought of the career which it seemed to open up, so far from elating me, cast me into the lowest depth, out of which I uttered my *miserere* and found no room for a *gloria in excelsis*. Who was I that I should continue to lead so great a multitude? . . . It was just then that the curtain was rising upon my life-work, and I dreaded what it might reveal. . . . This depression comes over me whenever the Lord is preparing a larger blessing for my ministry."[21]

On the connection of depression with overwork, Spurgeon said, "*In the midst of a long stretch of unbroken labour*, the same affliction may be looked for. The bow cannot be always bent without fear of breaking. Repose is as needful to the mind as sleep to the body. . . . Hence the wisdom and compassion of our Lord, when he said to his disciples, 'Let us go into the desert and rest awhile.' What! when the people are fainting? When the multitudes are like sheep upon the mountains without a shepherd? Does Jesus talk of rest? . . . Rest time is not waste time. It is economy to gather fresh strength. Look at the mower in the summer's day, with so much to cut down ere the sun sets. He pauses in his labour—is he a sluggard? He looks for his stone, and begins to draw it up and down his scythe, with 'rink-a-tink—rink-a-tink—rink-a-tink.' Is that idle music—is he wasting precious moments? How much he might have mowed while he has been ringing out those notes on his scythe! But he is sharpening his tool, and he will do far more when once again he gives his strength to those long sweeps which lay the grass prostrate in rows before him. Even thus a little pause prepares the mind for greater service in the good cause. Fishermen must mend their nets, and we must every now and then repair our mental waste and set our machinery in order for future service. . . . God's ambassador must rest or faint; must trim his lamp or let it burn low; must recruit his vigour or grow prematurely old. It is wisdom to take occasional furlough. In the long run, we shall do more by sometimes doing less."[22]

Speaking relative to the clergy, but with equal application to anyone else, Spurgeon continued his reasons for depression by speaking of those who are hurt by the disloyalty of another believer. "One crushing stroke has sometimes laid the minister very low. The brother most relied upon becomes a traitor. Judas lifts up his heel against the man who trusted him, and the preacher's heart for the moment fails him. We are all too apt to look to an arm of flesh, and from that propensity many of our sorrows arise. Equally overwhelming is the blow when an honoured and beloved member yields to temptation, and disgraces the holy name with which he was named. . . . Ten years of toil do not take so much life out of us as we lose in a few hours by Ahithophel the traitor, or Demas the apostate."[23]

Missionary Amy Carmichael once wrote: "The call to enter for the second time into any painful experience is a sign of our Lord's confidence. It offers a great opportunity." Then she goes on to quote the words: "'The most powerful thing in your life is your opportunity . . . it is also the most irretrievable.'"[24] Along the same line of thinking Spurgeon commented: "When troubles multiply, and discouragements follow each other in long succession, like Job's messengers, then, too, amid the perturbation of soul occasioned by evil tidings, despondency despoils the heart of all its peace. Constant dropping wears away stones, and the bravest minds feel the fret of repeated afflictions. If a scanty cupboard is rendered a severer trial by the sickness of a wife or the loss of a child, and if ungenerous remarks of hearers are followed by the opposition of deacons and the coolness of members, then, like Jacob, we are apt to cry, 'All these things are against me.' . . . Accumulated distresses increase each other's weight; they play into each other's hands, and, like bands of robbers, ruthlessly destroy our comfort."[25]

At this point in his discussion Spurgeon identifies one of the most difficult aspects of certain types of depression. "This evil [depression] will also come upon us, we know not why, and then it is all the more difficult to drive it away. Causeless depression is not to be reasoned with. . . . One affords himself no pity when in this case, because it seems so unreasonable, and even sinful to be troubled without manifest cause; and yet troubled the man is, even in the very depths of his spirit. If those who laugh at such melancholy did but feel the grief of it for one hour, their laughter would be sobered into compassion. The physician and the divine may unite their skill in such cases, and both find their hands full, and more than full."[26]

Seeming to refer to the sense of oppression that is always a factor in spiritual endeavor, Spurgeon continues: "Our work, when earnestly undertaken, lays us open to attacks in the direction of depression. Who can bear the weight of souls without sinking to the dust? Passionate longings after men's conversion, if not fully satisfied (and when are they?), consume the soul with anxiety and disappointment. To see the hopeful turn aside, the godly grown cold, professors abusing their privileges, and sinners waxing more bold in sin—are not these sights enough to crush us to the earth? . . . How can we be otherwise than sorrowful, while men believe not our report, and the divine arm is not revealed? All mental work tends to weary and to depress, for much study is a weariness of the flesh; but ours is more than mental work—it is heart work, the labour of our inmost soul. . . . Such soul-travail as that of a faithful minister will bring on occasional seasons of exhaustion, when heart and flesh will fail. Moses' hands grew heavy in intercession, and Paul cried out, 'Who is sufficient for these things?' Even John the Baptist is thought to have had his fainting fits, and the apostles were once amazed, and were sore afraid."[27]

Contemporary with what we know today of the causes of burnout, Spurgeon perceived an unnecessary form of depression to be that which was created from too much study and too little exercise. As the author of more than 200 works and preacher of hundreds of sermons, such depression was a continuing problem for Spurgeon: "I confess that I frequently sit hour after hour praying and waiting for a subject, and that is the main part of my study. Almost every Sunday of my life I prepare enough outlines of sermons to last me for a month."[28]

Thus "there can be little doubt that *sedentary habits* have a tendency to create despondency in some constitutions. Burton, in his 'Anatomy of Melancholy,' has a chapter upon this cause of sadness; and quoting from one of the myriad authors whom he lays under contribution, he says . . . 'Students are negligent of their bodies. Other men look to their tools: a painter will wash his pencils; a smith will look to his hammer, anvil, forge; a husbandman will mend his plough-irons, and grind his hatchet if it be dull; a falconer or huntsman will have an especial care of his hawks, hounds, horses, dogs, etc.; a musician will string and unstring his lute; only scholars neglect that instrument (their brain and spirits, I mean) which they daily use.'

"To sit long in one posture, poring over a book, or driving a quill, is in itself a taxing of nature; but add to this a badly ventilated chamber, a body which has long been without muscular exercise, and a heart burdened with many cares, and we have all the elements for preparing a seething cauldron of despair, especially in the dim months of fog—

> 'When a blanket wraps the day,
> When the rotten woodland drips,
> And the leaf is stamped in clay.'

"Let a man be naturally as blithe as a bird, he will hardly be able to bear up year after year against such a suicidal process; he will make his study a prison and his books the warders of a gaol, while nature lies outside his window calling him to health and beckoning him to joy. He who forgets the humming of the bees among the heather, the cooing of the wood pigeons in the forest, the song of birds in the woods, the rippling of rills among the rushes, and the sighing of the wind among the pines, need not wonder if his heart forgets to sing and his soul grows heavy. A day's breathing of fresh air upon the hills, or a few hours' ramble in the beech wood's umbrageous calm, would sweep the cobwebs out of the brain of scores of our toiling ministers who are now but half alive. A mouthful of sea air, or a stiff walk in the wind's face, would not give grace to the soul, but it would yield oxygen to the body, which is the next best.

> 'Heaviest the heart is in a heavy air,
> Ev'ry wind that rises blows away despair.'

"'The ferns and the rabbits, the streams and the trout, the fir trees and the squirrels, the primroses and the violets, the farmyard, the new-mown hay, and the fragrant hops . . . these are the best medicine for the hypochondriacs, the surest tonics for the declining, the best refreshments for the weary.' For lack of opportunity, or inclination, these great remedies are neglected, and the student becomes a self-immolated victim."[29]

In connection with his own ministerial duties, Spurgeon also recognized the isolation of leaders as a cause of depression. "Men of God who rise above their fellows into nearer communion with heavenly things, in their weaker moments feel the lack of human sympathy. Like their Lord in Gethsemane, they look in vain for comfort to the disciples sleeping around them; they are shocked at the apathy of their little band of brethren, and return to their secret agony with all the heavier burden pressing upon them, because they have found their dearest companions slumbering. No one knows, but he who has endured it, the solitude of a soul which has outstripped its fellows in zeal for the Lord of hosts: it dares not reveal itself, lest men count it mad; it cannot conceal itself, for a fire burns within its bones: only before the Lord does it find rest. Our Lord's sending out his disciples by two and two manifested that he knew what was in men; but for such a man as Paul, it seems to me that no helpmeet was found; Barnabas, or Silas, or Luke, were hills too low to hold high converse with such a Himalayan summit as the apostle of the Gentiles. This loneliness, which if I mistake not is felt by many of my brethren, is a fertile source of depression."[30]

Bible translator J. B. Phillips has shared his experience with this source of depression, combined with that resulting from burnout as well as from, I am sure, the oppression that arises from the spiritual warfare of doing a work for God. Says Phillips: "The hardest thing of all to bear is what I can only describe as a nameless mental pain, which is, as far as I know, beyond the reach of any drug, and which I have tried in vain to describe to anyone."[31] With poignancy he exclaims: "It would have been of inestimable comfort and encouragement to me in some of my darkest hours if I could have come across even one book written by someone who had experienced and survived the hellish torments of mind which can be produced. And, alas, I know very, very few clergy or ministers who would even know what the sufferer was talking about."[32]

While it is helpful to understand the causes of depression, it is more difficult to comprehend the delay in the cure.

Continues Spurgeon: "Winters are not usually long in our favoured clime, but some years have seen the earth covered with snow and fettered in ice for many a dreary month; so also many souls are soon cheered by the light of God's countenance; but a few find, to their own sorrow, that at times the promise tarries. When the sun sets we usually see him in the morning; but Paul, when in a tempest at sea, saw neither sun, moon, nor stars for three days: many a tried soul hath been longer than this in finding light. All ships do not make speedy voyages: the peculiar build of the vessel, the winds, the waves, and the mistakes of the captain, all affect the time of the journey. Some seeds send forth their germs in a few days; others abide long in darkness, hidden under the clods. The Lord can, when it is His good pleasure, send conviction and comfort as rapidly in succession as the flash of lightning and the clap of thunder; but at times He delays it for purposes which, though we know not now, we shall know hereafter."[33]

There are times when depression *is* the result of unconfessed and undealt-with sin. Much has been written on that particular cause of depression, to the point of relegating *all* depression to sin. But, says

Spurgeon, "we would carefully distinguish between those withdrawals which are evidences of an offence given to our Lord, and those which are designed to be trials of our faith. . . .

"Holy men may be left to walk in darkness. 'Sometimes Christians are guilty of acting a part which is *offensive* to their dear Saviour, and therefore He withdraws from them. Darkness spreads itself over them, thick clouds interpose between Him and their souls, and they see not His smiling face.'"[34]

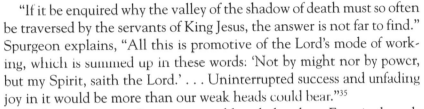

"If it be enquired why the valley of the shadow of death must so often be traversed by the servants of King Jesus, the answer is not far to find." Spurgeon explains, "All this is promotive of the Lord's mode of working, which is summed up in these words: 'Not by might nor by power, but my Spirit, saith the Lord.' . . . Uninterrupted success and unfading joy in it would be more than our weak heads could bear."[35]

By sharing his pain, Spurgeon was able to help others. Even in the pulpit, to a large congregation he once said: "I would go into the deeps a hundred times to cheer a downcast spirit. It is good for me to have been afflicted, that I might know how to speak a word in season to one that is weary."[36]

That such was true in Spurgeon's life was shown in a letter he received after a severe down period. Richard Day writes, "Here is a specimen showing how Spurgeon was able to comfort others with the same comfort whereby he was comforted. From Montreal came this rewarding letter.

"Oh, Mr. Spurgeon, that little word of yours, 'I am feeling low,' struck a chord which still vibrates in my spirit. It was to me like reading the Forty-second Psalm. I imagine there is nothing in your ministry to the saints that comes more tenderly to tried and stricken souls than just what you there express, 'I am feeling low.' The great preacher, the author of *The Treasury of David,* this man sometimes, aye, often, 'feels low' just as they do. In all their affliction he was afflicted—this is what draws hearts to Jesus; and the principle is just the same when the friends and intimates of Jesus 'feel low.' The fellow feeling, thus begotten, makes many wondrous kind.

Your friend in Jesus,
John Louson."[37]

"When our prayers are lowly by reason of our despondency," Spurgeon wrote, "the Lord will bow down to them, the infinitely exalted Jehovah will have respect unto them. Faith, when she has the loftiest name of God on her tongue, dares to ask from Him the most tender and condescending acts of love. Great as He is, He loves His children to be bold with Him. Our distress is a forcible reason for our being heard by the Lord God, merciful and gracious, for misery is ever the master argument with mercy."[38]

Indeed "stars may be seen from the bottom of a deep well when they cannot be discerned from the top of a mountain: so are many things learned in adversity which the prosperous man dreams not of. We need affliction, as the trees need winter, that we may collect sap and nourishment for future blossoms and fruit."[39]

"And yet again; this heaviness is of essential use to a Christian, if he would do good to others. Ah! There are a great many Christian people that I was going to say I should like to see afflicted—but I will not say so much as that; I should like to see them heavy in spirit; if it were for the Lord's will that they should be bowed down greatly, I would not express a word of regret; for a little more power to sympathize would be a precious boon to them, and even if it were purchased by a short journey through a burning, fiery furnace, they might not rue the day afterwards in which they had been called to pass through the flame. There are none so tender as those who have been skinned themselves. Those who have been in the chamber of affliction know how to comfort those who are there. Do not believe that any man will become a physician unless he walks the hospitals; and I am sure that no one will become a divine, or become a comforter, unless he lies in the hospital as well as walks through it and has to suffer himself. God cannot make ministers—and I speak with reverence of His holy name—He cannot make a Barnabas except in the fire. It is there, and there alone, that He can make His sons of consolation; He may make His sons of thunder anywhere; but His sons of consolation He must make in the fire, and there alone. Who shall speak to those whose hearts have been broken also, and whose wounds have long run with

the sore of grief? 'If need be,' then, 'ye are in heaviness through man-
ifold temptations.'"[40]

No matter what the cause of the depression or how long its cure is in
coming, our Lord is with us in the dark. "To the tearful eye of the sufferer the Lord seemed to stand still, as if He calmly looked on, and did
not sympathize with His afflicted one. Nay, more, the Lord appeared to
be afar off, no longer 'a very present help in trouble,' but an inaccessi-
ble mountain, into which no man would be able to climb. The presence
of God is the joy of His people but any suspicion of His absence is dis-
tracting beyond measure. Let us, then, remember that the Lord is nigh
us. The refiner is never far from the mouth of the furnace when the gold
is in that fire, and the Son of God is always walking in the midst of the
flames when His holy children are cast into them. Yet He that knows
the frailty of man will little wonder that when we are sharply exercised,
we find it hard to bear the apparent neglect of the Lord when He for-
bears to work our deliverance. . . . It is not the trouble, but the hiding of
our Father's face, which cuts us to the quick. . . . If we need an answer
to the question, 'Why hidest thou thyself?' it is to be found in the fact
that there is a 'needs-be,' not only for trial, but for heaviness of heart
under trial (1 Peter 1:6) for it is only *felt* affliction which can become
blest affliction. If we are carried in the arms of God over every stream,
where would be the trial and where the experience, which trouble is
meant to teach us?"[41]

Yet ultimately we cling to life even in the darkness. "He weakened
my strength in the way; he shortened my days. I said, O my God, take
me not away in the midst of my days. . . ." In relationship to the psalmist's
feelings and ultimate prayer, Spurgeon elaborated: the psalmist "pours
out his personal complaint. His sorrow had cast down his spirit, and even
caused weakness in his bodily frame . . . and [he] was ready to lie down
and die. . . . He [gave] himself to prayer. What better remedy is there for
depression? Good men should not dread death, but they are not forbid-
den to love life: for many reasons the man who has the best hope of
heaven, may nevertheless think it desirable to continue here a little
longer, for the sake of his family, his work, the church of God and even
the glory of God itself. [They say,] do not swirl me away like Elijah in a

79

chariot of fire, for as yet I have only seen half my days, and that a sorrowful half; give me to live till the flustering morning shall have softened into a bright afternoon of happier existence."[42]

Perhaps most comforting of all is the challenge to be like our Lord. Should we have no scar when he whom we worship also passed through the dark cloud of depression? Sometimes when we are engaged in God's work, we begin to act as though it is *our* work and he is joining *us*. But it is always *his* work and he is asking *us* to join *him*.

Several years ago when I was writing a book on bioethics called *Life on the Line*, I reached a point where I felt I could not go on writing. The research involved the knowledge of so much that was evil that I felt polluted in a way that nothing but the grace of God could cleanse. It was a Sunday afternoon. As I so often do when something is upsetting me, I began to read from the works of Amy Carmichael, in this case from *Gold Cord*, and the words were healing in their challenge. She was describing a time in her work in India when she, too, felt overwhelmed:

> At last a day came when the burden grew too heavy for me; and then it was as though the tamarind trees about the house were not tamarind, but olive, and under one of those trees our Lord Jesus knelt, and He knelt alone. And I knew that this was His burden, not mine. It was He who was asking me to share it with Him, not I who was asking Him to share it with me. After that there was only one thing to do: who that saw Him kneeling there could turn away and forget? Who could have done anything but go into the garden and kneel down beside Him under the olive trees?[43]

Explains Spurgeon: "It is a rule of the kingdom that all members must be like the head. They are to be like the head in that day when He shall appear. 'We shall be like Him, for we shall see Him as He is.' But we must be like the head also in His humiliation, or else we cannot be like Him in His glory. Now you will observe that our Lord and Saviour Jesus Christ very often passed through much of trouble, without any heaviness. When He said, 'Foxes have holes, and the birds of the air have nests, but the Son of Man hath not where to lay His head'; I observe no heaviness. I do not think He sighed over that. And when athirst He sat upon the well and said, 'Give me to drink,' there was no heaviness in all His thirst. I believe that through the first years of His ministry, although He might have suffered some heaviness, He usually passed over His troubles like a ship floating over the waves of the sea. But you will remember that at last the waves of swelling grief came into the vessel; at last the Saviour Himself, though full of patience, was obliged to say, 'My soul is exceeding sorrowful, even unto death'; and one of the evangelists tells us that the Saviour 'began to be very heavy.' What means that, but that His spirits began to sink? There is more terrible meaning yet . . . the surface meaning of it is that all His spirits sank with Him. He had no longer His wonted courage, and though He had strength to say, 'Nevertheless, not my will, but thine be done,' still the weakness did prevail, when He said, 'If it be possible let this cup pass from me.' The Saviour passed through the brook, but He 'drank of the brook by the way', and we who pass through the brook of suffering must drink of it too. He had to bear the burden, not with His shoulders omnipotent, but with shoulders that were bending to the earth beneath a load. And you and I must not always expect a giant faith that can remove mountains. Sometimes even to us the grasshopper must be a burden, that we may in all things be like our head."[44]

There are those who will insist on calling depression a sin and who will deny any possibility that our Lord could have experienced it. To these Spurgeon would say, "Sometimes you can not raise your poor depressed spirits. Some say to you, 'O! you should not feel like this.' They tell you, 'O! you should not speak such words, nor think such thoughts.' Ah! 'the heart knoweth its own bitterness, and a stranger intermeddleth not therewith.' Ay, and I will improve upon it, 'nor a friend either.' It is not easy to tell how another ought to feel and how another ought to act. Our minds are differently made, each in its own mold, which mold is broken afterward, and there shall never be another like it. We are all different, each one of us; but I am sure there is one thing in which we are all brought to unite in times of deep sorrow, namely, in a sense of helplessness. We feel that we can not exalt ourselves. Now remember our Master felt just like it. In the 22nd Psalm, which, if I read it rightly, is a beautiful soliloquy of Christ upon the cross, he says to himself, 'I am a worm, and no man.' As if he felt himself so broken, so cast down, that instead of being more than a man, as he was, he felt for a while less than man. And yet, when he could not lift a finger to crown himself, when he could scarce have a thought of victory, when his eyes could not flash with even a distant glimpse of triumph . . . then his God was crowning him. Art thou so broken in pieces, Christian? Think not that thou art cast away forever; for 'God also hath highly exalted him,' who did not exalt himself; and this is a picture and prophecy of what he will do for thee."[45]

Spurgeon's view of those who were depressed was a very tender one. Not only did he encourage the depressed but he encouraged others to be understanding of those so afflicted. Based on Isaiah 35:3 Spurgeon admonished: "It is the duty of all men to be careful of the sons of sorrow. There be some who from their very birth are marked by melancholy as her own. . . . Others there are who through some crushing misfortune are brought so low that they never hold up their heads again, but go from that time forth mourning . . . and among the flock of men it seems that there must necessarily be some who should more than others prove the truth of Job's declaration, 'man is born to trouble even as the sparks fly upwards.' It is the duty then of those of us who are more free than others from despondency of spirit to be very tender to those. . . . We do see every day that amongst the best of God's servants, there are those who are always doubting, always looking to the dark side of every providence, who look at the threatening more than at the promise, are ready to write bitter things against themselves, and often put the bitter for sweet, and the sweet for bitter, erring against their own spirits and robbing themselves of comforts which they might enjoy . . . wherever the Christian displays most his timidity and his dismay there we must be careful to apply the remedy of comfort."[46]

At another time Spurgeon implored: "Speak a kind word always; find out those who are weary. . . . Do not avoid them because they are melancholy, but rather pursue them. Hunt them out, do not let them be quiet in their nest of thorns, but if the Lord has given it to you to soar aloft into the clear blue ether, try to carry your friend with you, and lift him above the clouds. Suppose your house is on a hill, and he lives in the marsh, ask him to climb the hill and stay with you. . . . It is just possible that you may live in the upper storeys where you can see further and behold more of the blessed land. Ask him to come up from his cellar and walk on the roof of your palace, and scan the prospect through your telescope, '*Encourage him*.'"[47]

Then, once again to the one experiencing the depression: "The first qualification for serving God with any amount of success, and for doing God's work well and triumphantly, is a sense of our own weakness. . . . God will not go forth with that man who goeth forth in his own strength. . . . Your weakness is but the preparation for your being filled, and your casting down is but the making ready for your lifting up."[48]

Relating to his own experiences as a man with a comparatively happy lifestyle, Spurgeon comments: "I had been in a madhouse a dozen times if it had not been for my God. My feet had altogether gone into the chambers of despair, and I had ended this life, if it had not been for the faithful promises of the God that keeps and preserves his people. My life has not been a miserable, but a happy one; and yet I tell you that there have been times in it when I could not have done without my God. I do not understand what some of you, who are always at the pinch, do without God. There are many such here. You are poor; you are not often without sickness, you were born inheritors of maladies that make your life wretched; your children are sickly about you; it is as much as you can do by Saturday night to make ends meet; you are frequently in debt; you are constantly in trouble. Oh! I cannot tell what you do without God. Why, you have nothing here, and no hope of anything hereafter! Poor souls, I could weep for you to think that you are without God!"[49]

Refusing even to debate the issue of whether "good" Christians suffer from depression, Spurgeon challenges the Christian in how he or she handles that depression: "It is not necessary, I take it, to prove to you that Christian men have nights; for if you are Christians, you will find that *you* have them, and you will not want any proof, for nights will come quite often enough. I will, therefore, proceed at once to the subject . . . songs in the night, *their source*—God giveth them; songs in the night, *their matter*—what do we sing about in the night? songs in the night, *their excellence*—they are hearty songs, and they are sweet ones; songs in the night, *their uses*—their benefits to ourselves and others. . . .

"Any fool can sing in the day. When the cup is full, man draws inspiration from it; when wealth rolls in abundance around him, any man can sing to the praise of a God who gives a plenteous harvest. . . .

"It is easy to sing when we can read the notes by daylight; but the skillful singer is he who can sing when there is not a ray of light to read by . . . who sings from his heart, and not from a book that he can see, because he has no means of reading, save from that inward book of his own living spirit, whence notes of gratitude pour out in songs of praise. . . .

"It is not natural to sing in trouble. . . .

"Songs in the night come only from God; they are not in the power of man."[50]

Continues Spurgeon: "Martin Luther says, 'The devil can not bear singing.' That is about the truth; he does not like music. It was so in Saul's days: an evil spirit rested on Saul; but when David played on his harp, the evil spirit went away from him. This is usually the case: if we can begin to sing we shall remove our fears. I like to hear servants sometimes humming a tune at their work; I love to hear a plowman in the country singing as he goes along with his horses. Why not? You say he has no time to praise God; but he can sing a song—surely he can sing a Psalm, it will take no more time. Singing is the best thing to purge ourselves of evil thoughts. Keep your mouth full of songs, and you will often keep your heart full of praises; keep on singing as long as you can; you will find it a good method of driving away your fears."[51]

Ultimately, if Christ is our *example* in depression, he is also our *deliverer*. "Thus saith the Lord, '*Let him trust*. . . .'

"*I understand this verse to be a command to trust in the name of the Lord*. It is an order to trust in our God up to the hilt, for it bids us *stay* ourselves upon our God. We are not fitfully to trust, and then to fear; but to come to a stay in God, even as ships enter a haven, cast their anchors, and then stay there till the tempest is over-past. Let us say, 'This is my last dependence; this is my stay; and here will I remain for ever.'

". . . Did you ever hear of a captain of a vessel driven about by rough winds who wanted anchorage and tried to find it on board his vessel? He desires to place his anchor somewhere on board the ship where it will prove a hold-fast. He hangs it at the prow, but still the ship drives; he exhibits the anchor upon deck, but that does not hold the vessel; at last he puts it down into the hold; but with no better success. Why, man alive, anchors do not hold as long as they are on board a ship. They must be thrown into the deep, and then they will get a grip of the sea-bottom, and hold the vessel against wind and tide. As long as ever you have confidence in yourselves, you are like a man who keeps his anchor on board his boat, and you will never come to a resting-place. Over with your faith into the great deeps of eternal love and power, and trust in the infinitely faithful One. Then shall you be glad because your heart is quiet. Stay yourself upon your God, because he commands you so to do."[52]

"Oh, child of grief, remember the vale of tears is much frequented; thou art not alone in thy distress. Sorrow has a numerous family. Say not, I am *the* man that has seen affliction, for there be others in the furnace with thee. Remember, moreover, the King of kings once went through this valley, and here He obtained His name, 'the Man of sorrows,' for it was while passing through it He became 'acquainted with grief.'"[53]

No Scar?

Hast thou no scar?
No hidden scar on foot, or side, or hand?
I hear thee sung as mighty in the land,
I hear them hail thy bright ascendant star,
Hast thou no scar?

Hast thou no wound?
Yet I was wounded by the archers, spent,
Leaned Me against a tree to die; and rent
By ravening beasts that compassed Me, I swooned:
Hast thou no wound?

No wound? no scar?
Yet, as the Master shall the servant be,
And pierced are the feet that follow Me;
But thine are whole: can he have followed far
Who has nor wound nor scar?[54]

Furthermore, Spurgeon challenges Christians not to lose heart: "Let no man say, My case is hopeless; let none say, I am in the valley, and can never again know joy. There is hope. There is the water of life to cheer our fainting souls. It is certainly not possible for us to be in a position where Omnipotence cannot assist us. God hath servants everywhere, and where we think He has none His word can create a multitude. There are 'treasures hid in the sand,' and the Lord's chosen shall eat thereof. When the clouds hide the mountains, they are as real as the sunshine; so the promise and the providence of God are unchanged by the obscurity of our faith, or the difficulties of our position. There is hope, and hope at hand; therefore let us be of good cheer."[55]

However, even for those who walk closely with their Lord, "if the Christian did not sometimes suffer heaviness he would begin to grow too proud, and think too much of himself, and become too great in his own esteem. Those of us who are of elastic spirit, and who in our health are full of everything that can make life happy, are too apt to forget that all our own springs must be in Him. . . ."

For "in heaviness we often learn lessons that we never could attain elsewhere. Do you know that God has beauties for every part of the world; and He has beauties for every place of experience? There are views to be seen from the tops of the Alps that you can never see elsewhere. Ay, but there are beauties to be seen in the depths of the dell that ye could never see on the tops of the mountains; there are glories to be seen on Pisgah, wondrous sights to be beheld when by faith we stand on Tabor; but there are also beauties to be seen in our Gethsemanes, and some marvelously sweet flowers to be culled by the edge of the dens of the leopards. Men will never become great in divinity until they become great in suffering. 'Ah!' said Luther, 'affliction is the best book in my library,' and let me add, the best leaf in the book of affliction is that blackest of all the leaves, the leaf called heaviness, when the spirit sinks within us, and we cannot endure as we could wish."[56]

If the history of great men of God is any indication of the incidence of depression among the godly, then rather than being indicative of sinfulness or indifference to God, depression may often be an indicator that God intends to use and bless an individual.

Daniel seems to me to be as nearly as possible a perfect character.
. . . Sinner he was, doubtless, before the eye of God; he is faultless
towards man. His was a well-balanced character. [But,] . . . notice
that Daniel became the subject of a COMMON INFIRMITY.
He was full of fear on one occasion, and therefore, an angel
said to him, "Fear not." I am glad of this, because it teaches
us that even the best of men may be subject to very great fears.[1]

4

ANXIETY

While he was autographing books in a bookstore, Bible translator J. B. Phillips once experienced a panic attack of crippling
intensity. In his words: "I can well remember sitting in the
S.P.C.K. bookshop in Salisbury autographing . . . and being seized
by an utterly irrational panic at the thought of meeting people
whom I did not know. This mounted to such a pitch that by tea-
time I was obliged to ask my wife to drive me home."[2]

Anxiety and depression plagued him for a long period of his
life. In commenting on this period Phillips explained, "The
hardest thing of all to bear is what I can only describe as a nameless mental pain." Relating to his psychological treatment he
said, "I do not myself believe that there is any substitute for the
long unhurried conversations between the sufferer and the compassionate, trained psychiatrist."[3]

Emotional pain for the Christian, such as that described by
Phillips, is too often minimized or overspiritualized by fellow
Christians. When we do address such problems, as we did to
some degree in the last half of the twentieth century, we tend

to move from overspiritualization of emotional problems and even cold condemnation, to the opposite extreme of a weakened Christian commitment accompanied by a worship of psychology. Whether we are talking about Christians or the secular world, balance seems unpopular and difficult to find.

Spurgeon once preached: "Do not let us think of limiting the Holy One of Israel to any special mode of action. When we hear of men being led to break out into new ways of going to work, do not let us feel, 'This must be wrong'; rather let us hope that it is very probably right, for we need to escape from these horrid ruts, and wretched conventionalisms, which are rather hindrances than helps. Some very stereotyped brethren judge it to be a crime for an evangelist to sing the gospel; and as to that American organ,—dreadful! One of these days another set of conservative souls will hardly endure a service without such things, for the horror of one age is the idol of the next. Every man in his own order, and God using them all; and if there happens to be some peculiarity, some idiosyncrasy, so much the better. God does not make his servants by the score as men run iron into moulds; he has a separate work for each man, and let each man do his own work in his own way, and may God bless him."[4]

What is true in church order is also true in other areas. There are various ways of treating emotional problems, and let us be careful when we try to limit the Holy Spirit's guidance in these issues. Sometimes problems respond to spiritual or emotional treatment. For other problems there may be a physical basis. Often the integration of all three areas helps best.

Anxiety, depression, and the host of other negative emotions that have plagued mankind since the beginning have been spiritualized, psychologized, made into physical problems, and relegated to a host of other causes and cures. Psychotherapy has been almost worshiped by many— even those in church. At the same time it has been shunned and even damned by others. We have polarized to the point where we talk about "biblical counseling" as though therapy can only be "biblical" if it is totally devoid of any psychological thought. At the same time we have damned so-called "secular counseling" as though all mainstream psychological thinking is in error. We have throughout this ritual avoided balance as though it were the enemy. We have preferred the lies of extremes over the monotony of balance.

In Spurgeon's own time problems such as anxiety, when they manifested themselves in relatively minor ways, were considered socially acceptable because they were believed to have a physical source. Up to the sixties in the twentieth century they were considered psychological in origin and thereby stigmatized by society and church alike. Now as we begin the twenty-first century we seem to be going back once again to the position of the Victorians, a viewpoint arising this time out of the biochemical and genetic research that gives credence to the notion that some emotional problems are based in the biology of the person involved.

Obviously the cause and cure of an emotion like anxiety is not simple. Often there is no consistent diagnosis or cure. Perhaps the obvious reason is that there are many causes and cures for the many people so afflicted, people who are themselves vastly different from one another.

One of Spurgeon's most outstanding characteristics is that while he was fastidiously precise in his view of biblical truth, he could see that in areas relating to emotions there was great potential for differences in point of view. In dealing with emotions like depression and fear Spurgeon could envision any one or any combination of factors to be the cause or cure. The body, the mind, and the spirit could each or all be factors. While one could not always rule sin out, neither could sin automatically be cited as the cause.

As one reads Spurgeon on the subject of anxiety, it is impossible not to be reminded of C. S. Lewis's reference to *The Wind in the Willows* where Rat and Mole approach Pan: "'Rat,' he found breath to whisper, shaking, 'Are you afraid?' 'Afraid?' murmured the Rat, his eyes shining with unutterable love. 'Afraid? of Him? O, never, never. And yet—and yet—O Mole, I am afraid.'"[5]

Fear, like any other human emotion, is not always clear-cut. Indeed, it at times merges with other emotions like depression and particularly loneliness and isolation. In our fear, sometimes we begin to feel alone and abandoned. We may feel emotionally isolated, as though no one even begins to understand our fear. Yet uncommon as they may feel, these fears are truly common to mankind. At other times, we face situations in life that by their very nature are lonely: surgery, frightening medical tests and treatments, loss of job, poverty. Still, most of us experience some of these situations throughout our lifetimes. Others fall into even more unique circumstances that are not common to all mankind. Pilots who are held prisoner in enemy territory, people lost on a hiking expedition, or people who are kidnapped or held hostage have unique feelings of the terror of isolation. To all these Spurgeon would say as he did of the apostle Paul when he was locked up in a dungeon: "The next comfort for Paul was the reflection of the Lord standing by him. . . . He knows where he was and all about his condition. The Lord had not lost sight of Paul because he was shut up in the common gaol.

"You recollect the story of the Quaker who had come to see John Bunyan in prison and who said to him, 'Friend, the Lord sent me to thee, and I have been seeking thee in half the prisons in England.' 'Nay, verily,' said John, 'that cannot be, for if the Lord sent thee to me, thou would'st have come here at once. He knows I have been here for years.'

"'Thou, God, seest me' is a great consolation to one who delights himself in the Lord. . . . perhaps he is shut up in the narrow cell of poverty, or in the dark room of bereavement, or in the dungeon of mental depression. But the Lord knows in what ward His servant is shut up. He will visit those who cannot come forth. The Lord stood by Paul despite locks and doors; He asked no warden's leave to enter. . . . The Lord can come to His servants when nobody else can do so, when no one else can be allowed to be present because of contagion or the fear of excitement on the fevered brain. If we come into such a peculiar position where nobody knows our experience, no one having been tempted as we are, the Lord Jesus can enter into our special trial and sympathize in our peculiar grief. Jesus can stand by us side by side . . . for He has been afflicted in all our afflictions."[6]

Continues Spurgeon: "The Lord knows your troubles by His tender foresight before they come to you; He anticipates them before Satan can draw the bar. The Preserver of men will put His beloved beyond the reach of the arrow. Before the weapon is forged in the furnace and fashioned on the anvil, He knows how to provide us with . . . that which will turn the edge of the sword and break the point of the spear."[7]

Yet each of us has our own particular fears. Spurgeon had a fear of poverty, as by the way did C. S. Lewis. In describing this fear neither man seemed to think he was sinning. It was considered to be more a manifestation of humanness. Spurgeon once wrote, "During a very serious illness, I had an unaccountable fit of anxiety about money matters. One of the brethren, after trying to comfort me, went straight home, and came back to me bringing all the stocks and shares and deeds and available funds he had, putting them down on the bed: 'There, dear Pastor, I owe everything I have in the world to you, and you are quite welcome to all I possess.' Of course I soon got better and returned it all to my dear friend."[8] Truly "the strong are not always vigorous, the wise not always ready, the brave not always courageous, and the joyous not always happy."[9]

As a result of his own vulnerability in this area, Spurgeon is comforting regarding money: "If I might have any choice between having abundant wealth, or being brought to absolute dependence upon daily supplies; if, in the latter case, I could have greater power to exhibit and to exert faith in Christ, I must confess that I should prefer the mode of living which would give me most room to enjoy the luxury of depending upon my God. I believe it is more happy and more divine a life to live from hand to mouth, dependant upon the provinces of God, and having the confidence to trust Him, than it is to have all the abundance of this world, but to have nothing about which faith may exercise itself."[10] To fear and then to be able to comfort because of that fear is a theme emphasized by Spurgeon.

In a sermon where he personified fear in order to show its relevance to the church at large in his day, Spurgeon's words strikingly resemble the feelings of many as we begin the third millennium, the twenty-first century: "Pale-faced Fear will be found everywhere, she meddles with every matter, intruding into the bedchamber of Faith, and disturbing the banquets of Hope. Fear lodges with some as an abiding guest, and is entertained as though she were a dear, familiar friend. . . . Fear enquires 'Will God indeed bless us; for of late he has withheld his hand? There have been many hopeful signs, but they have disappointed us. We have expected the blessing long, we have thought we have seen the signs of it, but it has not come. . . . A thousand disappointments past lead us to fear that the blessing may not come.' Listen, O Fear, and be comforted. What if thou, too hasty and rash, hast misjudged the will of the Lord, is this any reason why he should forget his promise and refuse to hear the voice of prayer? Clouds have passed over the sky every day these many weeks, and we have said full often, 'Surely it must rain, and the thirsty fields must be refreshed,' but not a drop as yet has fallen; yet rain it must ere long. Even so is it with God's mercy. It may not come to-day, and tomorrow may not see it, but still he is not slack concerning his promise as some men count slackness. He has his own appointed time, and he will be punctual to it, for, while he never is before it he never is behind it: in due season . . . for 'God shall bless us.'

"'Yes,' says Fear, 'but we have seen so many counterfeits of the blessing. We have seen revivals in which intense excitement has seemed for a season to produce great results, but the excitement has subsided, and the results have disappeared. Have we not again and again heard the sound of trumpets, and the loud boastings of men, but vainglory was the sum of it?' This is most sorrowfully true. There is no doubt that much of revivalism has been a sham. . . . But this is no reason why there should not yet come a glorious and real revival from the presence of the Lord. . . .[11]

"But Fear replies, 'See how much there is in *the present* which is unlike a blessing, and which, instead of prophesying good, portendeth evil! How few there are,' saith Fear, 'who are proclaiming the gospel boldly and simply, and how many, on the other hand, oppose the gospel with their philosophies or with their superstitions.' But listen, O Fear, 'God shall bless us,' few though we be, for he saveth not by many nor by few. . . . Say not that Omnipotence can be short of instruments . . . if he wanted tongues to tell out of his love, he could make each stone a preacher, or each twinkling leaf upon the trees a witness for Jesus. It is not instrumentality that is necessary first and foremost, we need most the power which moves the instrumentality, which makes the weakest strong, and without which even the strongest are but weak. . . .

"But Fear findeth always room for murmuring, and therefore she saith, '*The future*, the black and gloomy future! What have we to expect from this wicked generation, this perverse people, but that we shall be given up once more to be devoured by the jaws of Antichrist, or to be lost in the mists of infidelity?' 'Our prospects are indeed appalling,' so Fear says, though I confess, not using her telescope, I discern no such signs of the times. Yet Fear saith so, and there may be reason in it; yet whatever that reason may be, it is counterbalanced in our mind by the belief that God, even our own God, will bless us. Why should he change? He has helped his church aforetime, why not now? Is she undeserving? She always was so. Does she backslide? She has done so ofttimes before, yet has he visited her, and restored her, and why not now? Instead of forebodings and fears, there seems to me cause for the brightest expectations, if we can only fall back upon the divine promise, and believe that God, even our own God, shall yet, in this very age bless us as he was wont to do in days of old. Remember the ship tossed with tempest on the Galilean lake. There was, indeed, a dreary out-look for the steersman of the boat. She must, ere long, be driven on the rocky headland, and she and her cargo must sink beneath the wave. Not so, not so, for see ye not walking upon the billows, which congeal to glass beneath his feet, the Man who loves the company within the vessel, and will not see them die? It is Jesus walking on the waves of the sea. He comes into the vessel, and immediately the calm is as profound as if wave had not lifted its head, nor wind had blown. So in the darkest times of the church's history, Jesus has always in due time appeared walking upon the waves of her troubles, and then her rest has been glorious. Let us not, therefore, be afraid, but casting fear away, let us rejoice with gladdest expectation. What can there be to fear? 'God is with us.'"[12]

Moving from the general anxiety of a specific age to the fears of individual people, Spurgeon illustrates the depths of fear that men and women experience by showing this reality in the lives of God's greatest saints, starting with the life of Christ as he walked on this earth as God incarnate. "And there appeared an angel unto him from heaven, strengthening him" (Luke 22:43 KJV). "I suppose that this incident happened immediately after our Lord's first prayer in the garden of Gethsemane. His pleading became so fervent, so intense, that it forced from him a bloody sweat. He was, evidently, in a great agony of fear as he prayed and wrestled even unto blood. We are told, by the writer of the Epistle to the Hebrews, that he 'was heard in that he feared.' It is probable that this angel came in answer to that prayer. This was the Father's reply to the cry of his fainting Son. . . .

"Scarcely had our Saviour prayed before the answer to his petition came. It reminds us of Daniel's supplication, and of the angelic messenger who was caused to fly so swiftly that, as soon as the prayer had left the prophet's lips, Gabriel stood there with the reply to it. So, brethren and sisters, whenever your times of trial come, always betake yourselves to your knees. Whatever shape your trouble may take,—if, to you, it should even seem to be a faint representation of your Lord's agony in Gethsemane, put yourselves into the same posture as that in which he sustained the great shock that came upon him. Kneel down, and cry to your Father who is in heaven, who is able to save you from death, who will prevent the trial from utterly destroying you, will give you strength that you may be able to endure it, and will bring you through it to the praise of the glory of his grace.

"That is the first lesson for us to learn from our Lord's experience in Gethsemane,—the blessing of prayer."[13]

Most instructive of all, however, for those who feel condemned under the weight of emotions like fear and depression is that he who was without sin could feel these emotions to the extreme. Our Lord's experience was no light affliction. His was that of intense fear and intense depression to the point of utter weakness.

"That he was exceedingly weak, is clear from the fact that an angel came from heaven to strengthen him, for the holy angels never do anything that is superfluous. They are the servants of an eminently practical God, who never does that which it is unnecessary for him to do. If Jesus had not needed strengthening, an angel would not have come from heaven to strengthen him. But how strange it sounds, to our ears, that the Lord of life and glory should be so weak that he should need to be strengthened by one of his own creatures! How extraordinary it seems that he, who is 'very God of very God,' should, nevertheless, when he appeared on earth as Immanuel, God with us, so completely take upon himself our nature that he should become so weak as to need to be sustained by angelic agency! . . .

"Here you can perceive how fully he shares the weakness of our humanity;—not in spiritual weakness, so as to become guilty of any sin;—but in mental weakness, so as to be capable of great depression of spirit; and in physical weakness, so as to be exhausted to the last degree by his terrible bloody sweat. What is extreme weakness? It is something different from pain, for sharp pain evidences at least some measure of strength; but perhaps some of you know what it is to feel as if you were scarcely alive; you were so weak that you could hardly realize that you were actually living. . . .

"It will help you to get an idea of the true manhood of Christ if you remember that *this was not the only time when he was weak*. He, the Son of man, was once a babe; and, therefore, all the tender ministries that have to be exercised because of the helplessness of infancy were necessary also in his case. Wrapped in swaddling bands, and lying in a manger, that little child was, all the while, the mighty God, though he condescended to keep his omnipotence in abeyance in order that he might redeem his people from their sins. Doubt not his true humanity, and learn from it how tenderly he is able to sympathize with all the ills of childhood, and all the griefs of boyhood, which are not so few or so small as some people imagine.

"Besides being thus an infant, and gradually growing in stature just as other children do, our Lord Jesus was often very weary. How the angels must have wondered as they saw him, who sways the sceptre of universal sovereignty, and marshals all the starry hosts according to his will, as he, 'being wearied with his journey, sat thus on the well' at Sychar, waiting for the woman whose soul he had gone to win, and wiping the sweat from his brow, and resting himself after having traveled over the burning acres of the land. The prophet Isaiah truly said that 'the everlasting God, the Lord, the Creator of the ends of the earth, fainteth not, neither is weary.' That is the divine side of his glorious nature. 'Jesus, therefore, being wearied with his journey, sat thus on the well.' That was the human side of his nature."[14]

Nor is the created above the Creator. Most people cannot in all honesty say that they are without fear. Some "who have attained to great strength and stability of faith, are nevertheless, at times, subjects of doubt. He who has a colossal faith will sometimes find that the clouds of fear float over the brow of his confidence. It is not possible, I suppose, so long as man is in this world, that he should be perfect in anything; and surely it seems to be quite impossible that he should be perfect in faith. Sometimes, indeed, the Lord purposely leaves his children, withdraws the divine inflowings of his grace, and permits them to begin to sink, in order that they may understand that faith is not their own work, but is at first the gift of God, and must always be maintained and kept alive in the heart by the fresh influence of the Holy Spirit."[15]

Furthermore, Spurgeon continued in a sermon preached on Sunday, April 3rd, 1859: "I think I shall be quite safe in concluding this morning, that there are some here who are full of doubting and fearing. Sure I am that all true Christians have their times of anxious questioning. The heart that hath never doubted has not yet learned to believe. As the farmers say, 'The land that will not grow a thistle, will not grow wheat;' and the heart that cannot produce a doubt has not yet understood the meaning of believing. He that never doubted of his state—he may, perhaps he may, too late. Yes, there may be timid ones here, those who are always of little faith, and there may be also great-hearts, those who are valiant for truth, who are now enduring seasons of despondency and hours of darkness of heart."[16]

Spurgeon goes on to give the example of Peter as he walks on the water towards his Master, who is telling him to come. Says Spurgeon: "I take it that Peter was a man of great faith. When others doubted, Peter believed. He boldly avowed that Jesus was the Christ, the Son of the living God, for which faith he received the Master's commendation, 'Blessed art thou, Simon Bar-jona: for flesh and blood hath not revealed it unto thee, but my Father which is in heaven.' He was of faith so strong, that at Christ's command he could tread the billow and find it like glass beneath his feet, yet even he was permitted in this thing to fall. Faith forsook him, he looked at the winds and the waves, and began to sink, and the Lord said to him, 'O thou of little faith, wherefore didst thou doubt?' As much as to say, 'O Peter, thy great faith is my gift, and the greatness of it is my work.'"[17]

Questions Spurgeon: "Why did Simon Peter doubt? He doubted for two reasons. First, because he looked too much to second causes, and secondly, because he looked too little at the first cause. The answer will suit you also, my trembling brother. This is the reason why you doubt, because you are looking too much to the things that are seen, and too little to your unseen Friend who is behind your troubles, and who shall come forth for your deliverance. See poor Peter in the ship—his Master bids him come; in a moment he casts himself into the sea, and to his own surprise he finds himself walking in the billows. He looks down and actually it is the fact; his foot is upon a crested wave, and yet he stands erect; he treads again, and yet his footing is secure. 'Oh!' thinks Peter, 'this is marvelous.' He begins to wonder within his spirit what manner of man *he* must be who has enabled him thus to tread the treacherous deep; but just then, there comes howling across the sea a terrible blast of wind; it whistles in the ear of Peter, and he says within himself, 'Ah!

here comes an enormous billow driven forward by the blast; now, surely, I must, I shall be overwhelmed.' No sooner does the thought enter his heart than down he goes; and the waves begin to enclose him. So long as he shut his eye to the billow, and to the blast, and kept it only open to the Lord who stood there before him, he did not sink; but the moment he shut his eye on Christ, and looked at the stormy wind and treacherous deep, down he went. He might have traversed the leagues of the Atlantic, he might have crossed the broad Pacific, if he could but have kept his eye on Christ, and ne'er a billow would have yielded to his tread, but he might have been drowned in a very brook if he began to look at second causes, and to forget the Great Head and Master of the Universe who had bidden him walk the sea. I say, the very reason of Peter's doubt was, that he looked at second causes and not at the first cause.

"Now, that is the reason why you doubt. Let me just probe you now for a while. You are in despondency about temporal affairs: what is the reason why you are in trouble? 'Because,' say you, 'I never was in such a condition before in my life. Wave upon wave of trouble comes upon me. I have lost one friend and then another. It seems as if business had altogether run away from me. Once I had a flood-tide, and now it is an ebb, and my poor ship grates upon the gravel, and I find she has not water enough to float her—what will become of me? And, oh! sir, my enemies have conspired against me in every way to cut me up and destroy me; opposition upon opposition threatens me. My shop must be closed; bankruptcy stares me in the face, and I know not what is to become of me.' Or else your troubles take another shape, and you feel that you are called to some eminently arduous service for your Lord, and your strength is utterly insignificant compared with the labour before you. If you had great faith it would be as much as you could do to accomplish it; but with your poor little faith you are completely beaten. You cannot see how you can accomplish the matter at all. Now, what is all this but simply looking at second causes? You are looking at your trouble, not at the God who sent your trouble; you are looking at yourselves, not at the God who dwells within you, and who has promised to sustain you. O soul! it were enough to make the mightiest heart doubt, if it should look only at things that are seen. He that is nearest to the kingdom of heaven would have cause to droop and die if he had nothing to look at but that which eye can see and ear can hear. What wonder then if thou art disconsolate, when thou hast begun to look at the things which always must be enemies to faith. . . .

"Peter sunk when he looked to outward providences, so must you. He would never have ceased to walk the wave, never would he have begun to sink, if he had looked alone to Christ, nor will you if you will look alone to him. . . .

"If Christ calls thee into the fire, he will bring thee out of it; and if he bids thee walk the sea, he will enable thee to tread it in safety."[18]

In a different context and with a different type of fear, Peter again is afraid. This time "the question is, 'Did not *I* see *thee* in the garden with him?' which leads me to observe that MANY OF US HAVE BEEN SEEN OF MEN IN OUR ASSOCIATION WITH OUR LORD JESUS CHRIST. We did not want to be observed: we were far from courting observation. There are some of the Lord's people who would like to go to heaven without being seen with the Lord Jesus in the streets by daylight. They would be saved, and yet never be seen with their Saviour. I do not think that the sin of this age, with most Christians, is obtrusiveness; far more likely it is unholy fear. Some think it modesty; but I question whether this is its real name. I will not call it cowardice, but I will take their own expression, and call it backwardness. They say they are of a 'retiring' disposition, which I interpret in a way very little to their credit. I have heard of a soldier who was of a very 'retiring' disposition when the battle was on, and he retired with great diligence as soon as the first shots were fired. I think I heard that he was hung up as a deserter and a coward. No good comes of a retiring disposition of that kind. We have that sort of 'retiring person' with us nowadays, but such people will have to answer for it when the Lord denies those who denied him."[19]

Looking at fear from still a different point of view Spurgeon speaks of another biblical figure. The Old Testament figure Hagar, who bore Abraham's son when he feared that his wife would not be able to do so, fled from her home once that child was born. Says Spurgeon: "You know the story of Hagar; of her being sent out from Abraham's tent with her son

Ishmael. It was necessary that they should be sent away from the child of promise. God, nevertheless, had designs of good towards Ishmael and his mother. Still he tried them. Whether we be saints or sinners, we shall meet with tribulation. Whether it is Sarah or Hagar, no life shall be without its affliction. To Hagar the affliction came in a very painful manner, for the little water that she had brought with her in her bottle was spent. She must give her child drink, or it would die, and then she by-and-by must follow. She laid the boy down, giving him up in despair, and began to weep what she thought would be her last flood of tears. Still there was no real cause for her distress. She need not have thirsted; she was close by a well. In her grief she had failed to see it. The distraction of her spirit had made her look everywhere except to one place, where she would have found exactly what she wanted. God therefore spake to her by an angel; and having done that he opened her eyes, and she saw a well of water, which, I suppose, had always been there. When she saw it, she went at once to it, filled her bottle, gave her child to drink, and all her sorrows were over. It seemed a very simple remedy for a very sad case. It is but an illustration of what is often happening in human life. Men and women come into sore trouble, and yet if they could see all around them they need not be in trouble. They actually come to death's door in their own judgment, and yet there really is, if they understood all things, no cause for their distress. They will escape out of their present trial as soon as ever their eyes are opened, for they will see that God has made provision for their necessities, prepared comfort for their griefs, and made such a way of escape from their fears that they need by no means give way to despair."[20]

Fearfulness in such circumstances is a normal state, and everyone experiences fear from time to time. Sometimes, as with Peter and Hagar, the answers are mainly spiritual. At other times, as with Spurgeon himself, the remedy could be as simple as another human being offering physical provision to alleviate his fears of poverty. Please note that Spurgeon did *not* turn down the offer, and he only returned the money when he felt better emotionally and physically.

Spurgeon had a noncondemning view of how fear can creep in. "Sometimes it is poverty, sometimes sickness, sometimes the recollection of the

101

past, and quite as often dread of the future. Even those who have faith in God may occasionally be weak enough to fear and be dismayed about common circumstances to which they ought to be indifferent, or over which they ought by faith to exult. Desponding people can find reason for fear where no fear is. A certain class of persons are greatly gifted with the mournful faculty of inventing troubles. If the Lord has not sent them any trial, they make one for themselves. They have a little trouble-factory in their houses, and they sit down and use their imaginations to meditate terror. They weave sackcloth and scrape up ashes. They know that they shall be bankrupt; there was a little falling off in their trade last week. They believe that they shall soon be too old for labour; it is true they are older than they were a month ago. They feel sure that they shall die in the workhouse; it is clear they will die somewhere. They feel certain about this dreadful thing and that, and fret accordingly. None of these things have happened to them yet, and in the judgment of others they are less likely to happen now than ever they were, but yet they convert their suspicions into realities, and torture themselves with them though they be but fancies. . . .

"Yet, I would not blame all those who are much given to fear, for *in some it is rather their disease than their sin, and more their misfortune than their fault.*"[21]

Going one step further, Spurgeon comments: *"even the strongest of God's servants are sometimes the subjects of fear."* And again Spurgeon draws from the lives of great saints. "David was a very strong man, and he overthrew Goliath, but we read that on one occasion when he was in battle, 'David waxed faint.'"[22] At another time, "David says, 'I am afraid.' Admire his honesty in making this confession. Some men would never have owned that they were afraid; they would have blustered, and said they cared for nothing; generally, there is no greater coward in this world than the man who never will own that he is afraid. But this hero of a thousand conflicts, this brave scion of the sons of men, honestly says, 'I am afraid.'"[23] "So the Lord's mightiest heroes sometimes have their fainting fits. We used to talk of our 'Iron Duke,' and there was one man in Scripture who was an Iron Prophet, and that was Elijah the Tishbite, and yet he sat down under the juniper-tree, and, I had almost said, whined out, 'It is enough; now, O Lord, take away my life; for I am not better than my fathers.' The best of men are but men at the best, and the strongest men are weak if God's mighty hand is for awhile withdrawn."[24]

David, the only person in the Bible whom God called a man after his own heart, suffered from a variety of emotions, ranging from joy and courage to depression and anxiety. Says Spurgeon: "his pilgrimage was so singularly varied. Some travel to heaven amid sunshine almost all the way there; and some, on the other hand, seem to have storms from beginning to end. But David's case differed from these, for he had both the storms and the sunshine. No man had fairer weather than the King of Jerusalem, yet no man ever plowed his way through soil that was more deep with mire, nor through an atmosphere more loaded with tempest than did this man of many tribulations."[25]

Another biblical figure who was great before God but subject to fear was Daniel, again in the Old Testament. Comments Spurgeon: "Daniel seems to me to be as nearly as possible a perfect character. If any one should ask me for what peculiar virtue I count him to be famous, I should hardly know how to reply. There is a combination in his character of all the excellencies. Neither do I think I could discover anything in which he was deficient. Sinner he was, doubtless, before the eye of God; he is faultless towards man. His was a well-balanced character. There is an equilibrium maintained between the divers graces, even as in John's character, which is also exceedingly beautiful. There is perhaps a touch of loveliness about the character of John, a tender softness that we do not find in Daniel; there is somewhat more of the lion in the prophet and of the lamb in the apostle, but still they are each of them perfect after his kind. All through Daniel's life you do not find a flaw; there is no break down anywhere. There was a great occasion in which he might have broken down, but God helped him through it. There he was, a business man for a long lifetime, a man bearing the burden of state, and yet never once any accusation could be brought against him of any wrong doing. A man of large transactions will usually be chargeable with something or other of wrong performed through his subordinates, even if he himself should be strictly upright; but here was a man rendered by grace so upright and so correct in all that he did, that nothing could be, even by his enemies, brought against him, except concerning his religion. A great mark of grace this, an ensign of piety far too rare. Many are Christians, and will we hope creep into heaven; but, alas! alas! alas! the less said about their inconsistencies the better. It is a special mark of a man greatly beloved, when he is consistent from the beginning to the end through the grace of God."[26]

Yet "Daniel became the subject of a COMMON INFIRMITY. He was full of fear on one occasion, and therefore, an angel said to him, 'Fear not.' I am glad of this, because it teaches us that even the best of men may be subject to very great fears. . . . Those fears on the part of Daniel were not the result of personal trial just then, they came to him indeed, when he had been highly honoured by revelations from God; but his fears sprang from *a sight of his Lord, and from a sense of his own unworthiness*. . . .

"Perhaps, too, Daniel's great fears had been awakened by *the disclosures that had been made to him* of the history of the nations, and especially of his own people. He had a peculiar anxiety for his own people. Did you ever get into that state, and begin to look upon the world, and upon the country, and upon the church, and then fall into a fit of trembling? . . . Daniel had seen the history of the world for a long period to come, therefore he was full of fear. And are you full of fear too? Well, it is a part of the lot of men whom God greatly loves that they should bear the troubles of the times, that they should be like Christ on the behalf of their age, and should bear the sins of men upon their hearts, and plead concerning them before the living God.

"I think too that Daniel's sorrow was occasioned partly by the repetition of those words to him: 'The vision is true, but the time appointed is long.' It seemed to come over and over to Daniel. 'The time is long.' I do not know any trouble that presses more heavily on my heart than that. It seems to be a dreadful long while since God has wrought a miracle—such a while since the church has had any great thing done in the midst of her."[27]

Obedience to God can sometimes be the means of alleviating fear. For example, John Bunyan, when confronted with punishment if he did not stop preaching, refused to give in to fear. Says Spurgeon: "What said Master John Bunyan, after he had lain in prison many years simply for preaching the gospel? The magistrates said to him, 'John, we will let you out, but you must promise not to preach again. There are the regular divines of the country; what have you, as a tinker [shoemaker], to do with preaching?' John Bunyan did not say, 'Well, now, I can see that this preaching is a bad thing. It has got me into prison, and I have had hard work to tag enough laces to keep my wife and that poor blind child of mine. I had better get out of this place, and stick to my tinkering.' No, he did not talk like that, but he said to the magistrates, 'If you let me out of prison to-day, I will preach again to-morrow, by the grace of God.' And when they told him that they would not let him out unless he promised not to preach, he bravely answered, 'If I lie in gaol [prison] till the moss grows on my eyelids, I will never conceal the truth which God has taught to me.'"[28]

In contrast, sometimes the very act of obedience engenders fear. The following example of obedience to God has contemporary implications. "Sometimes, there is a more powerful opposition still to the will of the Lord; that is, *when love of others would hinder us from obeying it.* 'If I do so-and-so, which I know I ought to do, I shall grieve my parents. If I carry out that command of Christ, the dearest friend I have will be very angry with me; he has threatened to cast me off if I am baptized. My old companions, who have been very kind to me, will all consider that I have gone out of my mind, and will no longer wish to have me in their company.' If a person has a genial heart, and a loving spirit, this kind of treatment is very trying, and there is a strong temptation to say, 'Well, now, how far can I go in religion, and yet just manage to save these fond connections? I do not wish to set myself up in opposition to everybody else; can't I, somehow or other, please God, and yet please these people too?' But, brethren and sisters, if we are indeed Christians, the supreme rule of our Lord's will drives us to say to him, 'Nevertheless, I will do whatever thou dost command.' Farewell, our best-beloved, if they stand in the way of Christ our Lord, for he said, 'He that loveth father or mother more than me is not worthy of me: and he that loveth son or daughter more than me is not worthy of me.' Everyone else and everything else must go, that we may keep company with Christ."[29]

With his usual sensitivity, Spurgeon encourages those who make decisions against their fears. "There are some people who seem as if they were born without nerves, or feeling, for they never appear to be downcast. But some of us, at times, shrink away, and seem to be dried up, as if the marrow were gone from our bones, and the strength from our hearts. At such a time as that, we know what Christ would have us do, but we hesitate to do it; we feel as if we could not,—not that we would not, but that we really could not. There is a want of courage,—a lack of confidence; we are timid, and cannot dash into the fray. Then is the time,—

when heart and flesh fail,—for us to take God to be the strength of our soul by resolving, let our weakness be what it may, that we will obey the command of Christ. When thy heart is faint, dear brother or sister, still follow Christ; when thou feelest as if thou must die at thy next step, still keep close at his heel; and if thy soul be almost in despair, yet hold on to him, and keep thy feet in his ways. If anyone, who feareth the Lord, still walketh in darkness, and hath no light, let him trust in the name of the Lord, and stay upon his God, for so shall his light break forth as the morning, and his heart shall be once more glad in the Lord."[30]

There are many opportunities to choose to behave contrary to our fears. For example, we also fear those who openly oppose us. "The Christian man does not like having enemies; if he could help it, he would not have a single one. He never willingly makes an enemy; and if he could destroy his enemies by turning them into friends, he would be delighted to achieve so great a victory. When, therefore, he sees that he has many enemies, and they are very cruel and very determined, then he is afraid.

"We are afraid, sometimes, when we think of the old enemy, our spiritual enemy, for we know his cunning. He has been so long tempting the saints that he knows his business well. We know what poor, foolish birds we are when he is the fowler, how soon we are taken in his net; and, therefore, at the prospect of being tempted again by him, we bow our knee to our great Father, and we cry, 'Lead us not into temptation, but deliver us from the evil one.'"[31]

Spurgeon shows his sensitivity for those who fear a variety of the what-ifs of the future. "We know the present, and we dread the unknown to-morrow. . . . This fear of that which is new is more powerful still when we are called to enter upon new labours. We become accustomed to our present service, which at first was difficult; continual exercise therein has made it easy to us, and, therefore, when the Lord calls us to something else, we are afraid to venture. We feel as if we were quite competent for the work we are now doing, whereas we ought to know that even there 'our sufficiency is of God,' and we are not able even in that to do anything as of ourselves; but we are afraid to sail upon seas which we have never navigated before, even though our unerring Pilot steers the ship in that direction. Like Jonah, we would sooner go to Tarshish than bear testimony for God in the streets of Nineveh; and, like the man of God at Horeb, we complain that we stammer and are slow of speech, and we are ready to forego the honour of the Lord's service if we may escape its responsibilities. . . .

"And, beloved, when this fear takes the shape of a foreboding of coming trial, it is even more common and crushing. We have sometimes to look forward to a period of sickness. Already it may be the disease has commenced to prey upon us; already consumption has weakened our strength by the way, or a more acutely painful disease is tearing at our vitals, and, therefore, we naturally expect that month after month our pain will greatly increase, and come to an alarming height. When death appears to be near, we persist in imagining that there is something terrible about departing out of this world unto the Father. Though tens of thousands of Christians have passed away with songs upon their lips, yet are we still afraid to ford the stream; though Jordan's banks have been made to ring ten thousand times with triumphant shouts, yet still we linger shivering there, and think it a dreadful thing to die. Forebodings, then, of pain, decay, and death, too often haunt us because we have not passed that way heretofore.

"To many the fear of poverty is very bitter; they dread the infirmities of old age; they are dismayed in prospect of the desertion of friends, or the loss of beloved relatives in whom their heart is wrapt up. All these things, because as yet we are new to them, are apt to exercise an influence over our faith of the saddest kind."[32]

Like Spurgeon, at times most people fear poverty. "The man of God may be afraid, too, *because he sees want surrounding him*. The Christian must eat and drink, and though he is not to make this the great question of his life, yet he cannot look upon his little ones, and think that he will not have sufficient bread to fill their mouths, without being somewhat afraid. The natural side of the question must come up. He is not so hardened that he does not feel it; and when he sees want staring him in the face, for his own sake and for the sake of those about him, he is afraid."[33]

Once again says Spurgeon: "We have known some, too, who have been afflicted with *fear of want coming upon them as to pecuniary matters*. One says, 'The giant of poverty will surely seize me! I have not enough laid by to furnish me with a sufficient maintenance.' I have known some even dread because they had not enough for their own funeral; as if that would not be sure to be settled somehow. The living will surely take care to bury the dead. I have known others say, 'If I were to be out of work; if such-and-such a thing were to happen; if So-and-so were to die, what should I do?' Ah! and if we fret over all the 'ifs' that we can imagine, we shall certainly never be without fretfulness; but where is your dependence, Christian, for this world? Have you placed it upon man? Then I wonder not that you are full of fear; but why do you not trust your body where you trusted your soul? If you have trusted Jesus to be the Saviour of your immortal spirit, can you not also trust him to be the Provider for this poor flesh of the things which perish? God feeds the ravens; will he not feed you? Up till this moment, the commissariat of the universe has never failed, but the myriads of living creatures have received from his hand all they have required; then is he likely to forget you? He has never done so yet; your bread has been given you, your water has been sure, why should he change his custom, and leave his own dear child to starve?"[34]

Another common what-if is that of being left alone. "Many a man fears *because he is afraid of loneliness*. More or less we must be alone in the service of God. Christian companionship is a great comfort, but if a man becomes a leader in Israel, he becomes a lonely spirit to a certain degree. So, too, in suffering, there is a bitterness with which no stranger can intermeddle. A part of the road to heaven every man must tread with no companion but his God. Now, I know some of you are getting old, and your friends have died one by one, and you are saying, 'I shall be left quite alone.' Others of you have come up to London from some country village where you used to have many Christian friends; and there is no place so desolate as this horrid London, when a man dwells in its teeming streets, and meets not a friend among its millions of passers to and fro. I know well what your state of mind is. Or perhaps, you are going to the States, or Canada, or Australia, and the thought in your mind now is—'I cannot bear being separated from all I love.' Now, here is this precious word for you, 'Fear thou not; for *I* am with thee.' The Lord of Hosts is the best of company. His society is the angels' delight, and the bliss of glorified spirits. . . ."[35]

Related to loneliness, "Another fear comes over men, and that is, *that they may lose all they have in the world*, and they know very well that if they lose their property, they usually lose their friends. Like the swallows which come to us in the spring-time, and are gone when the summer has departed, such are our worldly friends; when our goods are gone they are gone. But here the second promise comes in, *'Be not dismayed, for I am thy God.'* Jonah's gourd was withered, but Jonah's God was not. Your goods may go, but your God will not. Those around you may rob you of your loose cash of present comfort, but your invested capital, your God, they cannot take from you. That was a sweet word of the child when he saw his mother month after month in her widow's weeds sitting down and weeping, because her husband was dead. 'Mother,' said he, 'is God dead?'"[36]

Inadequacy, too, can become a fear as one looks ahead at one's task. In that way it becomes another what-if. Says Spurgeon: "Another fear that every good man has at times, unless he is buoyed up by faith, *arises from a sense of personal weakness,* 'I have a battle to fight, and I am very weak; I have a work to do for God before I die, and I have not sufficient power to perform it.' Now, here comes the next word of the text, *'I will strengthen thee.'* The strength which I have to do my work with does not lie in me; if it did it would be all over with me. How little strength there is in this arm I sorrowfully know, but there is no man on earth who can tell me how much strength God might put, if he so willed, into that same arm."[37]

But Spurgeon offers this comfort: "He can make you so strong that you can endure anything. Why, he has done it up till now. If somebody had told you years ago that you would have passed through your last trouble, you would have said, 'I shall never be able to bear it.' But you have borne it. 'Ah!' your unbelief would have said, 'that will be the death of me.' But it has not been the death of you. You can at this very moment tell of the widow's God; you can sing of him who strengtheneth the weak against the strong, who delivers them that are ready to perish, and makes the faint heart to sing for joy. Here is a word, then, for timid, trembling workers for God. 'I will strengthen thee.'

"Then comes the next consoling promise, *'Yea, I will help thee.'* This is intended to meet the fear *that friendly succour will fail.* There are some who say, 'I believe that God can strengthen me personally, but I need to have those around me who will help me; I desire to see raised up in the church of God other ministers, other Christian workers; I want to have some at my side who will with equal earnestness and with greater talent contend for the truth.' Note, then, this word, *'I will help thee.'* I will not only give you strength to use yourselves, but I will exert my strength both in other men and in my providence to help you."[38]

In an interesting angle on the perspective of our fears as human beings, Spurgeon builds his idea upon a verse in Isaiah: "Who art thou, that . . . hast feared continually every day because of the fury of the oppressor, as if he were ready to destroy? and where is the fury of the oppressor?" (Isaiah 51:12, 13 KJV).

"Objects often influence us out of proportion to their value because of their nearness. For instance, the moon is a very small insignificant body compared with the sun, yet it has far more influence over the tides and many other matters in the world than the sun has, simply because it is so much nearer to the earth than the sun is. The life that is to come is infinitely more important than the life that now is, and I hope that, in our inmost hearts, we reckon that the things that are seen and temporal are mere trifles compared with the things which are not seen and eternal; yet it often happens that the less important matters have a greater influence over us than those which are far more important, simply because the things of earth are so much nearer to us. Heaven is infinitely more to be desired than any joy of earth, yet it seems far off, and hence those fleeting joys may give us greater present comfort. The wrath of God is far more to be dreaded than the anger of man, yet sometimes a frown or a rebuke from a fellow-creature will have more effect upon our minds than the thought of the anger of God. This is because the one appears to be remote, while, being in this body, we are so near to the other. Now, beloved, it will sometimes happen that a matter, which is scarcely worthy of the thought of an immortal spirit, will fret and worry us from day to day. There is some oppressor, as the text puts it, whom we dread and fear continually, yet we forget the almighty God, who is on our side, who is stronger than all the oppressors who have ever lived, and who has all people and all things under his control. The reason why we act thus is because we think of God as if he were far off, while we can see the oppressor with our eyes, and we can hear with our ears his threatening words. . . .

"'Thou hast feared continually every day because of the fury of the oppressor, as if he were ready to destroy, and where is the fury of the oppressor?' The probable meaning of this verse is that the oppressor never came, so that they never did feel the force of his fury; and, in like manner, many of God's people are constantly under apprehensions of calamities which will never occur to them, and they suffer far more in merely dreading them than they would have to endure if they actually came upon them. In their imagination, there are rivers in their way, and they are anxious to know how they shall wade through them, or swim across them. There are no such rivers in existence, but they are agitated and distressed about them. Our old proverb says, 'Don't cross the bridge till you come to it'; but these timid people are continually crossing bridges that only exist in their foolish fancies. They stab themselves with imaginary daggers, they starve themselves in imaginary famines, and even bury themselves in imaginary graves. Such strange creatures are we that we probably smart more under blows which never fall upon us than we do under those which do actually come. The rod of God does not smite us as sharply as the rod of our own imagination does; our groundless fears are our chief tormentors; and when we are enabled to abolish our self-inflictions, all the inflictions of the world become light enough. It is a pity, however, that any who are taught of God, and who have had faith in Christ given to them, should fall into so guilty and at the same time so painful a habit as this of fearing the oppressor who does not come, and who never will come."[39]

Perhaps no fear on earth is as great as the fear of death. For each of our lives is truly a vapor, and what then? Even for those of us who are guaranteed entrance to heaven because we have accepted Christ's sacrifice as our atonement for sin, there are doubts at times. And few people escape the fear of *how*. How will I die? How long will it take? Will I suffer?

Says Spurgeon: "Some even among God's people hardly dare think of dying. It is a dreary necessity with them that they must die, and they fret and trouble about it quite needlessly; but, beloved, if we had perfect peace with God, we should not fear dying. I have known some who have thought that they would rather be translated, but I would rather not. If I were walking out to-morrow evening, and I saw horses of fire and chariots of fire standing ready to take me up, I should feel a great deal more troubled about getting into a fiery chariot than about going home, and lying down to die. If my Lord and Master shall choose to let me live till he comes, and so prevent my death, his will be done, but the Spirit saith, 'Blessed are the dead which die in the Lord,' so let us be content with that blessedness. But there is a fear of death in some good people's minds, and they cannot always shake it off; yet, beloved, there is nothing in it. If you are in Christ, you will never know anything about dying. I do not believe that Christians feel anything in death. If there are pains, as there often are, they are not the pains of dying, but of living. Death ends all their pains. They shut their eyes on earth, and open them in heaven. They have shaken off the cumbrous clay of this mortal body, and found themselves disembodied, in a moment, before the throne of the Most High, there to wait till the trumpet of the resurrection shall sound, and they shall put on their bodies once again, transformed and glorified like to the body of their Lord. Get rid of that fear of death, beloved, for it is not becoming in a Christian. The believer's heart should be so stayed upon the Lord Jesus Christ, who is the resurrection and the life, that he should leave himself in his Heavenly Father's hands to live or die, or to wait till the Lord shall come, just as the Lord shall please."[40]

Yet "if, as a rule, you and I can think of death without any kind of fear, if no tremor ever crosses our minds, well, then, we must have marvelously strong faith, and I can only pray we may be retained in that strength of faith. For the most part, there is such a thing as terror in prospect of death; the fear is often greater in prospect than in reality; in fact, it is ever so in the case of the Christian. But yet, when we give ourselves up to fear for a time, we are grievously afraid.

"This, then, is the natural side of the question. A man may be a true believer, he may be a very David, and yet be afraid."[41]

There is a fear, however, which is legitimate and healthy. For some it has been overdone. But in our time it seems to be an unknown entity. When I was in high school we had a school verse that we recited every day: "The fear of the Lord is the beginning of wisdom" (Proverbs 9:10 KJV).

"What is this fear of God?" asks Spurgeon. "I answer, first, *it is a sense of awe of his greatness*. Have you never felt this sacred awe stealing insensibly over your spirit, hushing, and calming you, and bowing you down before the Lord? It will come, sometimes, in the consideration of the great works of nature. Gazing upon the vast expanse of waters,—looking up to the innumerable stars, examining the wing of an insect, and seeing there the matchless skill of God displayed in the minute; or standing in a thunderstorm, watching, as best you can, the flashes of lightning, and listening to the thunder of Jehovah's voice, have you not often shrunk into yourself, and said, 'Great God, how terrible are thou!'—not afraid, but full of delight, like a child who rejoices to see his father's wealth, his father's wisdom, his father's power,—happy, and at home, but feeling, oh, so little! We are less than nothing, we are all but annihilated in the presence of the great eternal, infinite, invisible All-in-all."[42]

"The fear of God also takes another form, that is, *the fear of his Fatherhood which leads us to reverence him*. When divine grace has given us the new birth, we recognize that we have entered into a fresh relationship towards God; namely, that we have become his sons and daughters. Then we realize that we have received 'the Spirit of adoption, whereby we cry, Abba, Father.' Now, we cannot truly cry unto God, 'Abba, Father,' without at the same time feeling, 'Behold, what manner of love the Father hath bestowed upon us, that we should be called the sons of God.' . . .

"In this childlike fear, there is not an atom of that fear which signifies being afraid. We, who believe in Jesus, are not afraid of our Father; God forbid that we ever should be. The nearer we can get to him, the happier we are. Our highest wish is to be forever with him, and to be lost in him; but, still, we pray that we may not grieve him; we beseech him to keep us from turning aside from him; we ask for his tender pity towards our infirmities, and plead with him to forgive us and to deal graciously with us for his dear Son's sake. As loving children, we feel a holy awe and reverence as we realize our relationship to him who is our Father in heaven,—a dear, loving, tender, pitiful Father, yet our Heavenly Father, who 'is greatly to be feared in the assembly of the saints, and to be had in reverence of all them that are about him.'

"This holy fear takes a further form when *our fear of God's sovereignty leads us to obey him as our King;* for he, to whom we pray, and in whom we trust, is King of kings, and Lord of lords, and we gladly own his sovereignty."[43]

Comments Spurgeon: "The fear of the Lord is a brief description for true religion. It is an inward condition, betokening hearty submission to our heavenly Father. It consists very much in a holy reverence of God, and a sacred awe of him. This is accompanied by a child-like trust in him, which leads to loving obedience, tender submission, and lowly adoration. It is a filial fear. Not the fear which hath torment; but that which goes with joy, when we 'rejoice with trembling.'

"We must, first of all, *be* in the fear of God, before we can remain in it 'all the day long.' This can never be our condition, except as the fruit of the new birth. To be in the fear of the Lord, 'ye must be born again.' The fear of the Lord is the beginning of wisdom, and we are taught therein by the Holy Spirit, who is the sole author of all our grace. Where this fear exists, it is the token of eternal life, and it proves the abiding indwelling of the Holy Ghost. 'Happy is the man that feareth alway.' 'The Lord taketh pleasure in them that fear him.' This holy fear of the living God is the life of God showing itself in the quickened ones."[44]

Ultimately, "It is not possible that mortal men should be thoroughly conscious of the divine presence without being filled with awe. I suppose that this feeling in unfallen Adam was less overwhelming because he had no sense of sin, but surely even to him it must have been a solemn thing to hear the Lord God walking in the garden in the cool of the day. Though filled with a childlike confidence, yet even innocent manhood must have shrunk to the ground before that majestic presence. Since the fall, whenever men have been favoured with any special revelation of God they have been deeply moved with fear. There was great truth in the spirit of the old tradition that no man could see God's face and live; for such a sense of nothingness is produced in the soul by consciousness of Deity that men so highly favoured have found themselves unable to bear up under the load of blessing. Isaiah cries, 'Woe is me! for I am undone; for mine eyes have seen the King, the Lord of hosts'; Daniel says, 'There remained no strength in me'; Ezekiel declares, 'When I saw it, I fell upon my face'; and John confesses, 'When I saw him, I fell at his feet as dead.' You remember how Job cried unto the Lord: 'I have heard of thee by the hearing of the ear: but now mine eye seeth thee. Wherefore I abhor myself, and repent in dust and ashes.' Angels, who climb the ladder which Jacob saw, veil their faces when they look on God; and as for us who lie at the foot of that ladder, what can we do but say with the patriarch, 'How dreadful is this place?' Albeit that it is the greatest of all blessings, yet it is an awful thing to be a favourite with God. Blessed among women was the Virgin Mother, to whom the Lord manifested such high favour, but for this very reason to her it was foretold, 'Yea, a sword shall pierce through thy own soul also.' Blessed among men was he to whom God spoke as a friend, but it must needs be that a horror of great darkness should come upon him. It is not given to such frail creatures as we are to stand in the full blaze of Godhead, even though it be tempered by the mediation of Christ, without crying out with the prophet—'I was afraid.' 'Who would not fear thee, O King of nations?'"[45]

In our desire to know God and to share him with others, and in our love for him as Father, Husband, and Friend, we have gone away from God as *God*. He is not "the man upstairs." He is not to be overfamiliarized or to be brought down to merely human level. He is God, and we are mortal beings, created in his image to worship him forever.

On two occasions in my life when I was confronted with what were to me impossible tasks, God met me in an almost mystical way, although I was not spared the agony of anticipation before the peace was finally given. Both times, a day or two before the event I had a sudden sense of God's presence and peace that brought me through with a serenity and a competence not of my own doing. This was not God's usual way with me. For I have found that God rarely duplicates his methods in meeting our needs. More often, he varies those methods so that we do not learn to depend on the method but on the One who uses the method.

Usually, God draws near quietly. *"What is the manner in which God draws near to his people in their time of trouble?* At times he draws near to us by a secret strengthening of us to bear up when we are under pressure. We may have no marked joys, nor special transports; but quiet, calm, subdued joy rules the spirit. To my mind, the best of states is the deep calm which comes of the peace of God which passeth all understanding. I care not so much for your brilliant and gaudy-coloured joys; your neutral tints of quiet joy suit my soul's eye far better. I will not ask to see the sun above me, but I will be content to feel that 'underneath are the everlasting arms.' Do you not remember that when the burden came you feared it, but did not feel it? for the shoulder had grown stronger: when the need came which you dreaded so terribly, it turned out to be no need at all; for he who refused the meal also removed the hunger, he who denied the garment took away the cold. The secret sustenance of the soul by God is very precious."[46]

"I will never leave thee nor forsake thee" was a Spurgeon antidote for fear. Unless there was obvious sin involved, while the fear or depression raged, he would not condemn. But he would challenge! He would encourage!

Spurgeon was free in sharing his own depressions and fears with those to whom he was speaking. Said Spurgeon: "We sometimes sit down, and imagine all manner of dreadful, dolorous things. I will not repeat what things I have said to myself, for I do not want you to know quite how foolish I sometimes am. But I have heard persons bemoaning themselves like this: 'Perhaps I may lose my situation. I may not get another. I may starve.' What then comes of, 'I will never leave thee, nor forsake thee'? Another says, 'I fear I shall live to be very old. I do not know how I shall be supported. I shall get into the workhouse, and have to be buried by the parish. I cannot bear to think of it.' Friend, do you not after all believe the Word, 'I will never leave thee, nor forsake thee'?

"I will tell you this morsel of my own faults: sometimes I have said, 'I suffer so much. I become so ill. I shall be so long away from the Tabernacle. The congregation will be greatly injured. Perhaps I shall never be able to preach again.' I have struggled to this pulpit when I could hardly stand, and when the service was over, and I have been weary, the wicked whisper has come, 'Yes, I shall soon be useless. I shall have to keep my bed, or be wheeled about in a chair, and be a burden instead of a help.' This has seemed a dreadful prospect; but 'I will never leave thee, nor forsake thee,' has come in, and I have shaken off my fears, and have rejoiced in the Lord my God.

"Suppose we were to lose our eyes, we should still see God, and God would see us. Suppose we were to lose our hearing, we should still hear our Father's voice. Suppose we should gradually fail in every faculty, the Holy Spirit would still comfort us, and be with us. Many children of God have been very happy in the most deplorable circumstances. And suppose we should die. Ah, well! that is the best thing that can be, for then we shall go home, to be with our heavenly Father for ever.

"I cannot under the influence of this grand text find room for doubt or fear. I cannot stand here and be miserable to-night. I am not going to attempt such a thing; but I cannot be despondent with such a text as this, 'I will never leave thee, nor forsake thee.' I defy the devil himself to mention circumstances under which I ought to be miserable if this text is true. Child of God, nothing ought to make you unhappy when you can realize this precious text."[47]

Using the same text Spurgeon emphasizes the need to *take* promises. "I have heard of a Sunday-school teacher who performed an experiment which I do not think I shall ever try with Sunday-school children, for it might turn out exactly as it did in his case. He had been trying to illustrate what faith was, and, as he could not get it into the minds of his children, he took his watch, and he said, 'Now, I will give you this watch, John. Will you have it?' John fell thinking what the teacher could mean, and did not seize the treasure. He said to the next, 'Henry, there is the watch. Will you have it?' The boy replied, 'No thank you, sir,' with a very proper modesty. He went by several boys, till at last a youngster who was not so wise or thoughtful as the others, but rather more believing, said, 'Thank you, sir,' and put the watch into his pocket. Then the other boys woke up to a startling fact: their companion had received a watch, and they had not. One of the boys enquired of the teacher, 'Is he to keep it?' 'Of course he is,' said the teacher, 'I put the watch before you, and said that I gave it to you, but none of you accepted it.' 'Oh!' said the boy, 'if I had known you meant it, I would have had it.' And all the boys were in a dreadful state of mind to think that they had lost the watch. Each one cried, 'I did not think you meant it, but I thought'; each one said, 'Please, teacher, I thought.' Each one had his theory except the simple little boy who believed what he was told, and got the watch. Now, I wish that I could always be such a simple child as literally to believe what the Lord says, and live by that belief. The apostle drives us to such practical faith when he says, 'Let your conversation be without covetousness; and be content with such things as ye have: for he hath said, I will never leave thee, nor forsake thee.'

"You smiled just now. I do not think that there was any harm in your doing so; but I will tell you what we must not smile at, and that is, I believe that nine out of ten of you do not believe that God has said to you, 'I will never leave thee, nor forsake thee.' You think you do, but you do not. You also have got some most powerful reason why you dare not take the watch—I mean the promise. You are so wise that you feel that you cannot expect the Lord to interfere in any way for you. No, no, no; either you are not worthy of it (which is quite correct), or else you do not like to take things quite so literally, or there is some other reason why you cannot literally accept the divine assurance. There are, perhaps, one or two fools among us who have got a hold of God's Word, and actually believe it to be a matter of fact; but I do not think that many are so simple. Those who do so are generally poor obscure persons, but I should greatly envy them if I were not one of their number. With all my heart I do believe that 'He will never leave me, nor forsake me.'

"When the service is over, I know who will go away with dancing feet, and sparkling eyes, to sleep sweetly through the night, and wake tomorrow morning fresh as the lark with a song on his tongue. It is that poor simpleton of a Christian who really believes his God, and says, 'Yes, he will never leave me, nor forsake me.' Though he has scarcely a shoe to his foot, though he has scarcely a copper in his pocket, and though he is brought very low, and has to live from hand to mouth, yet if he has grasped the promise, he has such a wellspring of delight within him that his soul shall be satisfied in time of drought, and in the days of famine he shall be filled to the full. Oh, to be full of that blessed folly which treats God as he ought to be treated, and believes what he says, and acts thereon, and finds it to be true! If you have a sham God, and a sham faith, and sham troubles; and sham experiences, why, you are yourself a sham altogether; but he that believes in a real God, and has such a real faith in God as a child has in its mother, shall find God's promises to be the verity of verities."[48]

With another insight into how to take the provision God gives us in handling anxiety, Spurgeon refers to being anointed with fresh oil. "Jehovah Jireh, the Lord has provided to this day; in the mount of the Lord shall it be seen. Ebenezer, hitherto the Lord hath helped us. Well, then, if he has done so up till now, so will he, for he is an unchangeable God; therefore let us be assured that we 'shall be anointed with fresh oil.' . . .

"How shall I hope to hold on to the end? Here is the answer to it—'I shall be anointed with fresh oil.' I am poor, but I shall receive my daily pension; I am weak, and I have no strength in reserve, but my strength is laid up in God. Imagine two Israelites talking together one day, and one of them says to the other, 'Your cupboard seems to be very empty, I fear you are improvident.' 'But,' says the other, 'do you know we gathered this morning an omer full of manna, and it exactly supplied my family. I have a wife and a troop of boys with mighty appetites, and very soon the omer which had been full was empty, but we look for more to-morrow.' 'Nothing in the house!' said the other, 'do you not feel distressed?' 'No, not at all.' 'Why not?' 'Because I believe the manna will fall to-morrow morning, and that there will be just as much as I shall want, so that I have no need to lay by any in store.' 'Very imprudent,' said the other; 'I believe we ought to make hay while the sun shines. If you will come to my house, I will show you the good stock of manna which I have carefully laid by.' 'No,' said the other, 'I do not care to see it just now; but I will tell you what I will do; I will come down to-morrow at dinner time and see it.' So the man gathered in the morning his own manna fresh, and his family have been satisfied with it and delighted, and after they have eaten he says, 'I will go down and see my rich friend's manna; he was much better off last night than I was.' He goes to his friend's door, but his friend does not seem pleased to see him. 'I have come to see your manna that you stored up so carefully.' But the other blushes, and owns that he has none to show. 'Why not?' his friend enquires. 'Well, the fact is, I do not want you to come into my tent at all. I must come forth from it myself. There is a most detestable smell all through the tent. I had to take away the manna and bury it, for it bred worms and stank.' 'Ah,' said the other, 'then after all I did well to live upon daily manna, and to have no stock in hand; and you did foolishly to lay by a store.' Now there may be some professors here who want to feel that they are strong enough for to-morrow, or that they have grace enough for next week: they want to have such a proportion of divine strength given them that they shall feel confident about themselves for years to come. All that will breed worms, and stink; all human confidence, glory, and pride must rot; but if you remain a poor sinner and nothing at all, daily depending on the bounty of God, you will have grace from heaven fresh and fresh, smelling of the hand which gives it every morning. Beloved, it calms our fears about our poverty when we remember that the granary of heaven is not exhausted, and that as each morning breaks we shall find the dew of grace lying about our tent.

". . . It is possible you are afraid of some great and grievous affliction. I know dear sisters who are aware that a certain disease is upon them which will one day come to such a point that either there will be a painful operation or else they may die. Dear friend, do not fret about it. You have not sufficient strength for what is coming, but you will be anointed with fresh oil. Nobody wants to-morrow's grace to-day. . . .

"Some of us, it may be, have been troubled about the future death of some dear one upon whom we depend, or whose life is very precious to us: we have buried them a hundred times over in our fears. Let us remember that when the trouble comes it will be time enough for us to be cast down by it; nay, we shall not be cast down, for God, who helpeth those who are cast down, will comfort us. 'I shall be anointed with fresh oil.'"[49]

Another approach Spurgeon takes in relating to fears is "fixedness of heart." Says Spurgeon: "The translators somewhat differ as to what this passage means; and some think it means preparedness of heart; 'my heart is fixed,' or, 'my heart is prepared.' Let it mean both, and then we shall have the whole truth, for he whose heart is fixed is prepared. Now in what respect is a Christian's heart fixed? I think, in many.

"First, the Christian's heart is *fixed as to duty*. He says within himself, 'It is my business so to walk as Christ also walked; it can never be right for me to do contrary to God's will. I have set the Lord always before me, and in integrity of heart will I walk all my way, wherever that way may lead.' Such a man is prepared for anything. Whatever trial comes he is prepared to meet it, because his soul is resolved that come gain, come loss, he will not be dishonest to make himself rich; he will not tell a lie to win a kingdom; he will not give up a principle to save his life. He has not to go, as some of you have, to the next neighbour to say, 'What am I to do? What is the best policy?' The Christian has no policy; he does right, and leaves consequences to God. . . .

"But, more comfortable than this, the Christian's heart is *fixed as to knowledge* and so prepared. There are some things which a believer knows and is quite fixed about. He knows, for instance, that God sits in the stern-sheets of the vessel when it rocks most. He believes that an invisible hand is always on the world's tiller, and that wherever providence may drift, Jehovah steers it. That re-assuring knowledge prepares him for everything. 'It is my Father's will,' saith he. He looks over the raging waters and he sees the spirit of Jesus treading the billows, and he hears a voice which saith, 'It is I, be not afraid.' He knows too that God is always wise, and, knowing this, he is prepared for all events. They cannot come amiss, saith he, there can be no accidents, no mistakes, nothing can occur which ought not to occur. If I should lose all I have, it is better that I should lose than have, if God so wills: the worst calamity is the wisest and the kindest thing that could occur to me if God ordains it. 'We know that all things work together for good to them that love God.' The Christian does not merely hold this as a theory, but he knows it as a matter of fact. . . .

"Further, there is another kind of fixedness, namely, *the fixedness of resignation.* . . .

"Beloved, when we gave ourselves to Christ, we gave him our person, our estate, our friends, and everything: we made a full surrender, and the only way to be right when affliction comes, is to stand to that surrender, in fact, to renew it every day. It is a good thing every morning to give all up to God, and then to live through the day, and thank him for renewing the daily lease. If you think you have mercies on a fifty years' lease, you will become discontented if turned out of the tenancy; but if you feel you are only as it were a daily tenant, you will feel grateful that the great Landlord has given you a new lease. The eyes of your body—are they given for ever? Their light may never know to-morrow's sun. Those lips, which you to-day give to God's service, may soon chill in silence. So is it with all you have. Then resign all to God, for if you give it all up to him every day, it will not be hard to give it up when he takes it away at last. If you have resigned it a thousand times before, it will only be a repetition of what you have rehearsed to yourself aforetime, and, therefore, are well taught in. Stand to your resignation, be fixed about that, and you will be prepared for the most evil tidings.

"Better still, let me remind you of one form of fixedness which will make you outride every storm, namely, *fixedness as to eternal things.* 'I cannot lose'—the Christian may say—'I cannot lose my best things.' When a carrier has many parcels to carry, if he has gold and silver or precious stones, he is sure to put them near himself. Perhaps he has some common goods, and these he ties on behind: some thief, it is possible, steals from the cart some of the common goods which were outside. 'Oh, well,' says the man when he gets home, 'I am sorry to lose anything, but my precious things are all right; I have them all safe; I thank God the thief could not run away with them.'"[50]

From a slightly different point of view, many of us play old tapes of bad things that happened in the past, or terrible things that could happen in the future. By cutting those tapes when they begin to play and focusing on positive realities we can conquer many of our fears.

Spurgeon suggests: "If we would exercise our memories a little more, we might, in our very deepest and darkest distress, strike a match, which would instantaneously kindle the lamp of comfort. There is no need for God to create a new thing, in order to restore believers to joy; if they would prayerfully rake the ashes of the past, they would find light for the present; and if they would turn to the book of truth and the throne of grace, their candle would soon shine as aforetime."[51]

For example: "You are very poor and have come down for wealth. This is very hard, still you are in good health. Just walk into the hospital, ask to be permitted to witness the work done in the operating room; sit down by one bedside and listen to the story of pain and weariness; and surely you will leave the hospital feeling, 'I thank God that with all my poverty I have not sickness to complain of, and therefore I will sing of the mercies which I enjoy.'"[52]

With Spurgeon there is no harshness in dealing with fears and depression or doubt. There are comfort and practical suggestions about how to deal with these feelings. He could be tough and exacting regarding sin, although never unloving, but he was gentle with human frailty. He did not believe that fear or depression could be eradicated. He did believe that at times they could be cured or at least diminished in their painfulness. And always he believed that the experience could be a source of comfort for others. Above all, he believed in God's power and God's timing.

He once said: "There is no saying what man can do when God is with him. Give God to a man, and he can do all things. Put God into a man's arm, and he may have only the jawbone of an ass to fight with, but he will lay the Philistines in heaps; put God into a man's hand, and he may have a giant to deal with, and nothing but a sling and a stone; but he will lodge the stone in the giant's brow before long; put God into a man's eye, and he will flash defiance on kings and princes; put God into a man's lip, and he will speak right honestly, though his death should be the wages of his speech. There is no fear of a man who has got God with him; he is all-sufficient; there is nothing beyond his power. And my brethren, what an opportune help God's is! God's help always comes in at the right time. We are often making a fuss because God does not help us when we do not want to be helped. 'Oh!' says one, 'I do not think that I could die for Christ; I feel I could not; I wish I felt that I had strength enough to die.' Well, you just won't feel that, because you are not going to die, and God will not give you strength to die with, to lay up till the dying time comes. Wait till ye are dying, and then he will give you strength to die. 'Oh!' says another, 'I wish I felt as strong in prayer as so-and-so.' But you do not want so much strength in prayer, and you shall not have it. You shall have what you want, and you shall have it when you want it; but you shall not have it before. Ah, I have often cried to God and desired that I might feel happy before I began to preach—that I might feel I could preach to the people. I could never get it at all. And yet sometimes God hath been pleased to cheer me as I have gone along, and given me strength that has been equal to my day. So it must be with you. God will come in when you want him—not one minute before, nor yet one minute later. 'I will help thee.' I will help thee when thou needest help!"[53]

Spurgeon could help others because he himself had suffered. The challenge of Charles Haddon Spurgeon regarding painful emotions is this: "He who said twice, 'Comfort ye, comfort ye, my people; speak ye comfortably unto Jerusalem,' may make you to be a Barnabas, a son of Consolation to those who are weary and ready to die. Is it not the duty of Christians to strengthen the weak hands and to confirm the feeble knees? Do not follow the way of the world. It is always, if a man is going down, 'Down with him; the moment he begins to reel, give him a push; send him over at once.' And it is so with some coarseminded professors. If they see a brother a little faint, they tell him something frightful—something about the dragons and the lions, or the giants that are in the road. Instead of that, my brother, help to prop up thy reeling friend for a little season, and it may be that in some brighter day with him, when thy dark hour shall come, he will repay with a mighty interest the little cheer which thou givest to him to-day. It is a good thing, however, to temper kindness with wisdom."[54]

When Manoah lost all courage after an angelic visitation, his wife, who was much braver, responded with wisdom. "You know Manoah's wife did not say, when she found that she knew more than her husband did, 'Why how silly you must be! What a stupid man to be frightened like this!' She did not begin, as I know some Christians would do who are stronger in faith than the weak ones, by scolding about the matter: but no, she used soft liniment for smarting wounds. She knew that it does not do to put stinging-nettles to a cut, and therefore she put soft salve where there had been a very deep wound. Let us do the same. It is time to talk of duty to a brother when you get him out of the ditch; but when you see a man down, I would hardly talk to him about the sin of tumbling in, but pull him out first and brush him clean, and then afterwards tell him to take heed that he fall not there again. I have sometimes had lessons given me about unbelief, when they were not, I think, very profitable. There should be a timeliness about our advice, and if we see a man in Manoah's plight, afraid of dying, we should use the discretion of Manoah's wife, and encourage and cheer his heart. . . . It is a divine thing to wipe tears from all eyes: perhaps thy faith is meant to be a handkerchief with which thou mayest wipe away the tears of thy brother."[55]

In an apparently unpublished piece, Spurgeon offers a panoramic view of the topic of anxiety, based on the Scriptures. He draws from a New Testament story to show how the presence of Christ himself can be an antidote for fear. In Mark 6 Christ has commanded his disciples to get into a boat and go to the other side of the Sea of Galilee. Christ had just performed the miracle of multiplying five loaves and two fishes with which to feed 5,000 people to whom he had been preaching. Christ waited for the crowds to disperse and then he went off alone to pray. Thus while he was on the land, the disciples were on the sea. Night came, and a great storm occurred. Christ saw them rowing and going nowhere because of the power of the waves; so he went to them, slowly walking across the water to them. Comments Spurgeon: "They had been unwilling to put out to sea, although it was probably calm enough at the time; but they did not wish to leave the Lord Jesus. He constrained them to go, and thus their sailing was not merely under His sanction but of His express command. They were in the right place and yet they met with a terrible storm. . . . You must not think you are in a wrong position because you are in trouble. Do not consider that adverse circumstances are proof that you have missed your road; for they may even be an evidence that you are in the right way."[56]

Furthermore, the disciples seemed to be making no progress against the storms around them: "Because the wind was dead against them, it was with difficulty that they could keep what little way they had made and not be blown back again to the starting place. Probably you have heard it said that if a Christian man does not go forward he goes backward. That is not altogether true, for there are times of spiritual trial where if a man does not go backward he may reckon that he is really going forward. 'Stand fast' is a precept which when well kept may involve as much virtue as 'press forward.' . . . The Christian man may make little or no headway, and yet it may be no fault of his. It is ours to row, but it is not ours to manage the wind. . . ."[57]

Continues Spurgeon: "When a believer groans in prayer and cannot pray, he has offered prayer, and when he [tries to win] men's hearts and does not win them, his zeal is as acceptable as if it convinced a nation. And when he would do good and finds evil present with him, there is good in the [effort]. If he threw up the oar and drifted with the wind, that would be another thing, but if our Lord sees him toiling and rowing, albeit no progress is made, He has never a word to say against His servants, but He will bid them 'Be of good cheer.' . . . Looking at the text, we see to our astonishment that they were afraid of Jesus Himself. They were not afraid of winds and storms, and waves and tempests, but they were afraid of their best friend. That is the point which He aims at by saying, 'Be of good cheer. It is I, be not afraid.'"[58]

Explains Spurgeon: "He was appearing for them—coming to their rescue—to still the tempest for them, but they were afraid of Him—of Him whom they loved and in whom they had a measure of confidence. So holden were their eyes, so hardened were their hearts, so ignorant were their minds, that they were afraid of their Lord—afraid of Him when He was giving them the best reasons for trusting Him. Before their eyes He was displaying Himself as Lord over all, master of wind and wave, and yet they were afraid of Him. The greatness of that power would have converted them had they understood the truth, but they did not consider the miracle of the loaves, and therefore they were in a state of perplexity, and were sore afraid."[59]

Furthermore, "He was displaying His power, but it was not in a dazzling and overwhelming manner. Admire the sacred gentleness which made

Him move as though He would have passed by them. . . . As when the morning breaketh by slow increase of light, so Jesus came to His timid followers. Even then He moved as though He would pass by, that they might not be alarmed by His appearing to bear down upon them as an adversary. . . . The fears of the humbling crew were sufficiently aroused by even seeing Him at a distance; they are so afraid that they cry out thinking that they saw a spectre; what would they have done had He not in gentleness to their weakness manifested Himself gradually to them. . . ."[60]

"The manifestation of the Christ of God in all His glory to us will have to be by degrees as long as we are in this body, and mayhap even in Heaven it may not be at the very first that we shall be able to endure the fullness of its joy: even there He may have to lead us to fountains of water which at the first we did not discover. . . ."[61]

Even so, it may seem amazing that "what the Lord was doing was after all nothing more than they knew. Twenty-four hours had not passed since they had seen Him perform a work of creation. For He had taken bread and fish and multiplied a mere handful . . . He there and then did make a festival to five thousand and leaves far more when all had eaten than had been in the store when first the loaves and fish were counted. After this they ought not to have been surprised that He should walk the water. To walk the water is to suspend a law, but to make loaves and fishes is to exercise the supreme power of creation which must forever remain with God Himself. Knowing this they might not have been astonished—not so soon at any rate. The memory of that festival ought not to have vanished quite so quickly from the most forgetful minds. Winds and waves ought not to have roared or washed out of them the confidence which that miracle should have inspired; and yet when they saw Him only doing a thing which they knew He could do, only doing something not a jot more difficult than He was accustomed to do, they cried out for fear."[62]

To encourage the disciples, Christ "assured them that He was not a disembodied spirit. He said, 'It is I' and that 'I' was a man who did eat and drink with them, a man of flesh and blood, whom they had seen and heard themselves. They were comforted when they knew that it was really no disembodied spirit but a man in flesh and blood. . . . As a real man Jesus reigns above; He is no phantom, no ghost, no spirit, but a risen man touched with the feeling of our infirmities, and pities us and loves us and feels for us; and in that capacity He speaks to us out of the glory of Heaven, and He saith, 'It is I, be not afraid.' . . .

"When our Lord met Paul on the road to Damascus, He says to him, 'I am Jesus,' but when He spoke to those who knew His voice and were familiar with Him, He did not give His name, but said, 'It is I.' They were sheep, and they have been long enough with the Shepherd to know His voice, and they had only to hear Him speak, and without a name being mentioned they perceived that it was the Lord. To this conclusion they came first, but as they blundered and [said], 'It is a spirit,' their loving Master corrected them by saying, 'It is I'—'It is Jesus.' . . . The comfort of the Lord's people lies in the person and character of Jesus. Here is their solace—'It is I.' But what a big 'I' it is. Compound in one all it is conceivable of goodness, and mercy, and grace, and faithfulness and love: add perfect humanity and infinite Godhead and all the sovereign rights, powers, and possessions of the Highest, and these are all contained in the one little letter 'I' when Jesus says, "It is I, be not afraid.' We have not reached the bottom of it yet. The Greek is . . . 'I am.' Literally rendered the word . . . was not 'It is I' but 'I am.' 'I am' would cheer them. Even Jehovah bade Moses to comfort Israel by saying 'I am.' The '"I am" has sent me unto you.' When Jesus said to those who came to take Him in the garden, 'I am,' they fell backward. Such was the power of the word. . . ."[63] "I am" was the composite of the entire Godhead.

"Believing reader, Christ saith 'I am.' . . . Alas, it is a dying, fleeting world, but there is One who is always the same. For Jesus says to you, 'I am.' Because I live, you shall live also. Be comforted whatever else is gone, wherever else the arrows of death may fly, Jesus and His eternal priesthood and unchanging nature shall live. 'I am,' blessed word and rich comfort to be heard amid the darkness of the night by weary mariners whose hearts had been sinking within them. Then the men knew that Jesus was not only 'I am' but 'Immanuel, God with us.' The 'I am' had come to the rescue and was in the ship with them. Here, dear reader, is your comfort and mine. We will not fear the supernatural or the unseen, for we see Jesus, and in Him we see the Father and are of good cheer.

". . . there are times when we are likely to need such comfort as this. . . . At certain periods diabolical influences seem paramount. The reins of nations seem to be taken out of the hands of the great government, yet it is not so. Look through the darkness and you shall see your Lord amid the hurricane, walking the waters of the politics, ruling national convulsions, governing, overruling, arranging all, making even the wrath of man to praise Him, and restraining it according to His wisdom. Above the howling of the blast I hear His voice sounding, 'It is I.' When men's hearts sink within them for fear and the rowers feel the blade of the oar ready to snap off by the strain of useless toil, I hear that word, it is the soul of music, 'It is I, be not afraid—I am ruling all things. I am coming to rescue thee. . . .

"Another time of need would surely be when we reach the swelling of Jordan. We shall near the spirit world; the soul will begin to slough off her material garment to enter on a new form of life. How shall we feel as we enter the unknown world! Shall we cry out as we salute the first inhabitant, 'It is a spirit.' It may be so,—but then a sweet voice will destroy death's terror and end all our alarms, and this shall be its utterance—'It is I, be not afraid.' . . . Our pain and dying throes are not unknown to Him. The disembodied state wherein the spirit sojourns for a while unclothed, He knows it all for He died, entered into the spirit land, and can sympathize with us in every step of the way. In what sweet company shall we pass through the Valley of Death Shade! Surely its gloom will turn to brightness, as the cavern wrapped in blackness is lit up with a hundred torches and a myriad of gems sparkle from roof and walls. . . . Jesus will be with us. . . .

"When Jesus is with a man, the storms have lost their power to trouble him. . . . Once more, there is a day coming when the Son of Man will be revealed in the clouds of Heaven. We know not when it will be, but we are solemnly warned that when men look not for Him, He will suddenly appear. He will come as a thief in the night to the mass of men, but as for believers, they are not in darkness: for them He will be a long-expected friend. There will be seen tokens—signs in the Heaven above and the earth beneath which we shall recognize. . . . What then will be our delight to hear Him say, 'It is I, be not afraid.' Lift up your heads ye saints, for the coming of the Lord draws nigh. To you it is not darkness, but day. To you it is not judgment and condemnation, but honor and reward. What blessing will be to catch the first glimpse of our Lord on the throne! Men will begin to wring their hands and weep and wail because of Him, but we shall know His voice and welcome His appearing. When the last trumpet rings out clear and loud, happy shall we be if we hear the gladsome sound, 'It is I, be not afraid.' Rolling earth and crumbling mountain, darkened sun and blackened moon, flames of fire and roll of earthquake, gathering angels and chariots of God—none of these things shall amaze us while Jesus whispers to our soul yet again, 'It is I, be not afraid.'"[64]

There is such a thing—I would God we might reach it—
as *the solitude of elevated piety*. In the plain everything is in
company, but the higher you ascend the more lone is the
mountain path. . . . When a man grows in grace he rises out
of the fellowship of the many, and draws nearer to God.[1]

5

LONELINESS

"I have to change my appointments so that I can get home to
the chat room," a young, attractive woman said to me in my
counseling office. "Apart from having to go to work and put in
an appearance at family gatherings, that's my life now." She soon
quit counseling, for rather than deal with the problems she had
with her stepdaughter and her husband, to say nothing of her
isolation from people where she worked, she found it easier and
even safer to handle the more protected relationships she was
developing on the Internet.

Matt is only fourteen but he's having a hard time making
friends at school. His grades are going down and at home he iso-
lates himself in his room. But he's meeting people, he's meeting
them in chat rooms where no one sees his acne, where if anyone teases him he can just leave, where everyone thinks he's an
adult, not a kid. Matt's parents both work, and his older brother
is totally involved in sports. So Matt is free to create his own little world of people he's never met.

Yet whether we go to a drive-in church or build our social life
around a computer monitor in our home, where we also pay bills,

do our banking, and Christmas shop for whatever flesh and blood friends we have left, the ultimate danger resulting from this high-tech lifestyle is loneliness. If we thought we were lonely in the sixties, I would suggest that the degree of loneliness we are experiencing as we go into the twenty-first century has reached epidemic proportions. No wonder scrapbooking is the number-one hobby in the nation as we scramble to find our roots in the middle of the social and spiritual hurricane in which we find ourselves.

Even those who still deal with the real world around them are not unscathed. Craig and Linda had been married for only three years when Linda found herself a widow. Craig was killed in a car accident while he was on his way home from a business trip, a three-hour drive away from home. Business trips had been the greatest source of pain in the marriage as far as Linda was concerned, particularly those near-to-home ones that had seemed to increase considerably over the last year. Craig was always considerate of Linda, but he seemed preoccupied—and obsessed with his work, or so she thought. When he died, she mourned the man she never knew.

Then the shock came. In looking through his papers Linda found letters, love letters. The address was from the town he always visited on "business" trips, the one three hours away. Then she found a reference to a chat room. There her search simply began rather than ended. Ultimately Linda found out that her husband had spent hours every day in chat rooms. Sometimes he met the women he encountered in these chat rooms in person; most of the time he didn't. Only one, the one three hours away, had involved a sexual encounter. But Linda soon realized that the man she had married had never really been hers. He had faked his relationship with her while his real life had been with people whom, for the most part, he'd never even met.

A caricature of what can occur in a fanatical depersonalization of human relationship is given to us in Colin Turnbull's description of the Ik, a tribe that used to live in the mountains separating Uganda, the Sudan, and Kenya. I first heard about the Ik on an old talk show with Dick Cavett and Colin Turnbull. The impression on me was a lifetime one. Its relevance to contemporary life seems to increase with the years.

Originally a hunting tribe cooperating in their work, the Ik were forced into becoming farmers by the creation of a national game reserve in Kenya. Drought and lack of technological knowledge about farming defeated them, and at the time Turnbull wrote about them, they had deteriorated into a tribe of fewer than two thousand, isolated from each other in an attempt to survive. Children were thrown out on their own at three. Old people were laughed at as they died. Family members took food from each other, even at the cost of causing death to a husband or a wife. There are no words for goodness left in their language, and there was no apparent desire for love or understanding. Loneliness was a way of life and as such was scarcely felt on a conscious level. Says Turnbull:

> There is no goodness left for the Ik, only a full stomach, and that only for those whose stomachs are already full. But if there is not goodness, stop to think, there is no badness, and if there is no love, neither is there any hate. Perhaps that, after all, is progress; but it is also emptiness.[2]

In relating the state of the Ik to the emotion of loneliness, Turnbull comments:

> Only Lokeléa *did* feel lonely, for although I detected signs, symptoms of loneliness, I think the others really felt nothing; though perhaps in reality that is the greatest loneliness of all. But Lokeléa felt deeply. I remember one night that really moved me with its beauty. There was a full moon and shortly after dark it rose above Meraniang and touched the summit of Morungole, already silhouetted by a burning bush fire on the far side. Slowly and peacefully that special silvery gleam spread down the side, leaving a shadow in the shape of the hills behind me. Over the glimmering stretch of park, at the base of Lotukoi, a tiny red glow told of a camp. I knew it was Lomer, gathering honey out in that vast expanse, and alone. I stayed awake a long time, and when I went to sleep it seemed only a few minutes before I heard Lokeléa. But it was half-past four in the morning, and the moonlight was gone and the beauty was gone, and outside was nothing but blackness of night and soul, cold and blustery. Lokeléa had awakened to find his wife and children were already awake with cold and hunger and were huddled over a fire. He gave out a cry of despair that, being Lokeléa, he turned to poetry and to song, asking how God could allow such unhappiness and misery to those he had let down from the sky; asking why he had retreated beyond their reach, leaving them without hope. He sang to himself and his wife and children for half an hour, and then fell into a silence that was even more bitter than the song.

For all around were others who also were cold and hungry, but who had lost all trust in the world, lost all love and all hope, who merely accepted life's brutality and cruelty because it was empty of all else. They had no love left that could be tortured and compelled to express itself as grief, and no God to sing to, for they were Ik.[3]

What struck Turnbull with violent force were the parallels between the Ik and Western culture in the twentieth century. Speaking of the Ik, he claims: "They were brought together by self-interest alone, and the system takes care that such association is of a temporary nature and cannot flourish into anything as dysfunctional as affection or trust. Does that sound so very different from our own society . . . ?"[4]

Continues Turnbull regarding our own system: "What has become of the Western family? The very old and the very young are separated, but we dispose of them in homes for the aged or in day schools and summer camps instead of on the slopes of Meraniang. Marital relations are barely even fodder for comedians, and responsibility for health, education and welfare has been gladly abandoned to the state. . . . The individualism that is preached with a curious fanaticism, heightened by our ever growing emphasis on competitive sports, the more violent the better, and suicidal recreations, is of course at direct variance with our still proclaimed social ideals, but we ignore that, for we are already individuals at heart and society has become a game we play in our old age, to remind us of our childhood."[5]

In speaking of the transitoriness of life and those we love even within the Christian community, Spurgeon says aptly: "I have come to look on friends and dear ones as passing shadows; I see written across their brows the word 'mortal'; but Jesus is the one friend who only hath immortality, and therefore can never be lost to me."[6]

At another time he shows great sensitivity to those in his congregation who for one reason or another are lonely. "Some here are very full of care, and doubts, and anxieties, and fears. 'Oh! sir,' you say, 'if you could come to my poor house, you would not wonder that I should feel anxious. I have had to part with much of my little furniture to provide myself with living; I am brought very low; I have not a friend in London; I am alone, alone in the wide world.' Stop, stop, sir! you are not alone in the world; there is at least one eye regarding you; there is one hand that is ready to relieve you. Don't give up in despair. If your case be ever so bad, God can see your care, your troubles, and your anxieties. To a good man it is enough to *see* destitution to relieve it; and for God it is enough to see the distresses of his family at once to supply their wants. If you were lying wounded on the battle-field, if you could not speak, you know right well your comrades who are coming by with an ambulance will pick you up, if they do but see you; and that is enough for you. So if you are lying on the battle-field of life, God sees you; let that cheer you: he will relieve you; for he only needs to look at the woes of his children at once to relieve them. Go on then; hope yet; in night's darkest hour, hope for a better morrow."[7]

Spurgeon, however, was talking here about the normal vicissitudes of life, the loneliness that results from things like misunderstanding, change in geographical location, and ultimately sickness and death. He could not have been able to comprehend a society where technology declares freedom from multiple tasks from washing dishes to shopping outside of the home while at the same time the people benefiting from these advances seem to have less time than ever just to *be*, to get in touch with their own thoughts, much less those of their real-life family and friends. Spurgeon would have had a hard time with a dial-a-prayer approach to intercession with a holy God. He might not have understood a people who go to church on Saturday night so they don't "ruin" their Sunday. He would have grieved over a world where God's people don't even have to do the time-consuming task of baking their own bread and yet consider an hour too long for a sermon. But he would have understood the resultant loneliness.

Spurgeon lived during the time of the Industrial Revolution in England. The London of his day was teeming with disillusioned people, many of whom had moved to the city to get the new jobs offered by the new technology of that time. Actually, in the sense that both the Victorian Age and the later years of the twentieth century have been times of great discoveries and technological advances, Spurgeon is particularly relevant to our needs now and in the immediate future. But as in our own time, new technology does not always work for the best if you are poor. The Victorians had the extremes of the rich and poor with very little in between. Child labor forced small children to work before the sun came up until after sunset, leaving many of them with no acquaintance at all with sunlight. For the poor, several families were crammed into a single room on nights when they could afford to pay for their small corner. Medical care existed mainly for the rich, and that was still practiced with a newly discovered and primitive method of anesthesia along with very little knowledge of any germ theory. Doctors simply didn't realize for a long time that when you used dirty bandages on open wounds or didn't thoroughly clean an operating room, disease would kill the patient even if the surgery was successful. Many children died before they grew out of infancy and widespread epidemics were not unusual—including a cholera epidemic in Spurgeon's own lifetime.

In Spurgeon's time people went to debtor's prison for not paying bills. The poor house existed for those who couldn't make it. There was no plumbing, so sewage filled the streets, spreading disease, especially to those who had no homes. Many women turned to prostitution as the only answer for survival, since apart from domestic service in wealthy households there was little that women could do to support themselves. In this way they took a major chance on dying from sex-related disease or even from violent crimes.

There was no welfare, no medical insurance, no civil rights laws, no Social Security benefits, no Medicaid or Medicare. There were no safety nets. Two centuries earlier John Donne had written in one of his sermons, "No man is an island entire in itself." But in nineteenth-century England Matthew Arnold stated the conditions more accurately for his time:

> . . . in the sea of life enisled,
> With echoing straits between us thrown,
> Dotting the shoreless watery wild,
> We mortal millions live *alone*.[8]

To that group of people and to such people that we are as we enter the twenty-first century Spurgeon was and is so painfully relevant. Loneliness is not the disease of our time, but it is perhaps the major condition of our time. As such it is the natural outcome of a society that depends far too much on technology and has lost its existential grip on life, even within the organized church.

Spiritually, Spurgeon's great antidote for loneliness was expressed in the words of our Lord: "I will never leave thee, nor forsake thee." Explains Spurgeon: "This particular text is an extraordinarily useful one, for, first, if you notice, *it covers all time*. 'I will never leave thee, nor forsake thee.' Well, if God will *never* leave me, he will not leave me now. If he will never leave me, no time is excluded from the word 'never.' However dark or however bright, it says 'never.' Suppose I am going to live till I am ninety or a hundred—what then? You will call me a poor old soul; but *he* has said, 'I will never leave thee.' Suppose I should be very sick indeed, and my reason should begin to fail? Even then 'he hath said, I will never leave thee.' Might there not occur a few minutes in which the Lord may forget me? Certainly not, 'for he hath said, I will never leave thee, nor forsake thee.' Is not this a blessed cover for the whole of life, and all the exigencies of it? It matters not how long we live; we cannot outlive—'I will never leave thee.' You that are familiar with the Greek text know that there are five negatives here. We cannot manage five negatives in English, but the Greeks find them not too large a handful. Here the negatives have a fivefold force. It is as though it said, 'I will not, not leave thee; I will never, no never, forsake thee.' Perhaps a verse of one of our hymns hits it off as nearly as can be:

> 'The soul that on Jesus hath lean'd for repose,
> I will not, I will not desert to his foes;
> That soul, though all hell should endeavour to shake,
> I'll never, no never, no never forsake.'

"Our text *covers all space*, as well as all time. Suppose we emigrate. Suppose we are compelled to go to a backwoods settlement of America or Canada, or away to Australia or New Zealand, this promise will go with us all the way 'I will never leave thee, nor forsake thee.' Suppose we have to take to sea, and lead the risky life of a sailor: we will sail with this at the mast-head—'I will never leave thee.' But suppose we should get into prison. Does not Jesus visit those who are prisoners for his name's sake? Hath he not said, 'I will never leave thee'? Suppose we go up in the world, and fall under great responsibilities, this goes up with us, 'I will never leave thee.' Suppose, more likely, we go down in the world, this goes down with us, 'I will never leave thee, nor forsake thee.'

"And then *it covers all circumstances*. 'I will never leave thee.' I may get to be a very childish old body. 'I will never leave thee.' But my dear children may all be dead, and I may be quite a solitary person. 'I will never leave thee.' But every friend may turn tail, and desert me. 'I will never leave thee.' But I may be in such a state that nobody will own me. 'I will never leave thee, nor forsake thee.'

"I find the first Greek word has something of this meaning, 'I will never sit loose by thee,' or 'I will never relax.' That is the root of the word. I will never let thee slip. I will never let thee go, as it were, from me though holding thee loosely.

"The other word has in it something of the idea of a person remaining in a spot and another person going away from him, and so forsaking him. The Lord seems to say, 'I will never leave thee where I cannot be with thee. I will never let thee stand alone. I will always be with thee.'

"This is a blessed, blessed promise. You see it takes in *all contingencies*, however serious. It takes in *all anticipations*, however doleful. It takes in *all suppositions*, and it includes *all actualities*. 'I will never leave thee, nor forsake thee.' . . .

"Some of you cannot bask in this sunshiny promise. It is not yours. The words are 'I will never *leave* thee.' This implies that God must be with us; and if he be not with us, the promise is not ours. You cannot take home to yourself the promise, 'I will never leave thee,' if you have nothing to do with God. 'I will not forsake thee'; does not this also take somewhat for granted? If the Lord has never been with you, if he has never forgiven you, if you have never sought his face, if you have never accepted his mercy in Christ Jesus, why, then the promise is not yours, and you have cause for trembling rather than for rejoicing! God is against you. He fits his arrow to the string. He prepares his bolts against you. Tremble, and submit yourself to him. Oh, that you would do so at once, and trust in Jesus, and live!"[9]

This promise of God was the anchor upon which Spurgeon stood when it came to loneliness. In another context, speaking of Hudson Taylor, who was the founder of the China Inland Mission (now OMF) and a contemporary of his, Spurgeon spoke similarly: "If you have nobody else to help you, go in his strength. I told you of a good woman who was speaking about Mr. Hudson Taylor years ago. She said, 'Poor Mr. Hudson Taylor! I do not think that he can depend upon any of the missionary societies to help him. He has nobody to trust to but God.' She said it in that kind of style too—'nobody to trust to *but God.*' And whom do you want to trust to but God?"[10]

In similar fashion Spurgeon speaks of the absolute sovereignty of God upon which we can rest in our loneliness, particularly since it is a loving sovereignty. In talking about that most famous of all human sufferers Spurgeon refers to Job's declaration that even if God slays him he will still trust in God. Remember that God had allowed Satan a free hand with Job, to take all he had but his life, in order to prove that Job did not trust God because of his earthly prosperity but in spite of it.

"*The terrible supposition before us is inclusive of all possible ills.* 'Though he slay me.' He means that if every form of evil up to actual death should come upon him, yet would he trust in God. Though he should lose all that he had in flock or field, in purse or portion, yet would he trust. In Job's case away went the oxen and the asses, away went the sheep, away went the camels, and away went all the servants, and each time as the messenger came breathlessly running in, he said, 'I only am left alone to tell thee.' At last the worst news of all came, for all his children were taken away at a stroke. All was gone, for his wife was as good as lost also, since she went over to the enemy, and said, 'Curse God and die.' Well saith Job, 'Though my troubles have left me bare of all but life, though nothing remains to me but this dunghill and the broken potsherd with which I scrape my sores, yet will I trust in the Lord.' . . .

"Job included in his supposition all kinds of pain. We can hardly imagine the bodily agony of Job when he was covered with sore boils from the sole of his foot unto his crown. None could approach him, the disease was so foul, neither could he endure to be touched. Yet he says, 'Though I have all these boils, and even should they grow worse, so that the pains I now endure should become unendurable, and should I suffer the very anguish of death itself, yet still would I put my trust in my God. Neither poverty, loneliness, nor fierce torment shall make me forsake the Lord, nor shall all put together cause me to doubt him.'"[11]

God was with Job in the loneliness of his loss. But he was also with him in the loneliness of his betrayal and criticism. Even his own wife had left him and joined those who urged him to confess his sin. Here was a man whom God called upright, suffering so that God could prove the reality of that uprightness to Satan, being told to confess his sins. Explains Spurgeon: "Job at that time also suffered from dishonour, for those who once looked up to him with respect now despised him in their hearts. . . . Poor Job was sorely galled with the scorn poured on him at a time when he deserved both sympathy and honour, but yet his faith cries, 'If I am more despised still, and forgotten as a dead man out of mind, yet will I trust in thee, my God.'"[12]

In the area of loneliness in friendship Spurgeon derives great comfort from Christ as our example, in this case as he faces the mock trial that will send him to the cross. In speaking of the loneliness that can be a liability of closeness to others, Spurgeon explains why that is true: "It is a grief to our hearts to be forsaken of good friends and loving friends. I do not know; but if you were sure that they had been hypocrites, you might almost be glad that they were gone; but your very knowledge that they were true at heart, as true as such poor things could be, increases the bitterness that they should leave you. You need not think, when this occurs in your experience, that any strange thing has happened to you, for Christ was thus left alone.

"Notice, that *he was left by every man*. 'Ye shall be scattered, every man to his own,' 'every man.' When the trial comes, does not John remain? Does not he remember that dear breast on which he leaned his head? Is John gone? Yes, 'every man.' Christ looked, and there was none to stand by him. He must confront his accusers without a single witness in his favour; every man was gone. Ah, this was a trial, indeed! But one true friend, a Damon or a Pythias, to be faithful to one another even unto death, and the trial is not so overwhelming. But, no; every man is gone to his own, and Christ is left alone; of the people there is none with him, not even one of those who had been his most intimate friends.

"What were they all at? Well, *every man was looking to his own safety:* 'Ye shall be scattered, every man to his own.' Is not that the very essence of selfishness and of meanness, 'Every man to his own'? This is all that Christ received from the best of his followers; they left him, and went every man to his own, to his own house, to see to his own security, to screen his own character, to preserve his own life. . . . Do you wonder if, sometimes, you find that your friends would take care of you only that they must take care of themselves? They would keep you, but then you cost too much; you are too 'dear' a friend! The expense of your friendship has to be looked at, and their income will not bear it. 'Every man to his own.' This also the Saviour had to feel."[13]

We too have a term to define what Spurgeon calls too "dear" a friend. We call it high-maintenance friendship. Now if that high-maintenance level is required due to self-indulgence rather than real need, we are not talking about the same situation which Spurgeon is describing here. Here we are talking about the loneliness of abandonment as it affected our Lord himself.

Continues Spurgeon: "Remember, this happened *when Christ's special hour was come*. 'The hour cometh,' Christ's hour, the hour of the power of darkness. It was then that they left him. When he did not need their friendship, they were his very good friends. When they could do nothing for him if they tried, they were his faithful followers. But the pinch has come; now might they watch with him one hour, now might they go with him amid the rabble throng, and interpose at least the vote of the minority against the masses; but they are gone. . . . alas, for friendship, when it fails when most it is needed. And it did fail the Saviour then.

"He was left, also, *in violation of every bond*. These men who left him were pledged to stand by him. They had given him a promise to die with him. These were his choice companions; he had called them from the fishing-smacks of Galilee, and made them his disciples. These were his apostles, the chief men in his new kingdom. They were to sit upon thrones, judging the twelve tribes of Israel. These, he had redeemed unto himself; these were to be partakers of his glory in the day of his appearing. Never were men bound to man as they were bound to Christ; and yet they left him alone. Dear friend, do not expect gratitude from your fellow-creatures; it is a very scarce thing in this world. The more you do for men, the less will be their return. I speak not now like one who thinks ill of my fellows; but I know that it is so, alas! in many instances; and if it be not your lot, you may thank God that it is not, and wonder why you are an exception to the rule. If, by-and-by, you shall come down in the world, and need the help of those you helped in days gone by, they will, as a rule, be the last to help you, and the first to tread you down. Certainly, with our Lord Jesus Christ, those who were nearest and who owed him most fled from him, and he derived from them no succour. It was 'every man to his own';

and they left him alone, to be bound and beaten by his unfeeling adversaries, and to be taken away to prison and to death."[14]

But Christ, our example, goes back to that most secure of all defenses against loneliness: "He says, 'Ye shall leave me alone: and yet I am not alone, because the Father is with me.'"[15] And then again: "This confidence in God not only kept him to his purpose, but it *sustained him in the prospect of the trial*. Notice how it runs: 'Ye shall leave me alone: and yet I am not alone.' Christ does not say, 'I shall not be alone.' That was true; but he said, 'I *am not* alone.' I love to read the experience of the child of God in the present tense, the gifts, and graces, and promises of God in the present tense: 'I am not alone.' 'The Lord *is* my Shepherd,' as well as 'I *shall not* want.' 'He *maketh* me to lie down in green pastures; he *leadeth* me beside the still waters.' He is doing everything for me now. The blessed Christ says that the prospect of God's being with him all through the trouble, and the presence of God with him now, is his comfort in the prospect of it."[16]

In the Garden of Gethsemane we see Christ even more fully as our example in loneliness. The reality of Christ's suffering without even any suggestion of sin is reassuring to those who see sin in every human frailty, every sign of emotional distress. And for those who feel that we, Christ's servants, should suffer less than he, the Master, Spurgeon has a special word: "Do you know anything about Gethsemane, and the bloody sweat, about Gabbatha, and the cry, 'Crucify him!' and about Golgotha, that scene of deadly woe? Will you follow him there when the many turn aside? Will you witness there that he alone hath the living word? You think it shall be all king's weather with you if you go with Christ. Know ye not that Christ leads us where the fiercest winds do blow, and where the stormy blast pitilessly hurls the sleet into our faces, and where we must perish if we live on earthly comforts?

". . . The disciple is not above his Lord, nor the servant above his Master. What will you have to share if you follow Christ? You will have to follow a friendless Man without a home, and often with no one to understand him. If you take him to be your Leader, you will have to travel over a rough road. Oh, may none of you ever profess Christianity for the sake of what you can get! I can assure you that, in these days, those who follow Christ for loaves and fishes will find the loaves very small and the fishes very full of bone.

"... For our Saviour had no home of his own. There were kind friends, like those at Bethany, who often entertained him, yet there were nights when the fox went to his lair, and the crow went to the wood, but the Saviour had to tarry till his head was wet with dew, and his locks with the drops of the night, for no man gave him shelter. Christ says ... 'You will be treated like that; you will lose many of your friends; those who are of your own household will become your enemies; those who now admire you will then abhor you; and those who now call you a fine fellow, and are pleased to entertain you, will then shut the door in your face. That is what you have to expect.' ... Many a man, when he has found that there is a cross as well as a crown, has foregone the crown because he could not bear the cross."[17]

But, asks Spurgeon: "What was *the reason for the special weakness of our Saviour when in the garden of Gethsemane?*"[18] It was many things. It certainly involved the fact that Christ was our sin bearer. "Probably, however, it was the sense of utter desertion that was preying upon his mind, and so produced that extremity of weakness. All his disciples had failed him, and presently would forsake him. Judas had lifted up his heel against him, and there was not one of all his professed followers who would faithfully cleave to him. Kings, princes, scribes, and rulers were all united against him, and of the people, there were none with him. Worst of all, by the necessity of his expiatory sacrifice, and his substitution for his people, his Father himself withdrew from him the light of his countenance; and, even in the garden, he was beginning to feel that agony of soul which, on the cross, wrung from him that doleful cry, 'My God, my God, why hast thou forsaken me?' And that sense of utter loneliness and desertion, added to all that he had endured, made him so exceedingly weak that it was necessary that he should be specially strengthened for the ordeal through which he had still to pass."[19]

Continues Spurgeon: "If you be real Christians you will have to endure the trial of cruel mockings. In some cases family ties are the source of far greater sorrow than comfort: truly is it written, 'A man's foes shall be they of his own household.' The coming of the gospel into a man's heart has often rendered him the object of hatred to those who loved him before."[20]

There is one area of loneliness that Spurgeon was eminently qualified to speak about, and that is the loneliness of taking a difficult stand against the flow of the crowd: the loneliness of greatness, the loneliness of power and influence.

"Many serpents lurk among the flowers of prosperity: high places are dangerous places; it is not easy to carry a full cup with a steady hand."[21]

In speaking to his students, who were training to be pastors of churches, Spurgeon once said words that apply to anyone in a place of leadership or, indeed, anyone who takes a stand that sets one apart from the crowd: "A minister fully equipped for his work, will usually be a spirit by himself, above, beyond, and apart from others. The most loving of his people cannot enter into his peculiar thoughts, cares, and temptations. In the ranks, men walk shoulder to shoulder, with many comrades, but as the officer rises in rank, men of his standing are fewer in number. There are many soldiers, few captains, fewer colonels, but only one commander-in-chief. So, in our churches, the man whom the Lord raises as a leader becomes, in the same degree in which he is a superior man, a solitary man. The mountain-tops stand solemnly apart, and talk only with God as he visits their terrible solitudes. Men of God who rise above their fellows into nearer communion with heavenly things, in their weaker moments feel the lack of human sympathy. Like their Lord in Gethsemane, they look in vain for comfort to the disciples sleeping around them; they are shocked at the apathy of their little band of brethren, and return to their secret agony with all the heavier burden pressing upon them, because they have found their dearest companions slumbering. No one knows, but he who has endured it, the solitude of a soul which has outstripped its fellows in zeal for the Lord of hosts: it dares not reveal itself, lest men count it mad; it cannot conceal itself, for a fire burns within its bones: only before the Lord does it find rest. Our Lord's sending out his disciples by two and two manifested that he knew what was in men: but for such a man as Paul, it seems to me that no helpmeet was found; Barnabas, or Silas, or Luke, were hills too low to hold high converse with such a Himalayan summit as the apostle of the Gentiles. This loneliness, which if I mistake not is felt by many of my brethren, is a fertile source of depression."[22]

***

Early on, Spurgeon realized that with leadership came criticism: "There are some of us who come in for a very large share of slander. It is very seldom that the slander market is much below par; it usually runs up at a very mighty rate; and there are persons who will take shares to any amount. If men could dispose of railway stock as they can of slander, those who happen to have any scrip here would be rich enough by to-morrow at twelve o'clock. There are some who have a superabundance of that matter; they are continually hearing rumours of this, that, and the other; and there is one fool or another who has not brains enough to write sense, nor honesty sufficient to keep him to the truth, who, therefore, writes the most infamous libels upon some of God's servants, compared with whom he himself is nothing, and whom for very envy he chooses to depreciate. Well, what matters it? Suppose you are slandered; here is a comfort: 'Thou God seest me.' They say that such-and-such is your motive, but you need not answer them; you can say, 'God knows that matter.' You are charged with such-and-such a thing of which you are innocent; your heart is right concerning the deed, you have never done it. well, you have no need to battle for your reputation; you need only point your finger to the sky, and say, 'There is a witness there who will right me at last—there is a Judge of all the earth, whose decision I am content to wait; his answer will be a complete exoneration of me, and I shall come out of the furnace, like gold seven times purified.'"[23]

With characteristic wisdom Spurgeon offered practical advice on how to handle such criticism when it degenerated to the point of slander. "*In the case of false reports against yourself, for the most part use the deaf ear.* Unfortunately liars are not yet extinct, and, like Richard Baxter and John Bunyan, you may be accused of crimes which your soul abhors. Be not staggered thereby, for this trial has befallen the very best of men, and even your Lord did not escape the envenomed tongue of falsehood. In almost all cases it is the wisest course to let such things die a natural death. A great lie, if unnoticed, is like a big fish out of water, it dashes and plunges and beats itself to death in a short time."[24]

In speaking of the loneliness of standing for truth, Charles Spurgeon had deep personal insight, especially toward the end of his life. In 1864 Spurgeon became involved in a controversy over baptismal regeneration based on the writings in *The Book of Common Prayer,* used by the Church of England. While Spurgeon was not known as a man who sought controversy, he was not likely to back down once he was confronted with issues he deeply believed in. Starting with his staunch conviction that baptism saved no one, the debate escalated and branched out into related issues with the result that friendships were affected.

The second great controversy of his life came in 1887–89 and was called the "Down Grade Controversy." This controversy was far more serious in its effect on Spurgeon. Within the Baptist Union to which Spurgeon belonged came reports that certain of the clergy were denying basic doctrines like the virgin birth and the divine inspiration of Scriptures. After much debate Spurgeon resigned from the Baptist Union, as did some others, including his own son Charles. But Spurgeon's brother James did not. Since James had worked closely with him in his various ministries, this deficiency in support deeply wounded Spurgeon. Spurgeon's bottom line in resigning can best be summed up in a line he wrote in his own magazine *The Sword and the Trowel:* "Fellowship with known and vital error is participation in sin."[25]

Some progress could perhaps have been made toward resolving the differences between Spurgeon and various members of the union if those who had given information, such as the names of those preaching error, to Spurgeon had allowed him to release those documents. But they would not, including the Secretary of the Baptist Union himself.

Spurgeon's resignation was formally accepted in 1888. Immediately, a vote of censure was passed against Spurgeon. The resolution was raised by a close friend of Spurgeon's, but at least his brother James was one of the five dissenters.[26]

In the next stage a statement of faith was drawn up. This resolution was moved by a man hostile to Spurgeon. He made it clear when he spoke he was defending liberal theology and was against Spurgeon's protests. Spurgeon's brother James seconded the motion, but not the speech. While there were issues in the resolution to which Spurgeon could have subscribed, overall it did not rise to the level of unmistakably sound theology in Spurgeon's view. The debate went on but the censure remained, while James tried to make peace between the two factions. Spurgeon's public view of his brother was one of disappointment but understanding. Yet inside he was crushed.

In 1915, twenty-two years after Spurgeon's death, the union voted on a measure to delete Spurgeon's censure. The effort failed, and to this day the censure stands.[27]

Furthermore, in 1930 Spurgeon's college rejoined the Baptist Union, followed a little later by the Metropolitan Tabernacle. During World War II the tabernacle was bombed heavily and was rebuilt for the second time (the first had been in 1898). In 1898 the seating capacity had been reduced from 6,000 to 4,000. In the second rebuilding, that capacity went from 4,000 to 1,600. In 1980 the capacity was again reduced so that the building now accommodates about 700 worshipers. The Metropolitan Tabernacle eventually withdrew once again from the Baptist Union. The college did not.[28]

On Thursday evening, April 18, 1889, Spurgeon preached with some direct references to the Down Grade Controversy. In a sad commentary on the organized church as he saw it, Spurgeon said: "The Deity of our Lord and his great atoning sacrifice, his resurrection, and his judgment of the wicked, never were moot points in the church; but they are questioned at this time. The work of the Holy Spirit may be honoured in words; but what faith can be placed in those to whom he is not a person, but a mere influence? God himself is by some made into an impersonal being, or the soul of all things, which is much the same as nothing. Pantheism is atheism in a mask. The plenary inspiration of Holy Scripture, as we have understood it from our childhood, is assailed in a thousand insidious ways. The fall of Adam is treated as a fable; and original sin and imputed righteousness are both denounced. As for the doctrines of grace, they are ridiculed as altogether out of vogue, and even the solemn sanctions of the law are scorned as bugbears of the dark ages. For many a year, by the grand old truths of the gospel, sinners were converted, and saints were edified, and the world was made to know that there is a God in Israel; but these are too antiquated for the present cultured race of superior beings. They are going to regenerate the world by Democratic Socialism, and set up a kingdom for Christ without the new birth or the pardon of sin."[29]

Furthermore, "the churches have now conceived the idea that it is their duty to amuse the people. . . . There may have been such a dreadful thing as Puritanic rigidity, but I have never seen it. We are quite free from that evil now, if it ever existed."[30]

At the end of a sermon that was an indictment upon the church of our own time as much as or more than it was of his own, Spurgeon best summed up the feelings he had, resulting from the Down Grade Controversy, when he said: "If the ministry of our pastors be not successful, we shall lose by its want of power. If the gospel is not preached our souls will not be fed. See to it that you do not encourage false doctrine, or wink at the modern apostasy. Suppose the gospel is not preached with saving power, then we shall have our children unconverted, and they will not be our joy and crown. There cannot be a deficiency in the pulpit without its bringing mischief to our households."[31]

The effect of the controversy on Spurgeon was so deep that he claimed it would take his life—and it did. For in 1892, a few months after he made that statement, Charles Haddon Spurgeon died at the age of fifty-seven—an old man yet still young.

Often the butt of cartoons and critical snippets in even the secular press, Spurgeon knew much of the loneliness of slander. Well before the Down Grade Controversy he preached: "If you will turn to the lives of any of the saints of God, you will discover that they were the victims of slanders of the grossest kind. . . . If you turn to the life of Whitefield— our great and mighty Whitefield—in more modern times, what was his character? Why, he was accused of every crime that even Sodom knew; and perjury stood up and swore that all was true. As for Wesley—I have heard that on one occasion he said that he had been charged with every crime in the calendar, except drunkenness; and when a woman stood up in the crowd and accused him of that, he then said, 'Blessed God, I have now had all manner of evil spoken against me falsely, for Christ's name sake.' You remember in the life of John Bunyan, that episode concerning Agnes Beaumont. The good man suffered this young woman to ride behind him on his horse to a meeting at Gamlingay, and for this his character was implicated in two charges, before a magistrate, which might have involved him in the crime of poisoning, and laid the foundation for villainous reports of uncleanness; yet John Bunyan was the purest and most heavenly-minded man who ever put his hand to paper; and he did put his hand to paper as no other man ever did who was not inspired. Now, this is not pleasant, but if you are a true Christian, and you are called to occupy a prominent post in the service of God, set your account for this; expect to lose your character; expect not to have the good opinion of any but your God, and those faithful ones, who like you, are willing to bear contempt. But what joy it is for all these holy men, to know that at the last God will plead the cause of their souls!

"There will be a resurrection of persons as they really were, not as they seemed to be and were misrepresented. At the last great day, there will be a resurrection of reputations—reputations which had been laid into the dark grave which calumny had digged, which had been covered with the sod of contempt, and over which there had been raised an epitaph of infamy. These reputations will all rise up. They have washed their robes and made them white; they are black no longer now. The men who were pointed at, and hooted, and despised, shall now go streaming up the shining way of fame and glory, amidst the loud shouts of praise which the great Avenger shall receive from assembled worlds. They shall awake to glory, while others rise to shame and everlasting contempt. Oh! what must it be to be in the last day plucked and stripped of your plumes? What will be the fate of the Pharisee?—of the hypocrite who will find all his fine feathers torn away, and himself left to hide his contemptible head in the caverns of the earth—but denied even that consolation—set out before the full blaze of day as an acknowledged liar before God and man? But how different the condition of the poor man who lived and died in undeserved contempt, but who wakes up to find himself a bright and shining spirit, and all his adversaries compelled to own that God has pleaded the causes of his soul, and has avenged him of his traducers.

"Thus, you see, our text is not a small one: the words are few, but full of meaning; and I have but very poorly set forth what our soul, I trust, feels to be the truth—'Thou hast pleaded the causes of my soul; thou hast redeemed my life.'"[32]

In the loneliness of slander or loss or betrayal, as indeed in so many painful circumstances in which we find ourselves, there are the angels. In a culture filled with open occult activity, which has even permeated the organized church, it is foolish to think that the counterfeit is all that is real. For what is Satanic activity but the counterfeit of the far greater power of God himself? Within the counterfeit has evolved a near deification of angels. Serious too is a church that seems to minimize the activity of Satan in its midst and therefore fails to deal aggressively with his influence, even as demonic activity in the guise of "New Age" makes inroads into the activity of the church. Thus to believe in angelic involvement in our lives without renouncing demonic power, as well as our own sin, is to court an overemphasis on subjective experience or even a Gnostic type of angel worship that is talked about in the Book of Colossians.

Speaking of angels, Spurgeon clarified their roles: "This, however, we know—that angels are set by God to be the *watchers* over his people. Jacob was asleep, but the angels were wide awake. They were going up and down that ladder while Jacob was lying there, steeped in slumber. So when you and I are sleeping, when the blessed God has put his finger on our eyelids, and said, 'Lie still, my child, and be refreshed,' there may be no policeman at the door, no body-guard to prevent intrusion, but there are angels ever watching over us. We shall not come to harm if we put our trust in God. 'I will lay me down to sleep, for thou makest me to dwell in safety.'

"These angels were also *messengers*. 'Are they not all ministering spirits?' and are they not sent with messages from God? To Jacob they had their errand. On more than one occasion angels bore him messages from the Most High. How far or how oft they bring us messages now I cannot tell. Sometimes thoughts drop into the soul that do not reach us in the regular connection of our thoughts. We scarcely know how to account for them. It may be they are due to the immediate action of the blessed Spirit, but they may, for aught we know, be brought by some other spirit, pure and heavenly, sent to suggest those thoughts to our soul. We cannot tell. The angels are watchers certainly, and they are messengers without a doubt.

"Moreover, they are our *protectors*. God employs them to bear us up in their hands, lest at any time we dash our foot against a stone. We do not see them, but unseen agencies are probably the strongest agencies in the world. We know it is so in physics. Such agencies as electricity, which we cannot perceive, are, nevertheless, unquestionably powerful, and, when put forth in their strength, quite beyond the control of man. No doubt myriads of spiritual creatures walk this earth, both when we sleep and when we wake. How much of good they do us it is impossible for us to tell. But this we do know—they are 'sent forth to minister to them that are heirs of salvation,' and they are in God's hands the means, oftentimes, of warding off from us a thousand ills which we know not of, and about which, therefore, we cannot thank God that we are kept from them, except we do so by thanking him, as I think we ought to do more often, for those unknown mercies which are none the less precious because we have not the sense to be able to perceive them. . . .

"There can be no spiritual powers which you or I have any need to fear. . . . Who can hurt the man whom God protects? Unseen powers and terrible they may be, but they cannot injure us, for there are other unseen powers more terrible still, the hosts of that Lord who is mighty in battle, and all these are sworn to protect the children of God. 'Thou hast given commandment to save me,' says David; and if God has charged his angels to protect and save his people from all harm, depend upon it they are secure."[33]

Continuing his thoughts on angels, Spurgeon preached at length, but with valuable insight: "*Each one of the saints is personally protected:* 'He shall give his angels charge over *thee*, to keep *thee* in all *thy* ways.' God takes a personal interest in every traveler along the right road, and charges his angels to keep him. . . .

"*This protection is perpetual,* as well as personal; God's angels are 'to keep thee *in all thy ways;*'—in thy ups and thy downs, in thy advancements and thy retirings;—to keep thee when thou art asleep, and when thou art awake;—to keep thee when thou art alone, and when thou art in company;—to keep thee if thou hast to preach, and to keep thee if thou hast to hear;—to keep thee if thou hast to serve, and to keep thee if thou hast to suffer. Thou always needest keeping, and thou shalt always have it, for the angels are charged 'to keep thee in all thy ways.'

"And how beautiful it is to remember that *all this keeping brings hon-our with it:* 'He shall give *his* angels charge over thee.' Notice that: 'He shall give *his* angels'—the very angels that wait upon God, and see his face;—the very angels that are the body-guard of the Eternal;—'He shall give *his* angels charge over *thee*.' 'Mark you,' says the Lord to Gabriel, or Michael, or whatever the angel's name may be, 'I charge you to take special care of that poor girl, for she is a daughter of mine. Take care of that poor man whom so many despise, for he is a prince of the blood imperial. He belongs to me; he is an heir of God, and joint-heir with Jesus Christ.' Oh, what amazing dignity this promise puts upon the very least and lowliest of the followers of the Lamb!

"Note just one more point, that *all these privileges come to us by Jesus Christ,* for Christ is that mystic ladder which Jacob saw, up and down whose wondrous rungs the angels came and went. The commerce between the saints and heaven is kept up by way of the person of the Lord Jesus Christ. Oh, what joy is this! If Christ is yours, angels are yours, and all the principalities and powers in the heavenly places will delight to take care of you."[34]

"Now, if anyone here is going home to a lonely room, I should like you to feel that you are not going there alone. Father and mother are away in the country, perhaps, and some of you young people feel quite alone in London; but, if you are believing in the Lord Jesus Christ, you are not alone, for the Lord of all the holy angels is with you, and an innumerable company of blessed spirits is round about you. Take comfort from this glorious truth. God's mysterious angelic agency, which you see not, and hear not, but which is most true and real, will form a cordon round about you to protect you in the midst of the temptations of this great city; and if you be but faithful to him, and keep in his ways, nothing shall hurt you between here and heaven. There may be many darts hurled at you, but the great shield of faith shall turn them all aside, or quench them for ever. You will have to encounter many temptations and trials, but you will be preserved amid them all. I heard a Primitive Methodist minister, speaking last Friday night, make use of a very strong expression while describing what a man could do by faith. He said, 'He can not only overcome a legion of devils, but he could kick his way through a lane of devils if he did but rest in God.' I have had that idea in my mind ever since I heard him use that expression; and I am sure that it is true, for some of us have had to do it already. Those devils are great cowards; so, when God once takes entire possession of a man, he need not fear even though all hell were let loose upon him. One butcher is not afraid of a thousand sheep; and one man, whom God makes strong, can put to rout all the hosts of hell, and he need not fear all the trials of life whatever they may be. 'If God be for us, who can be against us.'

"There are two or three thoughts which I think are worth remembering. The first is this. Dear brethren, we see, from this text, that *the lowest employment is consistent with the highest enjoyment.* The angels are our nurses: 'they shall bear thee up in their hands,' just as nurses hold up little children who are not able to stand by themselves. Those angels continually behold God's face, and live in the perfect bliss of heaven, yet they condescend to do such humble deeds as these. Dear brother, be like the angels in this respect; teach an infant class in the Sunday-school, yet keep your face bright with the light of God's countenance. Give away tracts, go and visit among the poor, look after fallen women, or do any other work for the Lord that needs to be done. Never mind what it is, but remember that the employment is all the more honourable because it appears to be so commonplace. Never was Christ grander, methinks, than when he washed his disciples' feet; certainly, never are we more like him than when we also are willing to wash their feet, or render any lowly service that they may need.

"The next thought is, *as angels watch over us, how cheerfully ought we to watch over one another!* How gladly you, who are older in the divine life, ought to watch over the younger ones of the Lord's family! If God enables you to have any of the joy of angels over repenting sinners, mind that you take some of the care which angels exercise over those who walk in God's ways. What can I, the pastor of this huge church, and my brother and all the elders, do by way of watching over five thousand of you? You must pastorize yourselves to a large extent. Watch over one another. 'Bear ye one another's burdens, and so fulfill the law of Christ.' Visit each other in your sicknesses; seek to bring back to Christ and the church all the backsliders whom you can find; labour for the good of one another; for, in this way only, can our task be done, and you shall be like the angels if you bear up the feeble ones in your hands lest they trip up and fall to their grievous hurt.

"Then, next, *how safe and happy we ought to feel when we know that God has charged the angels to take care of us!* Do not be afraid, my dear friend, when sickness comes into your house. Do not be alarmed, as perhaps you are, when you hear that there is fever next door to you. Remember the promise that precedes our text: 'Because thou hast made the Lord, which is my refuge, even the most High, thy habitation; there shall no evil befall thee, neither shall any plague come nigh thy dwelling.' But suppose it should seem right to the Lord to let the plague come to you, and suppose you shall die of it, well, you will the sooner be in heaven. Wherefore, comfort one another with the reflection that all is well with you as long as you keep in the way of duty.

"And, lastly, *how holy we ought to be with such holy beings watching over us!* If the angels are always hovering round you, mind what you are at.

Would you, my dear friend, have spoken as you did when you were coming in at that door yonder, if you had seen an angel standing by your side, listening to what you were saying? Oh, no; you are wonderfully decorous when there is somebody near whom you respect! How often your glib tongue is checked when there is some Christian man or woman, whom you highly esteem, within hearing! How many a thing is done that would not be done under the eye of one whom you love! It is not only true that 'a bird of the air shall carry the voice, and that which hath wings shall tell the matter'; but it is also true that there are angels watching over us evermore. Paul wrote to the Corinthians that a woman in the public assembly ought to have her head covered because of the angels,—a certain decorum was due because of the angels who were there; and I am sure that I may use the same argument concerning all our actions. Whether we are alone or in company, let us not sin, because angels are ever watching us, and the angels' Lord is also watching us. May he graciously keep us in his holy way; and if we are so kept, we shall be preserved from all evil while we are here; and, at last, we shall see his face with joy, and abide with him for ever. I would to God that all, who are now present, were in that holy way. I remind you once more that the entrance to it is by a door that has the blood-mark upon the lintel and the two door-posts: 'The blood shall be to you for a token.' 'Believe on the Lord Jesus Christ, and thou shalt be saved.'"[35]

In the ultimate validation of the ministry of angels, Spurgeon points once again to our Lord's agony in Gethsemane: "'My God, my God, why hast thou forsaken me?' . . . let us meditate for a little while upon OUR LORD'S STRENGTHENING: 'There appeared an angel unto him from heaven, strengthening him.'

"It is night, and there he kneels, under the olives, offering up, as Paul says, 'prayers and supplications with strong crying and tears unto him that was able to save him from death.' While wrestling there, he is brought into such a state of agony that he sweats great drops of blood; and, suddenly, there flashes before him, like a meteor from the midnight sky, a bright spirit that had come straight from the throne of God to minister to him in his hour of need.

"Think of *the condescension on Christ's part to allow an angel to come and strengthen him*. He is the Lord of angels as well as of men. At his bidding, they fly more swiftly than the lightning flash to do his will. Yet, in his extremity of weakness, he was succoured by one of them. It was a wondrous stoop for the infinitely-great and ever-blessed Christ of God to consent that a spirit of his own creation should appear unto him, and strengthen him.

"But while I admire the condescension which permitted one angel to come, I equally admire *the self-restraint which allowed only one to come*; for, if he had so pleased, he might have appealed to his Father, and he would at once have sent to him 'more than twelve legions of angels.' No, he did not make such a request; he rejoiced to have one to strengthen him, but he would not have any more. . . .

"How could the angel strengthen Christ? That is a very natural enquiry; but it is quite possible that, when we have answered that question as well as we can, we shall not have given a full and satisfactory reply to it. Yet I can conceive that, in some mysterious manner, an angel from heaven *may have actually infused fresh vigour into the physical constitution of Christ*. I cannot positively affirm that it was so, but it seems to me a very likely thing. We do know that God can suddenly communicate new strength to fainting spirits; and, certainly, if he willed it, he could thus lift up the drooping head of his Son, and make him feel strong and resolute again.

"Perhaps it was so; but, in any case, it must have strengthened the Saviour *to feel that he was in pure company*. It is a great joy to a man, who is battling for the right against a crowd who love the wrong, to find a comrade by his side who loves the truth as he loves it himself. . . .

"Next to that, was *the tender sympathy which this angelic ministration proved*. I can imagine that all the holy angels leant over the battlements of heaven to watch the Saviour's wondrous life; and now that they see him in the garden, and perceive, by his whole appearance, and his desperate agony, that death is drawing near to him, they are so astonished that they crave permission that at least one of their number shall go down to see if he cannot carry succour to him from his Father's house above. I can imagine the angels saying, 'Did we not sing of him at Bethlehem when he was born? Did not some of us minister to him when he was in the desert, and amongst wild beasts, hungry after his long fast and terrible temptation? Has he not been seen of angels all the while he has been on earth? Oh, let some one of us go to his relief!' And I can readily suppose that God said to Gabriel, 'Thy name means, "The strength of God," go and strengthen your Lord in Gethsemane,' 'and there appeared an angel unto him from heaven strengthening him'; and I think that he was strengthened, at least in part, by observing the sympathy of all the heavenly host with him in his season of secret sorrow. He might seem to be alone as man; but, as Lord and King, he had on his side an innumerable company of angels who waited to do his will; and here was one of them come to assure him that he was not alone, after all. . . .

"If we are despised and rejected of men, if we are deserted and defamed by those who ought to have dealt differently with us, even a tender look from a child will help to remove our depression. In times of loneliness, it is something even to have a dog with you, to lick your hand, and show you such kindness as is possible from him. And our blessed Master, who always appreciated, and still appreciates, the least service rendered to him,—for not a cup of cold water, given to a disciple, in Christ's name, shall lose its reward,—was cheered by the devotion and homage of the ministering spirit that came from heaven to strengthen him. I wonder if the angel worshipped him,—I think that he could do no less; and it must have been something to worship the blood-red Son of God. Oh, that any one of us could have paid him such homage as that! The time for such special ministry as that is over now; yet my faith seems to bring him back here, at this moment, just as if we were in Gethsemane. I adore thee, thou blessed eternal God,— never more God-like than when thou didst prove thy perfect manhood by sweating great drops of blood in the awful weakness of thy depression in the garden of sorrow!

"Peradventure, too, the angel's presence comforted and strengthened the Saviour *as being a sort of foretaste of his final victory.* What was this angel but the pioneer of all the heavenly host that would come to meet him when the fight was over? He was one who, in full confidence of his Lord's victory, had flown before the rest, to pay homage to the conquering Son of God, who would tread the old dragon beneath his feet. You remember how, when Jesus was born, first there came one angel who began to speak of him to the shepherds, 'and suddenly there was with the angel a multitude of the heavenly host praising God, and saying, Glory to God in the highest, and on earth peace, good will toward men.' The first angel had, as it were, stolen a march upon his brethren, and got before them; but, no sooner was the wondrous news bruited through heaven's streets, than every angel resolved to overtake him ere his message was completed. So, here again is one that had come as an outrider, to remind his Lord of his ultimate victory, and there were many more afterwards to come with the same glad tidings; but, to the Saviour's heart, that angel's coming was a token that he would lead captivity captive. . . .

"Yet once more, *is it not very likely that this angel brought the Saviour a message from heaven?* The angels are generally God's messengers, so they have something to communicate from him; and, perhaps, this angel, bending over the Saviour's prostrate form, whispered in his ear, 'Be of good cheer; thou must pass through all this agony, but thou wilt thereby save an innumerable multitude of the sons and daughters of men, who will love and worship thee and thy Father for ever and for ever. He is with thee even at this moment. Though he must hide his face from thee, because of the requirements of justice that the atonement may be complete, his heart is with thee, and he loves thee ever.' Oh, how our Lord Jesus must have been cheered if some such words as these were whispered into his ears! . . .

"*In your times of deepest need, you may expect the greatest comforters to come to you.* Let me remind you that an angel appeared to Joseph when Herod was seeking Christ's life. Then, later, angels appeared to Christ when the devil had been tempting him. And now, at Gethsemane, when there was a peculiar manifestation of diabolical malice, for it was the hour of the powers of darkness; then, when the devil was loose, and doing his utmost against Christ, an angel came from heaven to strengthen him. So, when you are in your heaviest trials, you shall have your greatest strength. Perhaps you will have little to do with angels till you get into deep trouble, and then shall the promise be fulfilled, 'He shall give his angels charge over thee, to keep thee in all thy ways. They shall bear thee up in their hands, lest thou dash thy foot against a stone.'"[36]

With the balance so characteristic of Spurgeon, however, we cannot stay with the comforting ministry of angels. For above all, there is the presence of God himself. In reference once again to Jacob in the Old Testament, Spurgeon declares: "Jacob was alone. He was a man that loved society. There are many signs of that. Perhaps, for the first time in his life, he was then out of the shelter of his tent, and away from the familiar voices of his beloved father and mother. He had always been his mother's son. Something about him had always attracted her. But now no one was within call. He might, perhaps, have heard the roar of the wild beast, but no familiar voice of a friend was anywhere near. It was a very lonely night to him. Some of us recollect the first night we were away from home—how dreary we felt as children. The same kind of home-sickness will come over men and women when they say to themselves, 'Now, at last, I have got out of the range wherein I have been accustomed to go, and I have got away from the dear familiar faces that made life so happy to me.' Yes, but it was just then that God appeared to him, and have not you found it so? Amidst darkest shades Christ appears to you. Have you not had times of real desolation of spirit, from one cause or another, in which the Lord has seemed more sweet to you than ever he was before? When all created streams have run dry, the everlasting fount has bubbled up with more sweet and cooling streams than it ever did at any other time. Well; recollect all those scenes, and the accompanying circumstances which made them seem so cheering, and then say, 'This God, even the God of Bethel, is still my God; and if I am at present in trouble, if I am as lonely now as I was then, if I am brought so low that literally I have nothing but a doorstep for my pillow; if I should lose house, and home, and friends, and be left like an orphan amidst the wild winds, with none to shelter me, yet, O God of Bethel, thou who wast the cover of my head and the protector of my spirit, wilt still be with me, the God of those early visitations in times of my dark distress.' Thus the God of Bethel by that visit cheered Jacob's heart."[37]

Continuing with the same theme regarding the presence of God as a comfort, Spurgeon urges a special turning to God in one's need. "On the other hand, if you do not come to Jesus, and commune with him of all that is in your heart, *you will lose his counsel and help, and the comfort that comes from them.* . . . There is many a child of God, who might be rich to all the intents of bliss, who continues to be as poor as Lazarus the beggar; he has hardly a crumb of comfort to feed upon, and is full of doubts and fears, when he might have had full assurance long ago. There is many an heir of heaven who is living upon the mere husks of gospel food when he might be eating the rich fare of which Moses speaks: 'Butter of kine, and milk of sheep, with fat of lambs, and rams of the breed of Bashan, and goats, with the fat of kidneys of wheat.' Very often, beloved, you have not because you ask not; or because you believe not, or because you do not confide in Jesus, and commune with him."[38]

"Sometimes, our naughty habit of *reticence towards Jesus is aggravated by our eagerness to tell our troubles to others.* In the time of trial, we often imitate king Asa, who, when he was sick, 'sought not to the Lord, but to the physicians.' It was not wrong to go to the physicians, but he should have gone to the Lord first. It is the same with many of you as it was with Asa, away you go to your neighbor over the fence, or you call in a friend, and have a talk with him in your own drawing-room, or you go to some great one, and tell him all your trouble; yet how much have you gained by doing so? Have you not often found that you would have been wiser if you had followed Solomon's advice, 'Go not into thy brother's house in the day of thy calamity'? Have you not also frequently discovered that, when you have talked over your griefs with your friends, they still remain? . . .

"You say that you want a friend; yet he who is the Friend that sticketh closer than a brother is neglected by you. Suppose the Lord Jesus Christ were to meet some of you, and you were to say to him, 'Good Master, we are in trouble;' and suppose he should say to you, 'Where have you been with your trouble? You have not been to me'; and you were to reply, 'No, Lord, we have been consulting with flesh and blood; we have been asking our friends to help us'; and suppose he were to say to you, 'And have they disappointed you?' and you had to reply, 'Yea, Lord, they have'; suppose he looked at you severely, and said, 'Where you have already gone, you had better go again. You went to your friends first; are you coming to me last? Am I to play the lackey to you, and do you only come to me after having tried all others?' Ah! if he did talk like that, what could you reply? Why, I think your only answer could be, and I trust your answer now will be, 'Jesus, Master, I have too much forgotten thee. I have not regarded thee as a real present Friend. I have gone to my neighbours because I could see them, and speak with them, and hear what they had to say to me; but I have thought of thee as if thou wert a myth, or, perhaps, I have not thought of thee at all. Forgive me, Lord, for I do believe that thou art, and that thy Word is true, which declares that thou art ever with thy people, and help me, henceforth, by thy grace, always to come to thee.'

"... Are you very grieved? Are you smitten of God, and afflicted? Then, brother, sister, you may well go to Jesus with your sorrows, for he is the Man of sorrows and acquainted with grief. He knows all about you, and all about your sorrows, too. There is not a pang that you have ever felt but he has felt the like. If you will only talk with him, you will find an open ear, and a sympathetic heart, and a ready hand, all placed at your disposal. 'What do you mean, sir? Do you mean that I am to sit down in my room, and tell Jesus all about my troubles?' Yes, I do mean just that; and as you would do if you could see him sitting in the chair on the other side of the fire, sit down, and tell it all to him. If you have a quiet and secluded chamber, speak aloud if that will help you; but, anyhow, tell it all to him, pour into his ear and heart the story which you cannot disclose to anyone else. 'But it seems so fanciful to imagine that I can really speak to Jesus.' Try it, beloved; if you have faith in God, you will discover that it is not a matter of fancy, but the most blessed reality in the world."[39]

Rarely has a society been so isolated. We avoid problems by going to extremes. If we are intruded upon or taken advantage of, we withdraw like the sea urchin, who finding himself alone on the beach at low tide, quickly draws in his tentacles when touched ever so gently by a foreign object. We find it hard to state reasonable boundaries, while at the same time acting under divine orders to extend ourselves for others when that is the right thing to do seems equally difficult. Every need cannot constitute a call. But at the same time we are called to be selfless and giving. We are called to follow the call of God rather than the impulse of the need of the moment or our own selfishness. But that kind of balance requires a close walk with God. Without it we flounder in a life of overextension or a self-occupation that turns into the me-ism so characteristic of our times.

Other factors, like constant mobility, the buying of services rather than friends and family helping each other, an absence of good Bible teaching, a focus on material goods and money as well as the worship of technological advances referred to at the beginning of this section, all contribute to the loneliness of our times.

Loneliness is not the same as aloneness. For one can be quite happy alone, while at the same time one can be lonely in a crowd. Loneliness implies that something is going wrong. It involves alienation or frustration or just overload in a time frame where information is given faster than it can be absorbed and demands seem to multiply in spite of time-saving devices and technologies.

Loneliness can be helped in all sorts of human ways: a friend's listening ear, the love of a child, a quiet walk by the sea with all of its predictability and reassurance. But ultimately our loneliness is dissolved in the presence of our Lord.

Not too long before his death, I received a letter from a prominent church leader. It was a warm, handwritten note relating to the publication of my book *Amma*, a book that was written about Amy Carmichael.

After his death I bought a book he wrote as he was going through those deep waters of a terminal illness. One thing stood out in particular. He talked about his resolve to spend the first hour of every day with his Lord and not to give that time to anyone else. For me, rather than fitting God in somewhere in the morning, I found that to put him as the first person of the day led to a whole different feeling about the so-called "quiet time." It became a daily appointment. It became routine. It became a meeting between me and God that I could look forward to. When a problem arose during the day, I could also say to myself, "Just let it go until morning when you can talk to your heavenly Father about this." Usually, after I talked to him—and listened—I regained a sense of calm. Indeed my whole life seemed to have a greater sense of calm, even when the answers weren't immediate.

Sometimes as I stand and watch the ocean in all of its majesty, and I see the waves crash on the shore and then retreat again, I am struck with the constancy of it all. The waves go out, but they always come back in. They don't change. So in our lives we never eradicate loneliness. It may retreat like the sea, and we feel it's really gone. When it comes crashing back, we may feel it will never go. But neither is true, because loneliness, apart from its increase in our time, has been and always will be a human state. Not until heaven will we eradicate it, for it is not a disease, it is a human condition.

Friends and family can help. Confidence and a fulfillment in a task help. But on this earth the only real relief is that daily living in the presence of our Lord Jesus Christ. Our appointment with him each day is the antidote to loneliness.

Once again in the words of Spurgeon: "If you have faith in God, you will discover that it is not a matter of fancy, but the most blessed reality in the world."[40]

We shall never rise to the highest spiritual state by having all rain and no sunshine. Although we may prefer it, we shall never attain to the fullest fruit-bearing by having all sunshine and no rain. God puts the one over against the other, the dark day of cloud and tempest against the bright day of sunshine and calm; and when the two influences work together in the soul, as they do in the natural world, they produce the greatest degree of fertility, and the best condition of heart and life.[1]

6

CHANGE

Today I received a letter from Mentone, France, from the retired Ambassador of Sweden Per Anger and his wife, Elena, wishing me health and happiness for this last year of the millennium. Over a hundred years ago that greatest preacher of perhaps all time, Charles Haddon Spurgeon, died in Mentone, France, in the year 1892. The same place, separated by a century, provided refuge to people who have become very special to me. Both escaped their own countries, Sweden and England, during the harsh winter weather and found respite in the warmth of southern France. There is continuity along with change. Greatness exists with human need. The place remains, the players change.

We are in the process of a major transition from one century to another, one millennium to the next. Not for a thousand years will that happen again. Indeed the twentieth century itself has been a major transition from horse and buggy to automobile, from outhouse to indoor plumbing, from candle to lightbulb, from information by word of mouth and printing press to television, computer, and the Internet.

I heard one prominent leader say resentfully that she didn't understand why time had to be marked by the advent of Christ. But it *is* measured by the birth of God made flesh, and the fact that time itself is marked by that one person, Jesus Christ, adds to all the evidence of the reality of the Christian faith. That reality doesn't change. God remains unchangeable. But one of the most unnerving as well as challenging aspects of human existence is change. New is scary; even good new is scary just because it is new and means change. For that reason, health experts have recommended that, when possible, change be spread out to avoid too much at any one time. Yet when that change is death or illness or unexpected expenditures of money bunching together at one time, the idea of planned change evaporates and one struggles to get through the pressure and survive. Try telling a man who has just lost his job that he should have planned better. Remind a person who has just lost every earthly possession in a hurricane that it is better not to lose everything at one time!

But often changing jobs, moving to a new house, and redecorating a home can be spread out so that the change and stress are not concentrated into one small time zone. Even in small ways, like spreading Christmas-gift shopping throughout the year or simplifying the entertainment of guests when other demands are pressing in, the pressure of everyday demands and change can be minimized and one is also left free in case "big" things like illnesses come unexpectedly. As one doctor once said to me, "Don't overextend so much that you live so on the edge that even a stopped-up drain is too much to handle." Change causes stress and too much stress, whatever its source, makes it difficult to handle change.

Whatever we say about change and however we view it, change is inevitable. It will happen, for life never remains static. The healthy will become ill. The strong will have moments of weakness. The wealthy may have reversals in their fortunes, and the poor may become affluent. For some their present suffering will yet be alleviated, while for others much suffering may come in the future. The woman who said to me, "I will never change again" was foolish, for everything earthly changes.

Spurgeon spoke of the inevitability of change: "We have many things in our possession at the present moment which can be shaken, and it ill becomes a Christian man to set much store by them. The poorest man amongst us has many providential blessings for which to be grateful this morning, but the richest amongst us has nothing earthly upon which he can depend. Wife and children make glad our hearth; we have a little place which may be very homely, but it is our home, and we love it. Some of you are prospering and thriving traders, others are merchants who have almost accumulated a competency; be grateful for all this, but do not forget that these are things which may be shaken. The cheek of the wife may grow pale, the lustrous eyes of the little ones may soon become dim, the house may be left a heap of ashes, the property may take to itself wings and fly away: there is nothing stable beneath these rolling skies; change is written upon all things.

"Yet, my brethren, some of us have certain 'things which cannot be shaken,' and I invite you . . . to read over the catalogue of them, that if the things which can be shaken should all be taken away, you may derive real comfort from the things that cannot be shaken, which will remain. In the first place, whatever your losses may have been, you enjoy *present salvation*. You are this morning standing at the foot of his cross, trusting alone in the merit of Jesu's precious blood, and no rise or fall of the markets can interfere with your salvation in him; no breaking of banks, no run upon your credit, can touch that. A sinner saved! I recollect the time when I thought that if I had to live on bread and water all my life, and to be chained in a dungeon all my days, I would cheerfully submit to that if I might but get rid of my sins; when sin haunted and burdened my spirit, I am sure I would have counted the martyr's death to be preferable to a life under the lash of a guilty conscience. Now, your sins are all gone, there is not one left in God's book; through Jesu's blood you are clean, and that is a comfort which cannot be removed. . . .

"In the next place, you are *a child of God* to-day. God is your Father. No change of circumstances can ever rob you of that. If you were a peer of the realm you might be degraded; if you have walked among the rich you might be thrust out from their society; father and mother might forsake you, but you can never lose this joyous fact, that you are an heir of God, joint-heir with Jesus Christ. Coming out of losses and poverty, stripped bare, you can say, 'He is my Father still. Naked came I out of my mother's womb, and naked shall I return thither; but to my Father shall I return, and in my Father's house are many mansions; therefore will I not be troubled.' You have this day another permanent blessing, namely, *the love of Jesus Christ.* He who is God and man loves you with all the strength of his affectionate nature. Now, nothing can rob you of that. You can look to the cross, and know that he who died on it died for you; and he who reigns in heaven reigns for you and pleads for you. No catastrophes can deprive you of that. . . .

"Beloved, you have another thing, namely this truth, that *whatever may happen to you, you have God's faithful promise which holds true that all things shall work for your good.* Do you believe this? . . . The ship rocks!— What a wave was that! What a sea the vessel shipped! She rocks again, the sails fly to ribbons. How the yards are snapping! The masts will go by the board. The frail bark will be wrecked; the danger is imminent, she must be wrecked. The rocks are ahead, and she must be dashed upon them! Not so, thou passenger in the ship of Providence, not so. Dost thou see who it is that is at the helm, and dost thou not know that he who steers the ship also wings the winds and gives force to the waves? God is not the God of the vessel only, but of the stormy sea also. Therefore go thou where thou mayest be quiet, betake thyself to the hinder part of the ship near to the steersman, and go to sleep in peace. . . .

"Once more, if everything should melt away, yet you have a '*city that hath foundations, whose builder and maker is God.*' Sometimes foreign princes when they have been afraid of a revolution have invested all their money in the English funds, and then they have said, 'Now come what may, my prosperity is safe.' Ah, well, it is a blessed thing to invest all your wealth in the heavenly funds, and then let the earth go to ruin, our treasure is safe. Let the world, like an old water-logged hulk, go down if she will, it is a wonder that she keeps afloat so long—let her go, I am in the life-boat which can never sink; and soon shall be on shore where tempests cannot blow. Oh, to rest in assured hope, the hope that maketh not ashamed, the hope that shall never be confounded; the hope that when days and years are passed, we shall see the face of Jesus and dwell with him for ever! Courage, brethren, our best portion and richest heritage remains, and cannot be moved. Rejoice in this, and be of good cheer this day."[2]

In summary Spurgeon says, "How few families are long without severe trials: hardly a person escapes for any long season without tribulation. With impartial hand sorrow knocks at the door of the palace and the cottage." In this world change and even pain are inevitable. Yet great comfort lies in the fact that *"your troubles are all apportioned to you by divine wisdom and love."*[3]

With his characteristic understanding of human nature Spurgeon speaks of exceptions to the idea that most of us dislike change: "Some spirits are given to change, and would almost leap from the pan into the fire, but others of us take root deeply and dread transplanting."[4]

Yet for that vast majority of us who dislike too much change, especially when it is thrust upon us, Spurgeon offers comfort as well as practical help. For even when there is "good" change the stress can be difficult. Those who suddenly acquire great fortunes have new anxieties about changes in people's attitude toward them, or they face heavy taxes, or they fear loss. When they were poor they knew who their friends were. Now they are not sure. Taxes used to be simple; now they are complicated. And when they were poor they had little to lose, while now they have much to lose.

Very often, however, change does not come as a pleasant relief but as a problem, a source of pain. More often than not there is loss or discomfort. For while change can offer a better position or greater wealth, many times the change brings in something that is not only new but difficult. Says Spurgeon: "When the Lord calls us to a change of position, and brings out a new burden, he removes the older load. We shall not to-morrow be pressed with the weight of to-day. I do not know what my trials may be seven years hence, but I do know that the trials of the month of June, 1872, will not then disturb me. When we bow beneath the infirmities of age, we may rest assured that we shall not be annoyed by the temptations of boyhood, nor molested by the vexations of middle life. In advancing, there are prospects of gain as well as of loss.

"Moreover, although we have not passed this way heretofore, *the path runs in the right direction.*"[5]

Furthermore, "to-day's grief will only be new for to-day and for a little time to come; it will soon grow old if we live long enough, and we shall become as used to the new trial as to the old. . . . Press on, press on, ye warriors of the cross; the new foes shall be as the old. The novelty of sorrow is but of the hour; the hour will wear it out as it wears out itself, and we shall receive strength to bear up under all."[6]

Change that challenges our faith is often viewed in contemporary evangelical circles as punishment for sin. Yet as we look around us, can we honestly say that the friend who lost a loved one and a job in the same week is not walking with God while the couple enjoying their multiple inheritances are godly pillars of the church? Says Spurgeon: "In the autobiography of the famous Franké of Halle, who built, and, in the hand of God, provided for, the orphanhouse of Halle, he says, 'I thought when I committed myself and my work to God by faith, that I had only to pray when I had need, and that the supplies would come; but I found, that I had sometimes to wait and pray for a long time.' The supplies did come, but not at once. The pinch never went so far as absolute want; but there were intervals of severe pressure. There was nothing to spare. Every spoonful of meal had to be scraped from the bottom of the barrel, and every drop of oil that oozed out seemed as if it must be the last; but still it never did come to the last drop, and there was always just a little meal left. Bread shall be given us, but not always in quartern loaves; our water shall be sure, but not always a brook full, it may only come in small cups. God has not promised to take any of you to heaven without trying your faith. He will not fail you, but he will bring you very low. He will not forsake you, but he will test you and prove you."[7] The ultimate timing is in his hands.

And again: "God never left Paul, but I have seen the spot where Paul's head was smitten off by the headsman. The Lord never left Peter, but Peter, like his Master, had to die by crucifixion. The Lord never left the martyrs, but they had to ride to heaven in chariots of fire. The Lord has never left his church, but oftentimes his church has been trodden as straw is trodden for the dunghill; her blood has been scattered over the whole earth, and she has seemed to be utterly destroyed. Still, you know, the story of the church is only another illustration of my text; God has not failed her, nor forsaken her; in the deaths of her saints we read, not defeat, but victory; as they passed away one by one, stars ceasing to shine below, they shone with tenfold brilliance in the upper sky because of the clouds through which they passed before they reached their celestial spheres. Beloved, we may have to groan in a Gethsemane, but God will not fail us: we may have to die on a Golgotha, but he will not forsake us. We shall rise again, and, as our Master was triumphant through death, even so shall we through the greatest suffering and the most terrible defeats rise to his throne."[8]

"It is a mistake to think that our safety or our danger is according to our nearness to God, or our distance from him," Spurgeon warns. "A man who is near to God can stand on the pinnacle of the temple, and the devil may tempt him to throw himself down, and yet he will be firm as the temple itself. A man that is without God may be in the safest part of the road, and traverse a level way, and yet he will stumble. It is not the road, but the Lord that keepeth the pilgrim's foot. O heir of heaven, commit thou thy way unto God, and make him thine all in all, and rise above the creature into the Creator, and then shalt thou hunger no more, neither thirst any more, neither shall the heat nor the sun smite thee."[9]

"You who are God's favourites must not marvel at trials."[10] Spurgeon illustrates God's methods by comparing his people to precious stones. "The lapidary, if he takes up a stone and finds that it is not very precious, will not spend much care in cutting it; but when he gets a rare diamond of the first water, then he will be sure to cut, and cut, and cut again. When the Lord finds a saint whom he loves—loves much—he may spare other men trials and troubles, but he certainly will not this well-beloved one. The more beloved you are the more of the rod you shall have. It is an awful thing to be a favourite of heaven. It is a thing to be sought after and to be rejoiced in; but remember, to be of the King's council-chamber is a thing involving such work for faith that flesh and blood might shrink from the painful blessing. The gardener gets a tree, and if it is but of a poor sort he will let it grow as it wills, and take what fruit comes from it naturally; but if it be of a very rare sort, he likes to have every bough in its proper place, so that it may bear well; and he often takes out his knife and cuts here and cuts there, because, says he, 'That is a favourite tree, and it is one which bears such fruit that I would have much from it, and would leave nothing whatever that would cause it detriment.'"[11]

For "you must be very little acquainted with the history of the people of God if you think that they are strangers to these conflicts. There are some old mariners here that I could call up into the pulpit, if it were needed, to tell you that they have done business on great waters many years, and they have encountered many storms. You cannot expect to be upon these seas and not have tossings to and fro sometimes. The strongest faith that ever was in this world has sometimes faltered. Even Abraham had times when his faith was exceeding weak, though, indeed, at other times it staggered not at the promise through unbelief. David was a great man in battle, but he waxed faint, and had like to have been slain. So you will find the bravest of God's servants have their times when it is hard to hold their own; when they would be glad to creep into a mouse-hole, if they could there find themselves a shelter. But this is the point, dear brothers and sisters—no soul that rests in Jesus will ever be wrecked. You may have the tempests and tossings, but you will come to land; be sure of that."[12]

Sometimes when we plead for our adverse circumstances to change, God simply makes us content where we are. "Many saints have found riches in poverty, ease in labour, rest in pain, and delight in affliction. Our Lord can so adapt our minds to our circumstances, that the bitter is sweet, and the burden is light. Paul speaks of the saints 'as sorrowful, yet always rejoicing.'"[13]

Speaking of his own life in a letter that was read at the Metropolitan Tabernacle on Lord's Day, January 17, 1875: "After enduring much intense pain, I am now recovering, and, like a little child, am learning to stand, and to totter from chair to chair. The trial is hot, but does not last long, and there is herein much cause for gratitude. My last two attacks have been of this character. It may be the will of God that I should have many more of these singular seizures, and if so I hope you will have patience with me. I have done all as to diet, abstinence from stimulants, and so on, which could be done, and as the evil still continues, the cause must be elsewhere. We call the evil 'gout' for want of a better word, but it differs widely from the disorder which goes under that name. On the last two occasions I had an unusual pressure of work upon me, and I broke down. My position among you is such that I can just keep on at a medium pace if I have nothing extra, but the extra labour overthrows me. If I were an iron man you should have my whole strength till the last particle had been worn away, but as I am only dust, you must take from me what I can render, and look for no more. May the service which I can render be accepted of the Lord.

". . . Wounded on the battle-field, I raise myself on my arm and cry to those around me, and urge them to espouse my Master's cause, for if we were wounded or dead for his sake all would be gain. By the splendour of redeeming love, I charge each believer to confess his Lord, and live wholly to him."[14]

For Spurgeon, his physical and emotional pain provided a built-in source of change. He could work, then he could not; and frequently the changes from health to unhealth came unforeseen. That change was his constant enemy. Yet the very enemy of ill health that plagued so much of his life was what made him such a great man of faith. For his strength was most certainly from God.

While a negative change in circumstances does not necessarily imply punishment for sin, it can be God's way of preparing us for service. It is God's sandpaper. Comments Spurgeon: "When I met with a man that never had an ache or a pain, or a day's sickness in his life, I used to envy him; but I do not now, because I feel very confident that he is a loser by his unvarying experience. How can a man sympathize with trouble that he never knew? How can he be tender in heart if he has never been touched with infirmity himself? If one is to be a comforter of others, he must know the sorrows and the sicknesses of others in his measure. It was essential to our Lord, and, certainly, what was essential to him is necessary to those who are to be shepherds of others, as he was. Now, it may be that by nature some of us are not very sympathetic; I do not think Job was: it is possible that though he was kind, and generous to the poor, yet he was rather hard, but his troubles taught him sympathy. And, perhaps, the Lord may send you trouble till you become softer in heart, so that afterwards you will be one who can speak a word in season to the weary. As you sit down by the bedside of the invalid, you will be able to say, 'I know all the ins and outs of a sick man's feelings, for I have been sore sick myself.' When God has wrought that in you, it may be he will turn your captivity."[15]

Furthermore, we have all encountered those false comforters, who sound spiritual but who feel that everyone ought to just pull themselves up by their bootstraps and go on. These comforters measure out their help by what they feel should be enough, not by what the need demands. Spurgeon had little tolerance for such so-called comfort: "Some men have no more feeling than granite. They will say about the collection to-day, 'I shall not give anything to the hospitals. Let the people take care of themselves. If they were more thrifty they would have a little laid by for a rainy day, and would not need to have hospitals provided for them.' This gentleman can supply wagon-loads of the same sort of hard material. I know you, my friend, I have known you, too, a long time. I was going to say, 'I would be happy to attend your funeral'; but I will not say so, lest it seem that I am hardening myself under your influence; and besides, there are so many of your order, that one more or less is of no great consequence."[16]

Of the same type of person in relation to physical pain and its vicissitudes Spurgeon says, "There is the furnace of *physical pain*. How soon is the strong man brought low! We who rejoiced in health are in a few moments made to mourn and moan, not in weakness merely, but in pain and anguish. He only thinks little of pain who is a stranger to it."[17] There are other afflictions that many who do not suffer in the same way cannot or will not understand. "The child sickens, the wife is gradually declining, the husband is smitten down with a stroke, friend after friend departs as star by star grows dim. We bitterly cry with Job, 'Lover and friend hast thou put far from me, and mine acquaintance unto darkness.' Then added to this there will crowd in upon us *temporal losses and sufferings*. The business which we thought would enrich, impoverishes. We build the house, but providence plucks it down with both its hands. We hoist the sail and seek to make headway; but we are driven by a back wind far from the desired haven. 'Except the Lord build the house, they labour in vain that build it.' I cannot multiply the description of these

170

crosses which our heavenly Father in his mysterious providence lays upon his beloved ones. Certain is that, like the waves of the sea, the drops of rain, the sands of the wilderness, and the leaves of the forest the griefs of the Lord's people are innumerable. Into the central heat of the fire doth the Lord cast his saints, and mark you this, he casts them there because they are his own beloved and dearly loved people. I do not see the goldsmith putting dross into the furnace—what would be the good of it? It would be a waste of fuel and labour. But he thrusts the crucible full of gold into the hottest part of the fire and heaps on coals till the heat is terrible. Some of you have no crosses; you are like Moab, 'settled on your lees'; 'you are not emptied from vessel to vessel,' because ye are reprobate, and God careth not for you: but the pure gold is put into the furnace to make it purer still. As silver is purified in a furnace of earth seven times, simply because it is silver, so are saints afflicted because of their preciousness in the sight of the Lord. Men will not be at such pains to purify iron as they will with silver; for when iron is brought to a tolerable degree of purity it works well, but silver must be doubly refined, till no dross is left. Men do not cut common pebbles on the lapidary's wheel, but the diamond must be vexed again, and again, and again with sharp cuttings, and even so must the believer."[18]

At times the same selfishness that leaves others alone in their pain is so absorbed in its own pain that for an entirely different reason the pain of others is ignored. "Too many people are so *wrapped up in their own grief* that they have no room in their souls for sympathy. Do you not know them? The first thing when they rise in the morning, is the dreadful story of the night they have passed. Ah, dear! and they have not quite eaten a hearty breakfast, before their usual pain is somewhere or other coming over them. They must have the special care and pity of the whole household. All the day long the one great business is to keep everybody aware of how much the great sufferer is enduring. It is this person's patent right to monopolize all the sympathy which the market can supply, and then there will be none to spare for the rest of the afflicted. If you are greatly taken up with self, there is not enough of you to run over to anybody else. How different this from our Lord, who never cried, 'Have pity upon me! Have pity upon me, O my friends!' He is described as 'endur-

171

ing the cross, despising the shame.' So strong was he in love, that, though he saved others, himself he could not save; though he succoured the afflicted, none succoured him."[19]

Furthermore, "men who are *wrapped up in their own glories are not sympathetic*. Is it not a fine thing to spend life in contemplating one's own magnificence? Those who are amazed at their own greatness have no thought to spare for the suffering. 'No,' says the man, 'the masses must obey the laws of supply and demand, and get on as well as they can. Let them do as I have done. I might have been as poor as they are, if I had shown as little push and enterprise as they do.'"[20]

As we journey through this life to our final abode in heaven, we will pass through much change, some of which will be painful, for "a Christian man is seldom long at ease."[21] We can waste that change or we can grow. We can just get by or we can minister to others. But if we are to help others through their pain, if we are to be true comforters, we will need to get into their skin and come from where they come from. If something that we feel would not hurt us hurts another person, that does not mean the other person's pain is not real. Indeed we ourselves may complain about things that hurt us which may in turn seem insignificant to someone else. We suffer differently from each other based on our personalities and backgrounds as well as our present circumstances. Sometimes even fatigue can make us more sensitive to pain or conflict. Just look at a tired child who hasn't had a nap.

A small child sat contentedly on the floor eating the remains of her dish of ice cream. With a deliberate slowness she savored every bite of her favorite dessert. In a manner that was as hurried as the child was slow, an adult grabbed her dish and started to take it to the kitchen. When the child wailed in protest, the adult admonished her and threatened punishment. Another adult stepped in quietly, held the child, and allowed her to finish her two remaining bites. To one person, two bites of ice cream seemed silly to worry about. To the child, two bites of ice cream meant a lot and the person taking it from her seemed unfair. The incident is so illustrative of our Father's comfort to us. God understands trivia, small hurts, as well as the catastrophic events that occur in our lives. Others may not always comprehend our needs, but down to the smallest trivial detail God understands. And we Christians are to have the mind of Christ.

With God nothing relating to human souls is a trifle. No transition is too small for him to notice. No imperfection is too faint for him to ignore. Says Spurgeon: "I was in a diamond-cutting factory at Amsterdam, and I noticed that there were huge wheels revolving, and a great deal of power being developed and expended; but when I came to look at the little diamond,—in some cases a very small one indeed,—upon which that power was being brought to bear, it seemed very remarkable that all that power should be concentrated upon such a little yet very precious object. In a similar style, all the wheels of providence and nature, great as they are, are brought to bear, by divine skill and love, upon a thing which appears to many people to be of trifling value, but which is to Christ of priceless worth; namely, a human soul."[22]

God has high expectations for his church as that body of Christ helps those who are wounded. For "if you have been helped as well as converted, you are especially bound to lay yourself out to help others. When a person who has been very despondent, comes out into comfort, he should look out for desponding spirits, and use his own experience as a cordial to the fainting. I do not think that I ever feel so much at home in any work as when I am trying to encourage a heart which is on the verge of despair, for I have been in that plight myself. It is a high honour to nurse our Lord's wounded children. It is a great gift to have learned by experience how to sympathize. 'Ah!' I say to them, 'I have been where you are!' They look at me, and their eyes say, 'No, surely, you never felt as we do.' I therefore go further, and say, 'If you feel worse than I did, I pity you indeed; for I could say with Job, "My soul chooseth strangling rather than life." I could readily enough have laid violent hands upon myself, to escape from my misery of spirit.' In talking to those who are in that wretched condition, I find myself at home. He who has been in the dark dungeon knows the way to the bread and the water. If you have passed through depression of mind, and the Lord has appeared to your comfort, lay yourself out to help others who are where you used to be. If you are in prison, and you get out, do not enjoy your own liberty alone, but hasten to set free another captive. Are your chains broken? Then be a chain-breaker in the Lord's name." Indeed, "God will not send his babes to a church that is not prepared to nurse them."[23]

In another apparently unpublished work Spurgeon says, "Some speak lightly of a believer's comfort, but God thinketh not so, for He cries: 'Comfort ye, comfort ye my people.'"[24] To comfort each other is a direct command of God.

Sometimes, however, things happen that obliterate normal life for a time. These are not trivia by anyone's viewpoint. They are indeed crushing blows. Sometimes they represent changes we knew were inevitable, but we hoped they would not come for a long time. Such was the case for me when my mother was killed in a car accident. Her death had been a lifelong dread of mine, but never in my worst nightmares had I thought it would be accompanied by so much unexpected trauma. Yet God was more than enough.

Spurgeon shows unusual insight in such matters: "A very heavy affliction has fallen upon you, and yet to your surprise it has not crushed you as you feared it would have done. Years before you had looked forward to the stroke with agonizing apprehension, and said, 'I shall never bear it'; but you did bear it, and at this moment you are thankful that you had it to bear. The thing which you feared came upon you, and when it came it seemed like a feather weight compared with what you expected it to be; you were able to sit down and say, 'The Lord gave, and the Lord hath taken away; blessed be the name of the Lord.' Your friends were surprised at you: you had been a poor, wretchedly nervous creature before, but in the time of trial you displayed a singular strength such as surprised everybody. Most of all you surprised yourself, for you were full of amazement that in weakness you were made so strong. You said, 'I was brought low, and he helped me.' You could not doubt his Deity then: anything which would rob him of glory you detested, for your heart said, 'Lord, there is none that could have solaced my soul in this fashion save only the Lord God Almighty.' Personally I have had to cry out, 'It is the Lord!' when I have seen his wonders in the deep. 'O my soul, thou hast trodden down strength.' My soul shall magnify my Lord and my God, for 'he sent from above, he took me; he drew me out of many waters. He brought me forth also into a large place: he delivered me, because he delighted in me.'"[25]

The ministry of consolation that can arise from the painful vicissitudes of life can bear fruit even after our death. "'How could you bear your long imprisonment so well?' said one to the Landgrave of Hesse, who had been shut up for his attachment to the principles of the Reformation. He replied 'The divine consolations of martyrs were with me.'"[26]

But if there is challenge as well as ministry in change that brings sorrow, there is also challenge in the transition from obscurity to success. That is why the sandpaper of sorrow so often is the prerequisite to success: "Many of us are not fit to receive a great blessing till we have gone through the fire. Half the men that have been ruined by popularity have been so ruined because they did not undergo a preparatory course of opprobrium and shame. Half the men who perish by riches do so because they had not toiled to earn them, but made a lucky hit, and became wealthy in an hour."[27]

There is a secret preparation that God puts a person through when he is to succeed. For "when a man is brought forward by God, he is often one whom everybody criticizes, finds fault with, and declaims as an impostor, but the banter he is exposed to serves as ballast for his mind. When he comes off with success he will not be spoiled with conceit, for the grace of God will make him bow with gratitude. The sword that is meant for a princely hand, to split through skull and backbone in the day of battle, must be annealed in the furnace again and again: it cannot be fit for such desperate work until it has passed through the fire full many a time. Do not ask to be appreciated. Never be so mean as that. Appreciate yourself in the serenity of conscience, and leave your honour with your God."[28]

Furthermore, "if you have preached or taught, or done work for Christ with little success until now, do not infer that you will always be unsuccessful. Regret the lack of prosperity, but do not relinquish the labour of seeking it. You may reasonably be sorrowful, but you have no right to despair. Non-success is a trial of faith which has been endured by many a trusty servant who has been triumphant in the issue. Did not the disciples toil all night, and catch nothing? Did we not read just now of some who cast the net, and yet took no fish? Did not our Lord say that some seed would fall on stony ground, and some among the thorns, and that from these there would be no harvest? What good did Jeremiah do? I have no doubt he laboured, and God blessed him, but the result of his

175

preaching was that he said, 'The bellows are burned in the fire.' He had blown up the fire till he had burnt the bellows, but no man's heart was melted. 'Woe is me!' said he. 'Oh that my head were waters, and mine eyes a fountain of tears!' I do not know what was the result of Noah's ministry, but I do know that he was a preacher of righteousness for a hundred and twenty years, and yet he never brought a soul into the ark except his own family. Poor preaching we may count it judging by the influence it exerted: and yet we know that it was grand preaching, such as God commanded. Do not, then, grudge the time, or the strength, you lay out in the service of our great Lord because you do not see your efforts thrive, for better men than you have wept over failure."[29]

"Did it never strike you that you may be now employed in breaking up ground and preparing the soil from which other labourers who come after you will reap very plentifully. Perhaps your Master knows what a capital ploughman you are. He has a large farm, and he never means to let you become a reaper because you do the ploughing so well. Your Master does not intend you to take part in the harvest because you are such a good hand at sowing; and as he has crops that need sowing all the year round he keeps you at that work. He knows you better than you know yourself. Perchance if he were once to let you get on the top of a loaded wagon of your own sheaves, you would turn dizzy and make a fall of it; so he says, 'You keep to your plowing and your sowing, and somebody else will do the reaping.' Peradventure when your course is run you will see from heaven, where it will be safe for you to see it, that you did not labour in vain nor spend your strength for nought. 'One soweth and another reapeth.' This is the divine economy. I think that every man that loves his Master will say, 'So long as there does but come a harvest, I will not stipulate about who reaps it. Give me faith enough to be assured that the reaping will come, and I will be content.' Look at William Carey going to India, his prayer being 'India for Christ.' What did Carey live to see? Well, he saw good-speed enough to rejoice his heart: but certainly he did not see the fulfillment of all his prayer. Successive missionaries have since gone and spent their life on that vast field of enterprise. With what result? A result amply sufficient to justify all their toil, but, as compared with the millions that sit in heathendom, utterly inadequate to the craving of the church, much less to the crown of Christ. It does not much matter how any one man fares. The mighty empire will revert to the world's Redeemer, and I can almost trace in the records of the future the writing of 'These be the names of the mighty men whom David had,' as the valiant deeds of his heroes are chronicled by our Lord. When old St. Paul's cathedral had to be taken down in order to make room for the present noble edifice, some of the walls were immensely strong and stood like rocks. Sir Christopher Wren determined to throw them down by the old Roman battering-ram. The battering-ram began to work, and the men worked at it for hours and hours, day after day, without apparent effect. Blow after blow came on the wall; tremendous thuds that made the bystanders tremble. The wall continued to stand till they thought it was a useless operation. But the architect knew. He continued working his battering-ram till every particle of the wall felt the motion, and at last over it went in one tremendous ruin. Did anybody commend those workmen who caused the final crash, or ascribe all the success to them? Not a bit of it. It was the whole of them together. Those who had gone away to their meals, those who had begun days before, had as much honour in the matter as those who struck the last blow. And it is so in the work of Christ. We must keep on battering, battering, battering, and at last—though it may not be for another thousand years—the Lord will triumph. Though Christ cometh quickly he may not come for another ten thousand years, but in any case idolatry must die, and truth must reign. The accumulated prayers and energies of ages shall do the deed, and God shall be glorified. Only let us persevere in holy effort, and the end is sure. When a certain American general was fighting they said, 'What are you doing?' He said, 'I am not doing much, but I keep pegging away.' That is what we must do. We cannot do much at any one time, but we must keep on. We must keep on pegging away at the enemy, and something will come of it by-and-by.

"... Whether I prosper in life or not is not my question. To bring souls to Christ is my main endeavour, but it is not the ultimate proof of my ministry. My business is to live for God, to lay aside self, and give myself up wholly to him, and if I do that I shall be accepted whatever else may happen."[30]

Yet for all the preparation there are times in the lives of some when there is ultimately an almost unexpected clear-cut transition from obscurity to fame. Such was true of Mary, the mother of Jesus. "Mary knew also that she was *to be famous*. 'All generations shall call me blessed.' But do notice how she balances her fame with another fame. She says, 'Holy is his name, and his mercy is on them that fear him.' She magnifies the name of the Lord. If he has given her a measure of honour, she lays it at his feet. Mind you do the same. Be not so vain as to be lifted up with a little success. We have all passed through this test of character, and in the fining-pot how few of us have borne the fire without loss! Perhaps you have preached a sermon and God has blessed it; the congregation is increased, and crowds are gathering; the probability is that the devil whispers, 'You are a capital preacher. Well done! You put your point admirably: God is blessing you. There must be something admirable in your character and abilities.' Away, away, thou fiend of the pit! This is ruinous pride! But suppose, dear brother, that the fiend will not go away while he finds you musing upon your success, what are you to do? Try him with this—'My soul doth magnify the Lord.' Praise the name of the Lord that ever he should make use of such a poor, unsuitable instrument as yourself. Give him all the honour and all the glory, if honour and glory there be, and see if the arch-enemy does not take to flight, for God's praises are abhorrent to the devil.

"In whatever capacity you are serving the Lord, if he puts any honour upon you, mind you give it all back to him. . . .

"Mary had faith, and yet, at the same time she must have been *awe-stricken* by the revelation. That she should give birth to the Son of the Highest must have utterly abashed and overwhelmed her. Now both these states of mind are here—faith and awe. Faith says, 'I know that the angel's message is true, and therefore my soul doth magnify the Lord.' Awe says, 'What a solemn thing it is that God should come to dwell in my breast! My soul doth magnify the Lord.' Thus in these words confidence and reverence have met together, assurance and adoration have kissed each other. Here is faith with its familiarity, and devotion with its godly fear."[31]

When we succeed, when we reach the pinnacle of success, or as we are merely comfortable in our family, our church, our lives, it is important to remind ourselves once again of the inevitability of change. Cherish those happy moments and do not forget those who are down when you are up. For transitions in life will continue and, at best, life on this earth is short. "Children may bear our name, and yet a fourth generation shall quite forget that we ever sojourned in this region."[32]

For this reason we who go from change to change are obligated to think of those who are down when we are happy and content. In the time of our success we must *"notice those who are cast down*. We are such foolish creatures that, sometimes, when the Lord trusts us with a happy experience, we begin to grow mightily proud, and we look down upon his tried and afflicted people. Even among those who do know the Lord, if they have a very charming experience, and enter into high fellowship with God, there is a tendency to begin to think that the poor doubting and fearing ones are very much to be censured and blamed, or, at any rate, that they are to be ignored, and left to themselves. 'Well,' says someone, 'really it quite depresses me to talk with old Mrs. So-and-so. I could not keep my joy if I were to go and try to encourage that young man who is always so cast down.' Ah, my dear friend, but if you begin to talk like that, it may not be long before you will even envy that old lady you now despise, and wish you were half as hopeful of salvation as that young man whom you just now condemned! . . . The duty of a happy Christian is to take notice of those who are not so joyous as he is, to seek them out, to condescend to men of low estate. When thou hast abundant provision in thy house, it is thy duty to send portions to those for whom nothing is prepared. Mind that thou attendest to this matter, lest thy Lord should put thee on short commons, too, and make thee feel a little more as thou oughtest to do towards the afflicted."[33]

There is no reason, however, to feel depressed about being happy or guilty when life goes right. Joyfulness is a blessing, not a sin, and we are meant to enjoy it when it comes our way. "There are some now-a-days who would like to strike out everything from mortal life which gives pleasure. We have societies now which are *anti* to every mortal thing that is pleasant and agreeable, and if there remains one solitary enjoyment to mortal men in this vale of tears, which has not some society opposed to it, I have no doubt some genius will commence a crusade against it to-morrow. The theory is, that all wholesome things are nasty, and that all gratifications are deadly. I wonder they do not make the parish pump run with wormwood tea, and paint the meadows a dun colour. Then, when we have abstained from all that is either beautiful or agreeable, and reduced ourselves to the condition of the savage who eats acorns and lives in a cavern, we shall have climbed somewhat near perfection. Now I do not believe in this theory for ordinary life, much less for spiritual life. Men used of old to anoint the heads of their guests to give them pleasure, and they were never blamed for it; and the Lord intends that his people should have the richest pleasures in their souls. He is the happy God, and would have those round about him happy. He never intended this world to be a great workhouse, a vast drill-shed, or a convict settlement, so arranged that labour should banish joy, and a crushing sense of subjection should chase away love. He has made this world to be a happy lodging for his dear children, till he shall call them home, and he has provided for their delight many enjoyments, lawful and commendable, beneficial and spiritual. I believe the Lord intended his people to be the happiest people under the sun. When I see certain of them repining, complaining, fretting, worrying, and calling that state of mind 'experience,' I pray, 'The Lord save me from that experience, and give me to have his joy fulfilled in me.' Our Lord Jesus was sorrowful, not as our example, but as our substitute; he was put to grief that we might be joyous; he bore our load that we might have no load to carry. He was full of cares for us, that we might have no care, but might rejoice in him all our days. 'Let the children of Zion be joyful in their King.' 'Rejoice in the Lord always, and again I say, Rejoice.'"[34]

7

TRANSITION

On New Year's Day each year I have a dinner party for a few close friends. We exchange Christmas presents and catch up with the events of the past year, as a group, rather than on the one-to-one basis of other encounters throughout the year. One friend, a theologian, always closes with the kind of prayer that challenges one for the New Year.

This year that same friend and I spent time looking at some books, and I gave that friend my grandfather Benson's journal to read, mainly pointing out the closing remarks. I had found the journal not too long ago, wedged in between some old books. It was written in Swedish, so I wasn't even sure whose journal it was. When a consul general of Sweden who is a friend of mine offered to have it translated, I was delighted. When it turned out to be my grandfather's record of his life, I was ecstatic.

Alfred Benson was born in a farming province in Sweden in 1859. The journal records his life from that time until 1919, when he died in Necedah, Wisconsin, from the 1918 flu. I was speaking at the Scandinavian Seaman's Church the night the consul general handed me the translated copy. It was my first real introduction to my grandfather, since he had died long before I was born. That night as I finally settled down to read it, I had a heightened sense of expectation. Who was this man who was so interwoven in my life and yet so unknown to me?

On New Year's Day as I shared that journal with my friend I read him the words which my grandfather had written right before his death, the last entry in his journal:

> March 7th, 1919. I am with you and shall keep you wherever you go. . . . God is powerful and lets all grace prevail (2 Cor. 9:8). On this day I give myself [anew] to you. Do with me what you will. My body is weak underneath the burden of a long illness. Jesus is my healer in this time. At five p.m., March 7, 1919, I give myself anew to you to treat me as you find good. Jesus, give me the grace to rest quietly in your hands.[2]

After he had read through this journal, my friend turned to me and said: "Your grandfather's life reads like one day. It was all lived before God." He had said more clearly what I had felt more vaguely. My grandfather's life was seamless. It consisted of continuity, of a constant walk before God.

In 1877, on April 5, Alfred had come to know Christ. At the time he was still in Sweden. He wrote:

> It was the spring of 1877. April fifth of that year was for me a day of joy, as it was for the other villagers who loved the Lord. I accepted Jesus as my Savior, after a long period of worry about my soul. It was a preacher in my home parish who spoke strongly about the necessity of salvation. Before I went to hear the sermon I prayed to the Lord that he would show me what hindered me from receiving the consolation from Jesus. Then I became certain that I would be saved that very night. After the sermon I left without saying anything to anyone, and I was very sad. I had not walked far, however, when it was as if I was awakened from a long sleep, and I heard the words: "Blessed are the poor in spirit, because Heaven belongs to them." I cannot describe how happy I was, and my body became so light—it was as if a heavy burden had fallen from my shoulders. When I came home, we thanked and praised the Lord for the grace he had shown me, and that he had listened to my mother's prayers. [She had died two years earlier.][3]

As he spoke of the next few years before he immigrated to America at the age of twenty-one, he made one statement that describes his whole life and perhaps is the quality that makes it so seamless, indeed like one day: "I noticed that as soon as I turned my thoughts away from it [the Scriptures], I became worried and distraught. As soon as I read some truth from the Scripture I was solaced."[4]

At the end of his life his death was but a transition from one sphere of living to another, from one phase of eternal life to another. Birth, childhood, adulthood, old age, death—they are all different phases of a life that is eternal. When they are lived before God, the changes from one phase to another become truly seamless transitions. In that sense all of life is a gradual transition, each, including old age and death, a step forward according to God's plan.

A young woman who came close to dying in childbirth described herself as feeling the awesomeness of God coming over her until she realized that death "was just a transition." She could almost sense leaving her body and knew that if she died she wouldn't stop living even for a moment. The sense of the awesomeness of God was so great that, apart from her relationships with certain people and her desire to finish God's work through her, this world didn't matter anymore.

The transition of death is not reserved for the old. The young woman described above almost died in her youth. Others do die. But as we go on in life, certain markers indicate that we are moving through various transitions. The other day my granddaughter declined to watch a cartoon she used to like. She let me know that she's a kid now, not a toddler. She's outgrown the younger cartoons.

At the latter end of life some of us feel Christmas comes more quickly after Thanksgiving than it used to when we were kids and it seemed that Christmas would never come. Heaven seems a little richer, as the old preachers used to say, as people *we* know pass through that transition. On a practical level, the knees wear out and we start to evaluate our life tasks by limited time rather than feeling that we have forever to accomplish our tasks. We reminisce a lot and in general begin to sound more as our parents did when we were young and thought they were so ancient. The young seem younger every year, and old age starts later. These are markers, signposts that the time of old age is indeed coming upon us.

Spurgeon defines this time of transition well: "I cannot imagine or dream that I need offer any apology for preaching to aged people. If I were in sundry stupid circles where people call themselves ladies and gentlemen, and always want to conceal their ages, I might have some hesitation; but I have nothing to do with that here. I call an old man, an old man, and an old woman, an old woman; whether they think themselves old or not is nothing to me. I guess they are, if they are getting anyway past sixty, on to seventy or eighty. Old age is *a time of peculiar memories, of peculiar hopes, of peculiar solicitudes, of peculiar blessedness, and of peculiar duties*; and yet in all this, God is the same, although man be peculiar. First, *old age is a time of peculiar memory*; in fact, it is the age of memory. We young men talk of remembering such-and-such things a certain time ago; but what is our memory, compared to our father's? Our father looks back on three or four times the length of time over which we cast our eyes. What a peculiar memory the old man has!"[5]

"The aged man, too, hath *peculiar hopes*. He hath no such hopes as I or my young friends here. He hath few hopes of the future in this world; they are gathered up into a small space, and he can tell you, in a few words, what constitutes all his expectation and desire. But he has one hope, and that is the very same which he had when he first trusted in Christ; it is a hope 'undefiled, that fadeth not away, reserved in heaven for them that are kept by the power of God through faith unto salvation.'"[6]

"Again, old age is a time of *peculiar solicitude*. An old man is not anxious about many things, as we are; for he hath not so many things for which to concern himself. He hath not the cares of starting in business, as he once had. He hath no children to launch out in business. He hath not to cast his anxious eyes on his little family. But his solicitude hath somewhat increased in another direction. He hath more solicitude about his bodily frame than he once had. He cannot now run as he used to do; but he must walk with more sober gait. He fears every now and then that the pitcher will be 'broken at the cistern;' for 'the noise of the grinders is low.' He hath no longer that strength of desire he once possessed; his body begins to totter, to shake, and to quiver. The old tenement has stood these fifty years; and who expects a house to last for ever? A bit of mortar has gone off from one place, and a lath out of another; and when a little wind comes to shake it about, he is ready to cry out, 'The earthly house of my tabernacle is about to be dissolved.' But I told you before, this peculiar solicitude is but another proof of divine faithfulness; for now that you have little pleasure in the flesh, do you not find that God is just the same? and that, though the days are come when you can say, 'I have no pleasure in *them*,' yet the days are not come when you can say, 'I have no pleasure in *him*;' but, on the contrary,

> Though all created streams are dry,
>   His goodness is the same;
> With this you still are satisfied,
>   And glory in his name.

. . . I tell you, even your bodily pains are but proofs of his love; for he is taking down your old tenement stick by stick, and is building it up again in brighter worlds, never to be taken down anymore.

"And remember, too, there is another solicitude—a failure of mind, as well as of body. There are many remarkable instances of old men, who have been as gifted in their old age as in their youth; but with the majority the mind becomes somewhat impaired, especially the memory. They cannot remember what was done yesterday, although it is a singular fact that they can remember what was done fifty, sixty, or seventy years ago. They forget much which they would wish to remember; but still they find that their God is just the same; they find that his goodness does not depend on their memory; that the sweetness of his grace does not depend upon their palate. When they can remember but little of the sermon, they still feel that it leaves as good an impression on their heart as when they were strong in their memories; and thus they have another proof that God, even when their mind faileth a little, carries them down to their hoar hairs, their old age, and that to them he is ever the same.

"But the chief solicitude of old age is death. Young men may die soon, Old men *must* die. . . . A greyheaded old sinner is a greyheaded old fool; but an aged Christian is an aged wise man. But even the aged Christian hath peculiar solicitudes about death. He knows he cannot be a long way from the end. He feels that, even in the course of nature, apart from what is called accidental death, there is no doubt but in a few more years he must stand before his God. He thinks he may be in heaven in ten or twenty years; but how short do those ten or twenty years appear! He does not act like a man who thinks a coach is a long way off, and he may take his time; but he is like one who is about to go on a journey, and hears the post-horn blowing down the street, and is getting ready. His one solicitude now is, to examine himself whether he is in the faith. . . . But still, beloved, mark, God's faithfulness is the same; for if he be nearer death, he has the sweet satisfaction that he is nearer heaven; and if he has more need to examine himself than ever, he has also more evidence whereby to examine himself, for he can say, 'Well, I know that on such-and-such an occasion the Lord heard my prayer; at such-and-such a time he manifested himself to me, as he did not unto the world,' and, though examination presses more upon the old, still they have greater materials for it. And here, again, is another proof of this grand truth. 'Even unto old age I am the same,' says God; 'and even to hoar hairs will I carry you.'

"And now, once more, old age hath its *peculiar blessedness*. Some time ago I stepped up to an old man whom I saw when preaching at an anniversary, and I said to him, 'Brother, do you know, there is no man in the whole chapel I envy so much as you!' 'Envy me,' he said—'why, I am eighty-seven.' I said, 'I do, indeed; because you are so near your home, and because I believe that in old age there is a peculiar joy, which we young people do not taste at present. You have got to the bottom of the cup, and it is not with God's wine as it is with man's. Man's wine becomes dregs at the last, but God's wine is sweeter the deeper you drink of it.' He said, 'That's very true, young man,' and shook me by the hand. I believe there is a blessedness about old age that we young men know nothing of. I will tell you how that is. In the first place, the old man has a good experience to talk about. The young men are only just trying some of the promises; but the old man can turn them over one by one, and say, 'There, I have tried that, and that, and that.' We read them over and say, 'I *hope* they are true;' but the old man says, 'I *know* they are true.' And then he begins to tell you why. He has got a history for everyone, like a soldier for his medals; and he takes them out, and says, 'I will tell you when the Lord revealed that to me; just when I lost my wife; just when I buried my son; just when I was turned out of my cottage, and did not get work for six weeks; or, at another time, when I broke my leg.' He begins telling you the history of the promises, and says, 'There now, I know they are all true.' What a blessed thing, to look upon them as paid notes; to bring out the old cheques that have been cashed, and say, 'I know they are genuine, or else they would not have been paid.'"[7]

"And I think there are peculiar joys which the old Christian has, of another sort; and that is, he has peculiar fellowship with Christ, more than we have. At least, if I understand John Bunyan rightly, I think he tells us that when we get very near to heaven there is a very glorious land. 'They came into the country of Beulah, whose air was very sweet and pleasant; the way lying directly through it, they solaced themselves there for a season. Yea, here they heard continually the singing of birds, and saw every day the flowers appear on the earth, and heard the voice of the turtle in the land. In this country the sun shineth night and day; wherefore this was beyond the valley of the Shadow of Death, and also out of the reach of Giant Despair; neither could they from this place so much as see Doubting-castle. Here they were within sight of the City they were going to: also here met them some of the inhabitants thereof: for in this land the shining ones commonly walked, because it was upon the borders of heaven. In this land also the contract between the Bride and the Bridegroom was renewed; yea, here, "as the bridegroom rejoiceth over the bride, so doth their God rejoice over them." Here they had no want of corn and wine; for in this place they met with abundance of what they had sought for in all their pilgrimages. Here they heard voices from out of the City, loud voices, saying, "Say ye to the daughter of Zion, Behold, thy salvation cometh! Behold, His reward is with him!" Here all the inhabitants of the country called them, "the holy people, the redeemed of the Lord."' There are peculiar communings, peculiar openings of the gates of paradise, peculiar visions of glory, just as you come near to it. It stands to reason that the nearer you get to the bright light of the celestial city, the clearer shall be the air. And therefore there are peculiar blessednesses belonging to the old, for they have more of this peculiar fellowship with Christ. But all this only proves that Christ is the same; because, when there are fewer earthly joys, he gives more spiritual ones. Therefore, again, it becomes the fact 'Even to old age I am he; and even to hoar hairs will I carry you.'

"And now, lastly, the aged saint has *peculiar duties*. There are certain things which a good man can do, which nobody else ought to do, or can do well. And that is one proof of divine faithfulness; for he says of his aged ones, 'They shall bring forth fruit in old age;' and so they do. I will just tell you some of them.

"*Testimony* is one of the peculiar duties of old men. Now, suppose I should get up, and say, 'I have not seen the righteous forsaken, nor his seed begging bread,' some one would reply, 'Why, you are not twenty-two yet; what do you know about it?' But if an old man gets up, and says,

'I have been young, and now am I old; yet have I not seen the righteous forsaken, nor his seed begging bread,' with what power that testimony comes!"[8]

"Now, you middle aged men, you are plunged in the midst of business, and are sometimes supposing what will become of you in your old age. But is there any promise of God to you when you suppose about to-morrows? You say, 'Suppose I should live to be as old as so-and-so, and be a burden upon people, I should not like that.' Don't get meddling with God's business; leave his decrees to him. There is many a person who thought he would die in a workhouse, that has died in a mansion; and many a woman that thought she would die in the streets, has died in her bed, happy and comfortable, singing of providential grace and everlasting mercy. Middle aged man! listen to what David says, again, 'I have been young, and now am old; yet have I not seen the righteous forsaken, nor his seed begging bread.' Go on, then, unsheathe thy sword once more. 'The battle is the Lord's'; leave thy declining years to him, and give thy present years to him. Live to him now, and he will never cast you away when you are old. Do not lay up for old age and keep back from the cause of God; but rather trust God for the future. Be 'diligent in business;' but take care you do not hurt your spirit, by being too diligent, by being grasping and selfish. . . .

"'And even to your old age I am he; and even to hoar hairs will I carry you; I have made, and I will bear; even I will carry, and will deliver you.'"[9]

In a summary of old age, Spurgeon refers to David in the Old Testament:

I will go in the strength of the Lord GOD: I will make mention of thy righteousness, even of thine only.—Psalm 71:16 (KJV)

"This is a psalm of David's old age. . . . This is the tenor of the psalm: he has been with his God, and he is now ready for anything. This grand old man, in his later days, is exposed to enemies quite as fierce as those which he had to encounter in his earlier times; but instead of gathering his friends together, and conversing with them, and seeking their counsel, he gets quite alone, and begins to cry, 'In thee, O Lord, do I put my trust: let me never be put to confusion.' Trusting alone in God makes us grandly independent towards men. The man of God shuts . . . the door: he realizes that the Lord is in the chamber with him, and he speaks to him, saying, 'Be thou my strong habitation, whereunto I may continually resort: thou hast given commandment to save me; for thou art my rock and my fortress.' He pours out his heart before God, and pleads with him, 'Cast me not off in the time of old age; forsake me not when my strength faileth. O God, be not far from me: O my God, make haste for my help.' It is a delightful sight: there are two in the room, though you can see only one with the natural eye. The man whom you can see, discerns another, a great and glorious One, and he talks with him 'as a man talketh with his friend.'"[10]

To many, years of agony are to be feared when they reach old age. Says Spurgeon: "Tottering on thy staff, leaning, feeble, weak, and wan; fear not the last hour; that last hour shall be thy best. . . . Weak as thou art, God will temper the trial to thy weakness; he will make thy pain less, if thy strength be less; but thou shalt sing in heaven, 'Victory! victory! victory!' There are some of us who could wish to change places with you, to be so near heaven—to be so near home. With all your infirmities, your grey hairs are a crown of glory to you; for you are near the end, as well as in the way of righteousness."[11]

Aging, according to Spurgeon, is a time of memories: "Be faithful to your Lord, dear friend, if you are now in prosperity; for thus you will be laying up a store of cheering memories for years to come. To look back upon a well-spent life will not cause an atom of legal boasting to an experienced believer; but it will justly create much holy rejoicing. Paul was able to rejoice that he had not run in vain, neither laboured in vain, and happy are we if we can do the same. If it be right for us to chasten our conscience on account of omissions, it must be lawful ground for thankful joy that our heart condemns us not, for then have we confidence towards God. If any one of us should fall into straitened circumstances, it will be a comfort to be able to say, 'When I was rich, I freely used my wealth for the Lord.' If we are ill, it will be a satisfaction to remember that, when we were in health, we used our strength for Jesus. These are reflections which give light in the shade, and make music at midnight. It is not out of our own reflections that the joy arises, but out of the witness of the Holy Spirit that the Lord is not unrighteous to forget our work of faith and labour of love."[12]

But yet it is a time of labor, for "'you are immortal till your work is done.' Possibly not one half of your work is even begun, and therefore you will rise again from sickness, you will soar above depression, and you will do more for the Lord than ever. It will yet be said to you, as to the angel of the church in Thyatira, 'I know thy works, and the last to be more than the first.'"[13]

Indeed Spurgeon felt deeply that all of one's life is a work for God. There is no room for "retirement" if by retirement we mean ceasing to do God's work. Explains Spurgeon: "Above all, have we made any progress as to *work for our Master?* Some, as they grow old, give up their work. I do not understand it. I must confess an inability of comprehending how any man who once preached the gospel can ever leave his ministry while his strength lasts. If the Master has once allotted you a field of labour, unless it be sheer inability, I cannot understand how you can ever cease to till the ground, or reap the sheaves."[14]

According to Spurgeon the years of one's life are to be numbered; they are to be taken seriously.

For the LORD thy God hath blessed thee in all the works of thy hand: he knoweth thy walking through this great wilderness: these forty years the LORD thy God hath been with thee; thou hast lacked nothing.— Deuteronomy 2:7 (KJV)

"The habit of numbering our days is a very admirable one. To do it rightly a man needs to be taught of God; and if we have not been so taught, it is well to offer the prayer, 'So teach us to number our days that we may apply our hearts unto wisdom.' Some men number their cattle, number their acres, number their pounds, but do not number their days, or, if they do, they fail to draw the inference from them which both reason and grace suggest—that we may apply our hearts unto wisdom. It is not wisdom to try to seem younger than you are, though I have known many attempt it. I have marked between census and census that the ages of certain persons have hardly increased ten years, as I thought they would have done by the lapse of time. The age of many whom we admire is a mystery inscrutable. What there can be to be ashamed of in advancing years I am at a loss to know, for old age commands reverence, and not ridicule. Wherefore sorrow because another year of trial is over, another year of labour ended, another milestone on the road to heaven left behind? Instead of regretting that we are so far on the voyage to the fair haven, we may rather rejoice and make our years at least as many as we can. If we pretend to be more juvenile than we are, uncharitable persons may possibly attribute it to vanity; it is a pity to give them such an opportunity. At the same time, ripe years are not to be trifled with. We have known some who have treated the fact that they are advancing in life with unbecoming levity; their grey hairs show that they are nearing the bounds of life, but they are as thoughtless as if they were yet in their minority, and so they are an incongruous mixture of the weakness of age, and the frivolity of youth."[15]

The later years of one's life are also to be years of increasing expectation. "Forty years of divine faithfulness should teach us also *a surer, quicker, calmer, and more joyous expectation of immediate aid in all lines of strait and trial:* we should learn not to be flurried and worried because the herds are cut off from the stall, and the harvest is withered, for we know from abundant proofs that 'The Lord will provide.' . . . I am often glad when I feel that none but my Lord can carry me through, for I am certain of his help. If we have still a batch of dough in the kneading trough which we brought out of Egypt the windows of heaven will not yet be opened, but when the last little cake has been baked the manna will fall around the camp. As long as we can feel the bottom of the river we have not reached the best waters to swim in. When the barley loaves and the few small fishes are all broken, then the miracle of multiplying begins."[16]

And as one reaches toward the end of life, there should be a sense of joyous preparation for the transition to heaven. "He is a ripe Christian, ripening for heaven; and you may add to this that he now becomes more *kind in spirit* than he was before. The asperities of his youth give way to cordial kindness in his old age. He learns to overlook faults which irritated him when he was younger; he learns to bear with the young and with the silly, for he remembers that he was once young and foolish too.

He has compassion for those that are out of the way, and a kind and encouraging word for the distressed, and he goes about with a beaming countenance, looking indeed like ripe fruit with a rich bloom upon it, a pleasant sight for the great husbandman."[17]

But for some, as they approach that great transition, they face earthly trials rather than joy. For these Spurgeon has a word of encouragement. "Dear brothers and sisters, there are some of you here to-day who have been very much and very sorely tried, for your path has been through fire and through water. You are servants of God, and in looking back you can say that you have been helped hitherto. Just now your health and your spirits are failing you; you are brought very low indeed. Permit your minister to take hold of your hand, and look you in the face. My dear brother, will you dishonour your God now? You say, 'No, God forbid that I should dishonour him.' My dear friend, you have now before you a noble opportunity—an opportunity which an angel might well envy you; you have a noble opportunity of honouring God in the fire. I will not speak lightly of your troubles; I will suppose them to be just as great as you say they are. But will you glorify him in them all? Come, you have trusted him many times, will you trust him now? Perhaps Satan has a commission from on high to try you, and sift you in his sieve. He has been before God, and your Lord has said to him, 'Hast thou considered my servant Job?' 'Ah,' says Satan, 'he serves thee now, but thou hast set a hedge about him and blessed him, let me but touch him;' and he has come down to you, and he has afflicted you in your estate, afflicted you in your family, and at last he has afflicted you in your body. Shall Satan be the conqueror? shall grace give way? O my dear brother, stand up now and say once more, once for all, 'I tell thee, Satan, the grace of God is more than a match for thee; he is with me, and in all this I will not utter one word against the Lord my God. He doeth all things well—well, even now, and I do rejoice in him.'

"The Lord is always pleased with his children when they can stand up for him when circumstances seem to belie him. Here come the witnesses into court. The devil says, 'Soul, God has forgotten thee, I will bring in my witness.' First he summons your debts—a long bill of losses. 'There,' says he, 'would God suffer you to fall thus, if he loved you?' Then he brings in your children—either their death, or their disobedience, or something worse, and says, 'Would the Lord suffer these things to come upon you, if he loved you?' At last he brings in your poor suffering body, and all your doubts and fears, and the hidings of Jehovah's face. 'Ah,' says the devil, 'do you believe that God loves you now?' Oh, it is noble, if you are able to stand forth and say to all these witnesses, 'I hear what you have to say, let God be true, and every man and everything be a liar; I believe none of you. You all say, God does not love me; but he does, and if the witnesses against his love were multiplied a hundredfold, yet still would I say, 'I know whom I have believed.'

> 'I know that safe with him remains,
>   Protected by his power,
> What I've committed to his hands,
>   'Till the decisive hour.'

He will bring me safe to heaven at last, unhurt by the way."[18]

As for those who wish for the "good old days," Spurgeon had a word of positiveness: "Somebody said to me the other day that he did not meet with such good old men now as we used to know in our youth, and I told him that the men were quite as good, but we were in among them, and therefore had less of the superstitious awe of our youth, and I added that I was myself surprised to find them as good as they are now that our view of them is so much nearer and so much more daring. No prophet has honour in his own country, nor among men of his own age. Distance lends enchantment in many cases. We have as good men among us now as ever lived, but we know more about them than of those who have departed, and we criticise them more severely. We are none of us able fully to compare the generations past with this present one, because we were not in those generations as we are in this. Men at a great distance may appear to be absolutely perfect, but when we get close to them, spots are manifest, and our judgment changes. Never let us fall into that silly state of mind, in which we say 'the dear good men are all gone: the faithful are all dead.' There are dear good men alive still, and there are more coming on. Do not let us be afraid that the Almighty will run short of servants. Let us not dream that he with whom is the residue of the Spirit will allow his cause to droop for want of qualified ministers, elders, deacons, or other workers. On the contrary, let us say, 'Bless the Lord, whose mercy endureth for ever.' We have learned that instead of the fathers shall be the children, and we will take as much delight in the young saints who are growing up as in former years we took in those mature, judicious, well instructed saints, whom the Lord our heavenly Father has taken home."[19]

The transitions of life do not always come in their expected order. Sometimes the young die, when their life may appear to have great potential. Why did Spurgeon himself die at the age of fifty-seven when he was so valuable in his service? Spurgeon was so aware that death could come at any age that he prepared his twin sons at an early age. "Early in the life of my boys I took them to the old churchyard of Wimbledon and bade them measure some of the little graves within that enclosure, and they found several green hillocks which were shorter than themselves. I tried thus to impress upon their young minds the uncertainty of life. I would have every child remember that he is not too young to die."[20]

Death, therefore, is the one transition in this life on earth that requires constant preparation. Spurgeon gives examples from the lives of the great preachers Wesley and Whitefield. Of Wesley he wrote: "Let us imitate Mr. Wesley's calm anticipation of his end. A lady once asked Mr. Wesley, 'Suppose that you knew you were to die at twelve o'clock to-morrow night, how would you spend the intervening time?' 'How, madam?' he replied, 'why just as I intend to spend it now. I should preach this evening at Gloucester, and again at five to-morrow morning; after that I should ride to Tewkesbury, preach in the afternoon, and meet the society in the evening. I should then repair to friend Martin's house, who expects to entertain me; converse and pray with the family as usual; retire to my room at ten o'clock; commend myself to my heavenly Father, lie down to rest, and wake up in glory.'

"Live in such a way that any day would make a suitable topstone for life. Live so that you need not change your mode of living, even if your sudden departure were immediately predicted to you."[21]

Then of Whitefield he commented: "It was said of Mr. Whitefield, that he never went to bed at night, leaving even a pair of gloves out of its place; he used to say that he would like to have everything ready in case he might be taken away. I think I see that good man standing, with a bedroom candle in his hand, at the top of the staircase, preaching Christ the last night of his life to the people sitting on the stairs; and then going inside the room, and commending himself to God; and going straight away to heaven. That is the way to die; but if you do not live like Wesley and Whitefield lived, you cannot die like Wesley and Whitefield died. May God grant us grace that we may be perfectly ready to die when the time for our departure is at hand!"[22]

Speaking of the idea of the sovereignty of God in the existence of each of our lives, Spurgeon says: "Our presence on earth in this day of grace was a matter altogether beyond our control. . . . The *continuance* of life is equally determined by God. He who fixed our birth has measured the interval between the cradle and the grave, and it shall not be a day longer or a day shorter than the divine decree. How many times your lungs shall heave and your pulses beat have been fixed by the eternal calculator from of old. What reflections ought to arise out of this! How willing we should be to labour on, even if we be weary, since God appoints our day and will not over-weary us, for he is no hard taskmaster. How glad we ought to be even to suffer if the Lord so ordains. . . . The Lord's time is best: to a hair's breadth thy span of life is rightly measured. God ordains all: therefore peace, restless spirit, and let the Lord have his way."[23]

Furthermore, "It were a sad sentence if we were bound over to dwell in this poor world for ever." Therefore, we can take hope in the fact that "we are immortal till our work is done."[24]

In a sermon preached with a special emphasis on death, Spurgeon elaborates: "He has ordained the hour in which I must expire. A thousand angels cannot keep me from the grave an instant when that hour has struck. Nor could legions of spirits cast me into the pit before the appointed time. . . .

"All our times are in his hand. The means, the way I shall die, how long I shall be in dying, the sickness and in what place I shall be seized with the contagion, all these are ordained."[25]

In another sermon Spurgeon preached: "All fruits do not get ripe and mellow at the same season. So with Christians. They are at a 'full age' when God chooses to take them home. They are at 'full age' if they die at twenty one; they are not more if they live to be ninety. Some wines can be drunk very soon after the vintage. Others need to be kept. But what does this matter, if when the liquor is broached it is found to have its full flavour? God never broaches his cask till the wine has perfected itself. There are two mercies to a Christian. The first is that he will never die too soon; and the second, that he will never die too late.

"First, he will never die *too soon*. . . . But say some, 'How useful might they have been had they have lived.' Ah! but how damaging they might have been! And were it not better to die than to do something afterwards that would disgrace themselves, and bring disgrace to the Christian character? Were it not better for them to sleep while their work was going on, than to break it down afterwards? We have seen some sad instances of Christian men who have been very useful in God's cause, but have afterwards had sad falls, and have dishonoured Christ, though they were saved and brought back at last. . . . The Christian dies well: he does not die too soon.

"Again, the Christian never dies *too late*. That old lady there is eighty years old. She sits in a miserable room, shivering by a handful of fire. She is kept by charity. She is poor and miserable. 'What's the good of her?' says everybody: 'she has lived too long. A few years ago she might have been of some use; but now look at her! She can scarcely eat unless her food is put into her mouth. She cannot move; and what good can she be?' Do not you find fault with your Master's work. He is too good a husbandman to leave his wheat in the field too long and let it shale out. Go and see her; and you will be reproved. Let her speak: she can tell you things you never knew in all your life. Or, if she does not speak at all, her silent unmurmuring serenity, her constant submission, teaches you how to bear suffering. So that there is something that you can learn from her yet. Say not the old leaf hangeth too long on the tree. . . . Hear what God says to each of us:—'Thou shalt come to thy grave in full age.' Cholera! thou mayest fly across the land and taint the air; I shall die in a 'full age.' I may preach to-day, and as many days as I please in the week, but I shall die at a full age. However ardently I may labour, I shall die at a full age. Affliction may come to drain my very life's blood, and dry up the very sap and marrow of my being. Ah! but affliction thou shalt not come too soon—I shall die at a full age. And thou waiting-man! and thou tarrying woman! thou art saying, 'O Lord, how long? how long? Let me come home.' Thou shalt not be kept from thy beloved Jesus one hour more than is necessary; thou shalt have heaven as soon as thou art ready for it. Heaven is ready enough for thee, and thy Lord will say, 'Come up higher!' when thou hast arrived at a full age—but never before nor after."[26]

As to whether we have a right to interfere with the timing of our death, Spurgeon is quite clear: "We have no business to pray that we may die. . . . We shall all in good time, unless the Lord shall come in the splendour of his Second Advent. If you and I had the choice of the time of our death, there would be just a tinge of the element of suicide about it, and that is the very worst form of murder. This is clearly our duty, to leave ourselves wholly and unreservedly in the hand of him to whom belong the issues of life; it is certainly our best course.

". . . Do not pray to get out of the battle; ask of God that you may never be a coward, but that you may bravely play the man in the day of danger. Do not seek to be screened from affliction. You need not even pray that you may not have prosperity; but you may entreat the Lord that prosperity may not make you proud, or worldly. . . .

"'I pray not that thou shouldest take them out of the world, but that thou shouldest keep them from the evil.' We need to be kept from the evil of *apostasy*, the evil of *worldliness*, from the evil of *unholiness*, from the evil of getting to be as men of the world are; that is the main point. I do not think that it matters much what the condition of man is so long as his heart is above his condition. I remember that St. Bernard, as he is usually called,—Bernard, of Clairvaux,—one of the holiest and humblest of men, was one day riding on a mule to a certain monastery; and one who saw him said, 'I think Bernard is getting proud, because he is riding on a mule, and sitting upon a cloth which has a fringe of gold lace to it.' Now Bernard was a man who cared nothing for that sort of thing; and when the other charged him with pride, he said, 'Perhaps it may be so, but I never noticed that I had any cloth at all.' Someone else had put that fine cloth upon the mule without his knowing anything about it, and he really thought that he was riding on the animal's bare back, for his mind was taken up with something far more important. If thou art rich, and thou hast a cloth with a gold fringe to it, do not be conscious of its existence; let thy soul rise above it. If thou art poor, and thou hast no saddle at all, do not notice thy lack; but let thy soul soar above such matters. Pray not that thou mayest be taken out of this or that, be it poverty or be it wealth, be it sickness or be it health;

but pray that thou mayest be kept from the evil of it, for there is an evil in every case."[27]

For those who suffer in body Spurgeon offers an incentive to wait for God's timing rather than begging to die. He had the right credentials to address suffering, for Spurgeon endured great physical pain. There were times when he could not turn at night unaided. In a day that knew nothing of anti-inflammatory drugs or other effective methods of pain management, Spurgeon suffered from diseases like gout, which caused swelling and pain. Explained Spurgeon: "Truly we that are in this tabernacle do groan. Does it not sometimes appear to the children of sickness as if this body were fashioned with a view to suffering; as if all its nerves, sinews, veins, pulses, vessels, and valves, were parts of a curious instrument upon which every note of the entire gamut of pain might be produced? Patience, ye who linger in this shattered tenement, a house not made with hands awaits you. Up yonder no sorrow and sighing are met with; the chastening rod shall fall no longer when the faultiness is altogether removed. As the new body will be without pain, so will it be superior to weariness. The glory-body will not yield to faintness, nor fall through languour. Is it not implied that the spiritual body does not need to sleep, when we read that they serve God day and night in his temple? In a word, the bodies of saints, like the body of Christ, will be perfect; there shall be nothing lacking and nothing faulty. If saints die in feebleness of age they shall not rise thus; or if they have lost a sense or a limb or are halt or maimed, they shall not be so in heaven, for as to body and soul 'they are without fault before the throne of God.' 'We shall be like him,' is true of all the saints, and hence none will be otherwise than fair, and beautiful, and perfect. The righteous shall be like Christ, of whom it is still true that not a bone of him shall be broken, so not a part of our body after its change shall be bruised, battered, or otherwise than perfect."[28]

Years ago I remember an old preacher of some renown saying to a large gathering: "I am not afraid of death, for that is to be with my Savior. But I don't look forward to the process." It was an honest statement. As Spurgeon put it: "To suffer, is the common lot of all men. It is not possible for us to escape from it. We come into this world through the gate of suffering, and over death's door hangs the same escutcheon."[29]

Continuing the same theme Spurgeon says, "To pass away into the glory-land is so bright a hope that death is swallowed up in the victory, but the death itself is a bitter thing, and therefore needs to be swallowed up in the victory, before we can bear it. It is a bitter pill, and must be drowned in a sweet potion ere we can rejoice in it. I am certain that no person, apart from sweet reflections of the presence of God and the heavenly future, could regard death otherwise than as a dreadful calamity. Even our Saviour did not regard his approaching death without trembling; the thought of dying was not in itself otherwise than saddening even to him; witness the bloody sweat as it streamed from him in Gethsemane, and that manlike putting away of the cup with, 'If it be possible let this cup pass from me.' As you think of that soul-conflict let it increase your idea of the Godlike love which took the cup with both its hands resolutely, and drank right on, and never stayed its dreadful draught till the Lord had drank damnation dry for all his people, swallowing up their deaths in his own most comprehensive death. It is no light thing to die. We speak too flippantly of death, but dying is no child's-play to any man, and dying as the Saviour died, in awful agonies of body and tortures of soul, it was a great thing indeed for his love to do. You may surround death if you please with luxury, you may place at the bedside all the dear assuagements of the tenderest love, you may alleviate pain by the art of the apothecary and the physician, and you may decorate the dying couch with the honour of a nation's anxious care, but death, for all that, is in itself no slight thing, and when borne for others it is the masterpiece of love."[30]

Indeed, various fears confront people, even Christian people, as they contemplate death. Says Spurgeon in the context of his time: "Alas! I shall die in a workhouse; I do not know what will become of me in old age, when these fingers cannot earn my daily bread. . . ." Or, "The Holy Ghost will withdraw from our church; our ministry will not be useful; our various works will fall to pieces; we shall see those who profess to be zealous go back to the world again. . . ." Or, "Then we dream dreadful things concerning our nation. According to the gloomy prophets, all England is going to the bad—not England alone, but all countries are hastening on to a general and everlasting smash. . . ." But, "Our refuge is in God; let the worst calamities occur to the world in years to come, we are secure. It must be well: it cannot be ill. 'Jehovah-Jireh.'"[31]

But there is purpose even in the dying process. "It is said of the old Baptist church over in the City that the members went to Smithfield early one morning to see their pastor burnt, and when some one asked the young people what they went there for, they said that they went *to learn the way*. That is splendid! They went to learn the way. Oh, go to the Master's cross to learn the way to live and die! See how he spent himself for you, and then sally forth and spend yourselves for him."[32]

The actual passing from this world to the next is full of mystery. Yet clearly there is also insight: "I do not doubt, also, that on dying beds men get foretastes of heaven which they never had in health. When Death begins to pull down the old clay-house, he knocks away much of the plaster, and then the light shines through the chinks. When he comes to deal with our rough garment of clay he pulls it to rags first; and then it is we begin to get a better view of the robes of righteousness, the fair white linen of the saints, with which we are always covered, though we know it not. The nearer to death, the nearer to heaven, with the believer; the more sick, the nearer he is to health. The darkest part of his night is indeed the dawning of the day; just when he shall think he dies he shall begin to live; and when his flesh drops from him, then is he preparing to be clothed upon with his house which is from heaven."[33]

In speaking of what happens in the process of dying and consequent resurrection of the body, we can also be comforted by our Lord's gentle treatment of us. Using the example of a child, Spurgeon says: "The child has to go to bed, but it does not cry if mother is going upstairs with it. It is quite dark; but what of that? The mother's eyes are lamps to the child. It is very lonely and still. Not so; the mother's arms are the child's company, and her voice is its music. O Lord, when the hour comes for me to go to bed, I know that thou wilt take me there, and speak lovingly into my ear; therefore I cannot fear, but will even look forward to that hour of thy manifested love."[34]

Further, we need not fear the deaths of loved ones:

Why should it be thought a thing incredible with you, that God should raise the dead?—Acts 26:8 (KJV)

"Concerning the souls of our believing friends who have departed this life we suffer no distress, we feel sure that they are where Jesus is, and behold his glory, according to our Lord's own memorable prayer. . . .

"Our main trouble is about their bodies, which we have committed to the dark and lonesome grave. We cannot reconcile ourselves to the fact that their dear faces are being stripped of all their beauty by the fingers of decay, and that all the insignia of their manhood should be fading into corruption. It seems hard that the hands and feet, and all the goodly fabric of their noble forms, should be dissolved into dust, and broken into an utter ruin. We cannot stand at the grave without tears; even the perfect Man could not restrain his weeping at Lazarus' tomb."[35]

"My brethren, it would not be a complete victory over sin and Satan, if the Saviour left a part of his people in the grave; it would not look as if he had destroyed all the works of the devil if he only emancipated their spirits. There shall not be a bone, nor a piece of a bone, of any one of Christ's people left in the charnel house at the last. Death shall not have a solitary trophy to show: his prison-house shall be utterly rifled of all the spoil which he has gathered from our humanity."[36]

"We do then really in very truth believe that the very body which is put into the grave will rise again, and we mean this literally, and as we utter it. We are not using the language of metaphor, or talking of a myth; we believe that, in actual fact, the bodies of the dead will rise again from the tomb."[37]

> But some man will say, How are the dead raised up? and with what body do they come? Thou fool, that which thou sowest is not quickened, except it die: and that which thou sowest, thou sowest not that body that shall be, but bare grain, it may chance of wheat, or of some other grain. but God giveth it a body as it hath pleased him, and to every seed his own body.—1 Cor. 15:35–38 (KJV)

". . . First, then, our text suggests the real *identity* of the resurrection body. The apostle uses the figure of a seed, a shriveled grain of wheat. It is put into the ground, there it dies, all the farinaceous part of it decays and forms a peculiarly fine soil, into which the life-germ strikes itself, and upon which the life-germ feeds. The seed itself dies, with the exception of a particle almost too small to be perceived, which is the real life contained within the wheat. By-and-by we see a green blade upstarting:

that grows, swells, and increases, until it comes to be corn in the ear, and afterwards the full corn in the ear. Now no one has any suspicion but that the same wheat arises from the soil into which it was cast. Put into the earth, we believe it springs up, and we are accustomed to talk of it in our ordinary language as being the very same seed which we sowed, although the difference is striking and marvelous. Here you have a plant some three feet high, bearing many grains of wheat, and there you had the other day a little shriveled grain; yet no one doubts but that the two are the same. So shall it be in the resurrection of the dead. The body is here but as a shriveled seed; there is no beauty in it that we should desire it. It is put into the grave, like wheat that is sown in the earth; there it rots and it decays, but God preserves within it a sort of life germ which is immortal, and when the trump of the archangel shall shake the heavens and the earth it shall expand to the full flower of manhood, which shall blossom from the earth, a far more glorious form than the manhood which was buried."[38]

"Some have said, 'But when men's bodies are dead, and are committed to the grave, they are often digged up, and the careless sexton mixes them up with common mould; nay, it sometimes happens that they are carted away from the churchyard, and strewn over the fields, to become a rich manure for wheat, so that the particles of the body are absorbed into the corn that is growing, and they travel round in a circle until they become the food of man. So that the particle which may have been in the body of one man enters into the body of another. Now,' say they, 'how can all these particles be tracked?' Our answer is, if it were necessary, every atom could be traced. Omnipotence and Omniscience could do it. If it were needful that God should search and find out every individual atom that ever existed, he would be able to detect the present abode of every single particle. . . . But recollect, this is not necessary at all, for, as I said before, the identity may be preserved without there being the same atoms. Just go back to the excellent illustration of our text. The wheat is just the same, but in the new wheat that has grown up there may not be one solitary particle of that matter which was in the seed cast into the ground. A little seed that shall not weigh the hundredth part of an ounce falls into the earth, and springs up and produces a forest tree that shall weigh two tons. Now, if there be any part of the original seed in the tree, it must be but in the proportion of a millionth part, or something less than that. And yet is the tree positively identical with the seed—it is the same thing.

And so there may only be a millionth part of the particles of my body in the new body which I shall wear but yet it may still be the same. It is not the identity of the matter that will make positive identity. And I shall show you that again. Are you not aware that our bodies are changing—that in about every ten years we have different bodies from what we had ten years ago? That is to say, by decay, and the continual wearing away of our flesh, there is not in this body I have here, a single particle that was in my body ten years ago, and yet I am the same man. I know I am precisely the same. So you. You shall have been born in America, and lived there twenty years; you shall suddenly be transferred to India, and live there another twenty years; you come back to America to see your friends—you are the same man, they know you, recognise you, you are precisely the same individual; but yet philosophy teaches us a fact which cannot be denied—that your body would have changed twice in the time you have been absent from your friends; that every particle is gone, and has had its place supplied by another; and yet the body is the same. So that it is not necessary there should be the same particles; it is not needful that you should track every atom and bring it back in order that the body should preserve its identity."[39]

In summary, Spurgeon uses a simple illustration: "Take another—one used of old by that mighty preacher, Chrysostom—there is an old house, a straight and narrow cottage, and the inhabitant of it often shivers with the cold in winter, and is greatly oppressed by the heat of summer; it is ill adapted to his wants, the windows are too small and very dark, he cannot keep his treasure safely therein; he is often a prisoner; and when I have passed by his house I have heard him sighing at the window: 'Oh, wretched man that I am, who shall deliver me from the body of this death.' The good master comes, the landlord of the house, he speaks to the tenant, and he bids him come away, 'I am about to pull down thy old house,' saith he, 'and I would not have thee here while I am pulling it stone from stone, lest thou be hurt and injured. Come away with me and live in my palace, while I am pulling thy old house to pieces.' He does so, and every stone of the old house is thrown down; it is levelled with the ground, and even the foundations are dug up. Another is built: it is of costly slabs of marble, the windows thereof are pure and clear, all its gates are of agate, and all its borders of precious stones, while all the foundations thereof are of chrysolite, and the roof thereof is of jasper. And now the master of the house speaks to the old inhabitant, 'Come back, and I will show thee the house which I have built for thee.' O what joy, when that inhabitant shall enter and find it so well adapted to his wants, where every power shall have full range, where he shall see God out of its windows, not as through a glass, darkly, but face to face, where he could invite even Christ himself to come up and sup with him, and not feel that the house is beneath the dignity of the Son of Man. You know the parable, you know how your old house, this clay body, is to be pulled down, how your spirit is to dwell in heaven for a little while without a body, and how afterwards you are to enter into a house not made with hands, eternal in the heavens, a mansion which is holy, incorruptible, and undefiled, and which shall never decay."[40]

And what will we be like in heaven? "Personality will be maintained. I do not doubt but what you will know Isaiah in heaven; and you will recognize the great preachers of the ancient Christian church; you will be able to speak with Chrysostom, and will talk with Whitefield. It may be you shall have for your companions those who were your companions here; those with whom you took sweet counsel, and walked to the house of God, shall be there with you, and you shall know them, and with transporting joy you shall there together tell your former trials and ancient triumphs, and the glories you are alike made to share.

"At Stratford-on-Bow, in the days of Queen Mary, there was once a stake erected for the burning of two martyrs, one of them a lame man, the other a blind man. Just when the fire was lit, the lame man hurled away his staff, and turning round said to the blind man, 'Courage, brother, this fire will cure us both.' So can the righteous say of the grave, 'Courage, the grave will cure us all; we shall leave our infirmities behind us.' What patience this should give us to endure all our trials, for they are not of long duration."[41]

For "it is not death to die: it is only undressing. These poor garments are dusty with toil, and withal, in some cases, they are ragged with age, and therefore we may be well content to put them off. 'Not for that we would be unclothed, but clothed upon with our house which is from heaven.' Dying—why, it is only going to our bed-chamber to sleep a while, and then to wake up, at the sound of the trumpet, in the likeness of our Lord. Dying—why to our souls it is the entrance into the joy of our Lord; it is passing into the ivory palaces, wherein they have made him glad, and wherein we shall be made glad in his blessed company."[42]

Therefore, "do not, my brethren, think of the cemetery with tears, nor meditate upon the coffin and the shroud with gloomy thoughts. You only sojourn there for a little season, and to you it will not appear a moment. Your body will sleep, and if men sleep all through a long night it only seems an hour to them, a very short moment. The sleeping-time is forgotten, and to your sleeping-body it will seem no time at all, while to your glorified soul it will not seem long because you will be so full of joy that a whole eternity of that joy would not be too long. But you shall rise again. I do not think we get enough joy out of our resurrection. It will probably be our happiest moment, or rather the beginning of the happiest life that we shall ever know. Heaven is not the happiest place. Heaven at present is happy, but it is not the perfection of happiness, because there is only the soul there, though the soul is full of pleasure; but the heaven that is to be when body and soul will both be there surpasses all thought. Resurrection will be our marriage-day. Body and soul have been separated, and they shall meet again to be re-married with a golden ring, no more to be divorced, but as one indissolubly united body to go up to the great altar of immortality, and there to be espoused unto Christ for ever and ever. I shall come again to this flesh, no longer flesh that can decay, no longer bones that ache—I shall come back to these eyes and these ears, all made channels of new delight. Say not this is a materialistic view of the matter. We are at least one-half material, and so long as there is material about us we must always expect joy that shall not only give spiritual but even material delight to us. This body shall rise again."[43] Notice that while the physical body sleeps, the soul never sleeps.

Many people whom I talk to agonize over whether we shall know each other in heaven. Says Spurgeon: "In this world we have had some good wine of sweet company. . . . Some of you can remember golden names that were very dear to you in the days of your youth—of men and women with whom you used to go up to God's house and take sweet counsel. . . . and you have friends still left, to whom you look up with some degree of reverence, while they look upon you with intense affection. There are some men that are comforters to your soul, and when you talk to them you feel that their heart answers to your heart, and that you can enjoy union and communion with them. But beloved, the good wine is kept till the last. All the fellowship with the saints that we have had here, is as nothing compared with what we are to enjoy in the world to come. How sweet it is for us to recollect, that in heaven we shall be in the company of the best men, the noblest men, the most mighty men, the most honourable and the most renowned. We shall sit with Moses, and talk with him of all his life of wonders; we shall walk with Joseph, and we shall hear from him of the grace that kept him in his hour of peril; I doubt not you and I shall have the privilege of sitting by the side of David, and hearing him recount the perils and the deliverances through which he passed. The saints of heaven make but one communion; they are not divided into separate classes; we shall be allowed to walk through all the glorious ranks, and hold fellowship with all of them; nor need we doubt but that we shall be able to know them all. There are many reasons which I could not now enumerate, for it would occupy me too much time, that seem to my mind to settle the point, that in heaven we shall know even as we are known, and shall perfectly know each other; and that indeed, makes us long to be there."[44]

And again: "A Christian has nothing to lose by death. You say he has to lose his friends. I am not so sure of that. Many of you have many more friends in heaven than on earth; some Christians have more dearly beloved ones above than below. You often count your family circle, but do you do as that little girl of whom Wordsworth speaks, when she said, 'Master, we are seven.' Some of them were dead and gone to heaven, but she would have it that they were all brothers and sisters still."[45]

Not only will we know each other in heaven but we will know. Our questions will be answered. "Up in heaven, too, we shall see our life as a whole, and we shall see God's dealings with us on earth as a whole. A great many matters which now appear mysterious and complex, concerning which we can only walk by faith, for our reason is baffled, will be so clear to us as to excite our joyous songs in heaven. 'Now I see why I was laid aside when I wanted to be busy in God's work: now I see why that dear child, whom I hoped to have had spared to me as a stay for my old age, was taken away; now I understand why my business was suffered to fail; now I comprehend why that foul mouth was allowed to be opened against me; now I comprehend why I was assailed with inward fears, and was suffered to go tremblingly all my days.' Such will be our confessions when the day dawns and the shadows flee away. Then we shall say and sing: 'He hath dealt wondrously with us.' We shall feel that the best was done for us that even Eternal Wisdom could devise, and we shall bless the name of the Lord."[46]

The triumph of the grave, however, is that "we must not make a mistake by imagining that *the soul* sleeps. . . . 'To-day shalt thou be with me in Paradise,' is the whisper of Christ to every dying saint."[47]

Furthermore, "the soul forgets not, and we have no reason to believe that the glorified are ignorant of what is going on below."[48]

Indeed, "in a few minutes I shall know more of heaven than an assembly of divines could teach me. . . . Worms devour the clay, but angels welcome the soul. There is general mourning wherever the good man was known; but mark ye, it is only in the dark that this sorrow reigns. Up there in the light, what are they doing? That spirit as it left the body found not itself alone. Angels had come to meet it. Angelic spirits clasped the disembodied spirit in their arms, and bore it upward beyond the stars—beyond where the angel in the sun keeps his everlasting watch—beyond, beyond this lower sky immeasurable leagues. Lo! the pearly gates appear, and the azure light of the city of bejeweled walls! The spirit asketh, 'Is yonder city the fair Jerusalem where they need no candle, neither light of the sun?' He shall see for himself ere long, for they are nearing the Holy City, and it is time for the cherub-bearers to begin their choral. The music breaks from the lips of those that convey the saint to heaven—'Lift up your heads, O ye gates, and be ye lifted up ye everlasting doors, that the blood-bought of the King of glory may come in!' The gates of pearl give way, the joyous crowds of heaven welcome their brother to the seats of immortality. But what next, I cannot tell. In vain the fancy strives to paint it. Jesus is there, and the spirit is in his arms."[49]

Still, some Christians fear that heaven will be dull. However, in a sermon preached in the Metropolitan Tabernacle on Lord's Day morning, February 7, 1892, in connection with Spurgeon's own death, the Reverend A. T. Pierson offers the opposite view: "When a saint of God falls asleep as to his body, and enters into the presence of his Lord, as to his spirit for evermore, the *labours*, the toils, the vexations of this world, he leaves behind him; but he carries with him into immortality his *service*.

He goes to carry on his work for God, for that is as immortal as God himself. He goes where no limitations exist, where no vexations and hindrances circumscribe his activity, where 'they rest not,' because they are never tired nor fatigued; where, as they wait on the Lord, they renew their strength, mount up with wings as eagles, run and are never weary, walk and never faint. The tireless and endless activity of a redeemed soul partakes of the tireless energy of an untiring God. Let us not suppose, for a moment, that when a man who has spent his life in seeking to serve God, who has stored his mind with all manner of accumulations, and, with the tension of persistent effort, sought to acquire and achieve all that is possible for his Master; who has laid the foundation-stone of great institutions, has scattered abroad throughout the world the testimony of his faith and his courage for his Master's sake—let us not suppose for a moment that, when such a man falls, as we say, at the blow of death, his service ceases. God is a better *οἰκονόμος*, economist, housekeeper, than that. He is no such wasteful keeper of his eternal house. When a saint departs to be with Christ, instead of leaving service behind, he enters of a new sphere of service, where, instead of sacrificing acquisitions and attainments, he rather finds an absolutely perfect scope for the exercise of them all; instead of ceasing to work for his Master, he rather begins his work anew in the tirelessness of celestial energy."[50]

When I was a little girl, my Aunt Lydia had a small calendar in her hallway, which read "Perhaps Today." As I was in the process of making place cards for my New Year's Day dinner on that last New Year's in the 1900s, I awoke abruptly one morning in December with words from the Book of Revelation, "Behold I come quickly." These words went on the cards.

For centuries this earth has waited for our Lord's return. "Perhaps Today" has been our cry. Spurgeon tells the story of a woman: "There is the wife at evening. It is past the proper hour for her husband to return. She goes to the window and looks out into the cold dark night, and then she goes back to the chair, and to the little one, and takes her needle and whiles away the time, but soon she is up again looking out of the window once more, and listening to every foot-fall in the street, or looking out from the open door. Why is not her spouse at home? How is it that he is away? She sits down again, she tries to ease her mind with household business, but every ticking of the clock, and every striking of the hour suggests to her, 'Why is he so long in coming?' See she is again drawing back the curtains and looking out into the black night for the hundredth time, longing for her husband, and why? because she takes delight in him, and wants to see his face. So when Christians look out into the dark world and say, 'When will he come?' and when they go to their labour, and say, 'Why are his chariot-wheels so long in coming?' and when they can cry with John, 'Come quickly, even so, come quickly, Lord Jesus,' and are waiting for and hasting unto the coming of the Son of man, then they prove that they have intense delight in him."[51]

But if he does not come today, and we die today? "When we gather up our feet in our last bed, we may utter this text in a full and sweet sense, 'I shall not die, but live.' When Wycliffe died as to his body, the real Wycliffe did not die. Some of his books were carried to Bohemia, and John Huss learned the gospel from them, and began to preach. They burnt John Huss, and Jerome of Prague; but Huss foretold, as he died, that another would arise after him, whom they should not be able to put down; and in due time he more than lived again in Luther. Is Luther dead? Is Calvin dead to-day? That last man the moderns have tried to bury in a dunghill of misrepresentation; but he lives, and will live, and the truths that he taught will survive all the calumniators that have sought to poison it. Die! Often the death of a man is a kind of new birth to him; when he himself is gone physically, he spiritually survives, and from his grave there shoots up a tree of life whose leaves heal nations. O worker for God, death cannot touch thy sacred mission! Be thou content to die if the truth shall live the better because thou diest. Be thou content to die, because death may be to thee the enlargement of thine influence. Good men die no dies the seed corn which thereby abideth not alone. When saints are apparently laid in the earth, they quit the earth, and rise and mount to heaven-gate, and enter into immortality. No, when the sepulchre receives this mortal frame, we shall not die, but live. Then shall we come to our true stature and beauty, and put on our royal robes, our glorious Sabbath-dress."[52]

And for those who are left? In a sermon preached on Sunday morning, December 22, 1861, at the Metropolitan Tabernacle, Spurgeon spoke of the death of Prince Albert, husband of Queen Victoria of England. Said Spurgeon: "And this, too, shall be our best comfort. God hath done it. What! shall we weep for what God hath done? Shall we sorrow when the Master hath taken away what was his own? 'The Lord gave, and the Lord hath taken away, blessed be the name of the Lord.' The gardener had a choice flower in his beds. One morning he missed it. He had tended it so carefully that he looked upon it with the affection of a father to a child, and he hastily ran through the garden and sought out one of the servants, for he thought surely an enemy had plucked it, and he said to him, 'Who plucked that rose?' And the servant said, 'I saw the master walking through the garden early this morning, when the sun was ris-ing, and I saw him bear it away in his hand.' Then he that tended the rose said, 'It is well; let him be blessed; it was his own; for him I held it; for him I nursed it; and if he hath taken it, it is well.' So be it with your hearts. Feel that it is for the best that you have lost your friend, or that your best relation has departed. *God* has done it."[53]

In a sermon intended for use immediately following Spurgeon's own death, Spurgeon used the following text:

> Go to now, ye that say, To day or to morrow we will go into such a city, and continue there a year, and buy and sell, and get gain: whereas ye know not what shall be on the morrow. For what is your life? It is even a vapour, that appeareth for a little time, and then vanisheth away. For that ye ought to say, If the Lord will, we shall live, and do this, or that. But now ye rejoice in your boastings: all such rejoicing is evil. Therefore to him that knoweth to do good, and doeth it not, to him it is sin.— James 4:13–17 (KJV)

Said Spurgeon: "'What is your life? It is even a vapour, that appeareth for a little time.' That cloud upon the mountain—you see it as you rise in the morning; you have scarcely dressed yourself before all trace of it has gone. Here in our streets, the other night, we came to worship through a thick fog, and found it here even in the house of prayer. But while we worshipped, there came a breath of wind; and on our way home a stranger would not have thought that London had been, but a few hours before, so dark with dirty mist; it had all disappeared. Life is even as a vapour. Sometimes these vapours, especially at the time of sunset, are exceedingly brilliant. They seem to be magnificence itself when the sun paints them with heavenly colours; but in a little while they are all gone, and the whole panorama of the sunset has disappeared. Such is our life. It may sometimes be very bright and glorious; but still it is only like a painted cloud, and very soon the cloud and the colour on it are alike gone. We cannot reckon upon the clouds, their laws are so variable, and their conditions so obscure. Such also is our life.

"Why, then, is it, that we are always counting upon what we are going to do? How is it that, instead of living in the eternal future, where we might deal with certainties, we continue to live in the more immediate future, where there can be nothing but uncertainties? Why do we choose to build upon clouds, and pile our palaces on vapour, to see them melt away, as aforetime they have often melted, instead of by faith getting where there is no failure, where God is all in all, and his sure promises make the foundations of eternal mansions? Oh! I would say with my strongest emphasis: Do not reckon upon the future. Young people, I would whisper this in your ears: Do not discount the days to come. Old men, whispering is not enough for you, I would say, with a voice of thunder: Count not on distant years; in the course of nature, your days must be few. Live in the present; live unto God; trust him now, and serve him now; for very soon your life on earth will be over."[54]

Furthermore, "We are glad that we do not know when our friends are to die; and we feel thankful that we cannot foretell when we shall depart out of this life. What good would it do us?"[55]

It was in Mentone, France, that Spurgeon died. Mentone, where he had so often recovered from illness but where he had also been isolated from his dear Susannah, who had for years been too ill to make the journey. This time it was different and Susannah had come with—a divine gift to a departing saint.

Up to the end controversy flew around him. Most of all there was still the pain of what he had gone through with those whom he had trusted in the Down Grade Controversy. In this way he reminds us of the apostle Paul, alone and ready to die. Yet there were accolades, too, messages of concern from people like the Prince of Wales and William Gladstone, and there was the companionship of his beloved wife. Near the end he said to her: "Oh Wifey, I have had such a blessed time with my Lord." And then, "My work is done." The last verse of Scripture which he was known to recite was, "I have fought the good fight. I have finished my course. I have kept the faith."[56] Once again he was in step with the apostle Paul.

Yet unlike Paul, when Spurgeon died there was grief, seemingly all over the world. Dignitaries, church leaders, children, adults, the poor, the rich—all joined in mourning the loss of this remarkable man of God.

In the summer of 1888 Spurgeon had preached on Hebrews 12:1–2 (KJV).

> Wherefore seeing we also are compassed about with so great a cloud of witnesses, let us lay aside every weight, and the sin which doth so easily beset us, and let us run with patience the race that is set before us, looking unto Jesus the author and finisher of our faith; who for the joy that was set before him endured the cross, despising the shame, and is set down at the right hand of the throne of God.

"The apostle saith, 'Let us run.' He has in his mind's eye the Olympic games, where all the different tribes of Greece were gathered together in general assembly to display the prowess of the race. Among the athletic exercises were foot-races. The apostle makes this foot-race an illustration of the Christian life. We must run with patience along the appointed course if we would win the prize of our high calling.

"He stands with us at the starting-point, and earnestly says to us, not 'Run,' but, 'Let us run.' The apostle himself is at our side as a runner. The presence of such a comrade is most inspiriting. It is good doing good things in good company. 'Let us run,' saith he, 'with patience the race that is set before us.' Who will back out of a race wherein so great a saint takes his place at our side? . . .

"Before we start, with a wave of the hand the apostle directs us to the spectators who throng the sides of the course. There were always such at those races: each city and state yielded its contingent, and the assembled throng watched with eager eye the efforts of those who strove for the mastery. Those who look down upon us from yonder heavens are described as 'so great a cloud of witnesses.' These compass us about. Thousands upon thousands, who have run this race before us, and have attained their crowns, behold us from their heavenly seats, and mark how we behave ourselves. This race is worth running, for the eyes of 'the nations of them which are saved' are fixed upon us. . . . Angels, and principalities, and powers, and hosts redeemed by blood, have mustered to behold the glorious spectacle of men agonizing for holiness, and putting forth their utmost strength to copy the Lord Jesus. Ye that are men, now run for it! If there be any spiritual life and gracious strength in you, put it forth to-day; for patriarchs and prophets, saints, martyrs, and apostles look down from heaven upon you."[57]

Now he too had joined that vital group of heavenly witnesses who cheer us on. Spurgeon with the apostle Paul. What a meeting that must have been.

In speaking of family members who have gone to heaven before us, my granddaughter said to me the other day: "I wish heaven could come to earth so we could see them all." The joy for us who remain is that Spurgeon, the apostle Paul, our own loved ones, and a vast host of others do see us and cheer us on. And above all it is God himself who calls us to run the race of life for him.

NOTES

Epigraph

1. C. H. Spurgeon, *The Metropolitan Tabernacle Pulpit* 47 (1901): 169.

Preface

1. C. H. Spurgeon, *The Metropolitan Tabernacle Pulpit* 9 (1863): 302.

Chapter 1: Body, Mind, and Spirit

1. C. H. Spurgeon, *The Metropolitan Tabernacle Pulpit* 36 (1890): 134.
2. C. H. Spurgeon, *The Metropolitan Tabernacle Pulpit* 9 (1863): 663.
3. Ibid., 669.
4. Ibid.
5. Ibid., 664.
6. Ibid.
7. Ibid.
8. The *Los Angeles Times* (September 10, 1997): 1.
9. C. H. Spurgeon, *The Metropolitan Tabernacle Pulpit* 38 (1892): 547.
10. C. H. Spurgeon, *The New Park Street Pulpit* 1 (1855): 98.
11. C. H. Spurgeon, *The Metropolitan Tabernacle Pulpit* 21 (1875): 119.
12. C. H. Spurgeon, *The Metropolitan Tabernacle Pulpit* 18 (1872): 515.
13. Ibid., 514.
14. Ibid., 514–15.
15. C. H. Spurgeon, *The Metropolitan Tabernacle Pulpit* 19 (1873): 385.
16. Ibid., 389.
17. C. H. Spurgeon, *The New Park Street Pulpit* 1: 99.
18. C. H. Spurgeon, *The Metropolitan Tabernacle Pulpit* 19: 389.
19. C. H. Spurgeon, *The Metropolitan Tabernacle Pulpit* 18: 681.
20. Ibid., 680.
21. Quoted in Rev. R. Shindler, *From the Usher's Desk to the Tabernacle Pulpit, The Life and Labors of Pastor C. H. Spurgeon* (London: Passmore and Alabaster, 1892), 25, 27–30.
22. Ibid., 35–36.
23. Ibid., 37.
24. Quoted in Russell H. Conwell, *Life of Charles Haddon Spurgeon* (Edgewood Publishing, 1892), 64–65.

25. Ernest W. Bacon, *Spurgeon: Heir of the Puritans* (Grand Rapids: William B. Eerdmans, 1968), 161.

26. W. Williams, *Personal Reminiscences of Charles Haddon Spurgeon* (London: The Religious Tract Society, 1895), 32.

27. C. H. Spurgeon, *The Metropolitan Tabernacle Pulpit* 62 (1916): 22.

28. C. H. Spurgeon, *The Metropolitan Tabernacle Pulpit* 11 (1865): 3–4.

29. Quoted in Williams, *Personal Reminiscences*, 45.

30. Ibid., 48.

31. *C. H. Spurgeon's Autobiography, Compiled from His Diary, Letters, and Records, by His Wife*, vol. 2 (London: Passmore and Alabaster, 1897), 289–90.

32. Janet Oppenheim, *Shattered Nerves: Doctors, Patients, and Depression in Victorian England* (New York: Oxford University Press, 1991), 42.

33. Ralph Waldo Emerson, "The American Scholar," *American Heritage*, ed. Leon Howard et al., vol. 1 (Boston: D. C. Heath and Company, 1955), 621.

34. C. H. Spurgeon, *The Metropolitan Tabernacle Pulpit* 12 (1866): 298–99.

35. C. H. Spurgeon, *The Metropolitan Tabernacle Pulpit* 19: 690.

36. C. H. Spurgeon, *The Metropolitan Tabernacle Pulpit* 21: 119.

37. C. H. Spurgeon, *The Sword and the Trowel* 7 (1883, 1884): 124–25.

38. Ibid., 474.

39. Ibid., 475.

40. Ibid., 476.

41. C. H. Spurgeon, *The Metropolitan Tabernacle Pulpit* 57 (1911): 266.

42. C. H. Spurgeon, *The Metropolitan Tabernacle Pulpit* 19: 76.

43. Ibid., 281.

44. C. H. Spurgeon, *The Metropolitan Tabernacle Pulpit* 24 (1878): 424.

45. C. H. Spurgeon, *The Metropolitan Tabernacle Pulpit* 51 (1905): 350–51.

46. Ibid., 354.

Chapter 2: *Confidence*

1. C. H. Spurgeon, *The Metropolitan Tabernacle Pulpit* 8 (1862): 577.

2. C. H. Spurgeon, *The Metropolitan Tabernacle Pulpit* 11 (1865): 515.

3. C. H. Spurgeon, *The Metropolitan Tabernacle Pulpit* 30 (1884): 351.

4. C. H. Spurgeon, *The Metropolitan Tabernacle Pulpit* 36 (1890): 469.

5. C. H. Spurgeon, *The Metropolitan Tabernacle Pulpit* 8: 57.

6. C. H. Spurgeon, *The Metropolitan Tabernacle Pulpit* 25 (1879): 86.

7. Ibid.

8. Ibid., 86–87.

9. C. H. Spurgeon, *The New Park Street Metropolitan Tabernacle Pulpit* 7 (1861): 61.

10. C. H. Spurgeon, *The Metropolitan Tabernacle Pulpit* 8: 304–5.

11. Ibid., 305.

12. Ibid., 572.

13. F. B. Meyer, *Exodus* (London: The Religious Tract Society, n.d.), 223.

14. C. H. Spurgeon, *The New Park Street Pulpit* 6 (1859): 399.

15. C. H. Spurgeon, *The Metropolitan Tabernacle Pulpit* 30: 674–75.

16. C. H. Spurgeon, *The Metropolitan Tabernacle Pulpit* 36: 477.

17. G. K. Chesterton, *Orthodoxy* (New York: Lane, 1918), 101.

18. C. H. Spurgeon, *The Metropolitan Tabernacle Pulpit* 36: 477.

19. Ibid., 221.

20. C. H. Spurgeon, *The New Park Street Pulpit* 6: 383.

21. C. H. Spurgeon, *The New Park Street Pulpit* 5 (1859): 463.

22. C. H. Spurgeon, *The Metropolitan Tabernacle Pulpit* 19 (1873): 194–95.

23. C. H. Spurgeon, *The Metropolitan Tabernacle Pulpit* 2 (1855): 351.

24. Ibid., 350.

25. C. H. Spurgeon, *The Metropolitan Tabernacle Pulpit* 19: 195.

26. Ibid., 309.

27. C. H. Spurgeon, *The Metropolitan Tabernacle Pulpit* 25: 93.

28. C. H. Spurgeon, "Be of Good Cheer," apparently unpublished ms. (1880).

29. Ibid.

30. Ibid.

31. C. H. Spurgeon, *The Metropolitan Tabernacle Pulpit* 8: 182.

32. C. H. Spurgeon, *The Metropolitan Tabernacle Pulpit* 13 (1867): 637.

33. Ibid.

Chapter 3: *Depression*

1. C. H. Spurgeon, *The Metropolitan Tabernacle Pulpit* 32 (1886): 344.

2. C. H. Spurgeon, *Lectures to My Students*, vol. 1 (Pasadena, Tex.: Pilgrim Publications, 1990), 167.

3. Ibid.

4. Ibid., 178.

5. C. H. Spurgeon, preface, "Be of Good Cheer," apparently unpublished ms. (1880).

6. C. H. Spurgeon, *Sermons*, vol. 18 (New York: Funk & Wagnalls, n.d.), 351–52.

7. Ibid., 353.

8. Ibid.

9. Ibid., 353–54.

10. C. H. Spurgeon, *The Saint and His Savior* (London: Hazell, Watson, & Viney Ltd., 1895), 35.

11. Spurgeon, *Lectures*, vol. 1: 178.

12. Ibid.

13. Ibid., 168.

14. Ibid., 168–69.

15. Charles H. Spurgeon, *Treasury of David*, vol. 2a (Grand Rapids: Zondervan, 1966), 3–4 .

16. C. H. Spurgeon, *Sermons*, vol. 11, (New York: Funk & Wagnalls, n.d.), 80.

17 Ibid., 81.

18. Richard E. Day, *The Shadow of the Broad Brim* (Philadelphia: The Judson Press, 1934), 177.

19. Ibid., 96.

20. C. H. Spurgeon, *Sermons*, vol. 2 (New York: Funk & Wagnalls, n.d.), 136.

21. Spurgeon, *Lectures*, vol. 1: 172–74.

22. Ibid., 174–75.

23. Ibid.

24. Amy Carmichael, *Gold by Moonlight* (Ft. Washington, Pa.: Christian Literature Crusade), 101.

25. Spurgeon, *Lectures*, vol. 1: 176.

26. Ibid., 177.

27. Helmut Thielicke and John W. Doberstein, trans., *Encounter with Spurgeon* (Grand Rapids: Baker, 1975), 216.

28. Ernest W. Bacon, *Spurgeon: Heir of the Puritans* (Grand Rapids: William B. Eerdmans , 1968), 78.

29. Spurgeon, *Lectures*, vol. 1: 171–72.

30. Ibid., 170–71.

31. J. B. Phillips, *The Price of Success* (Wheaton: Harold Shaw, 1984), 202.

32. Ibid., 201.

33. Spurgeon, *The Saint and His Savior*, 36–37.

34. Ibid., 276.

35. Spurgeon, *Lectures*, vol. 1: 177–78.

36. Day, *Shadow*, 178.

37. Ibid., 178–79.

38. Spurgeon, *Treasury of David*, vol. 2a: 463.

39. Spurgeon, *The Saint and His Savior*, 250.

40. C. H. Spurgeon, *The New Park Street Pulpit* 4 (1858): 461.

41. C. H. Spurgeon, *Treasury of David*, vol. 1a: 110.

42. C. H. Spurgeon, *Treasury of David*, vol. 2b: 257.

43. Amy Carmichael, *Gold Cord* (Ft. Washington, Pa.: Christian Literature Crusade, 1957), 31.

44. C. H. Spurgeon, *The New Park Street Pulpit* 4: 460.

45. Spurgeon, *Sermons*, vol. 2: 147.

46. C. H. Spurgeon, *The New Park Street Pulpit* 5 (1859): 145–46.

47. C. H. Spurgeon, *The New Park Street Pulpit* 9 (1863): 608.

48. C. H. Spurgeon, *The New Park Street Pulpit* 3 (1857): 390–91.

49. Spurgeon, *Sermons*, vol. 11: 206–7.

50. Spurgeon, *Sermons*, vol. 2: 169–70.

51. Ibid., 182–83.

52. Spurgeon, *Sermons*, vol. 18: 364–66.

53. Spurgeon, *The Saint and His Savior*, 247.

54. Amy Carmichael, "No Scar," *Toward Jerusalem* (Ft. Washington, Pa.: Christian Literature Crusade, 1961), 85.

55. Spurgeon, *The Saint and His Savior*, 251–52.

56. C. H. Spurgeon, *The New Park Street Pulpit* 4: 460–61.

Chapter 4: *Anxiety*

1. C. H. Spurgeon, *The Metropolitan Tabernacle Pulpit* 19 (1873): 8.

2. J. B. Phillips, *The Price of Success* (Wheaton: Harold Shaw, 1984), 202.

3. Ibid.

4. C. H. Spurgeon, *The Metropolitan Tabernacle Pulpit* 21 (1875): 331.

5. C. S. Lewis, *The Problem of Pain* (New York: Macmillan, 1943), 9.

6. C. H. Spurgeon, "Be of Good Cheer," apparently unpublished ms. (1880).

7. Ibid.

8. Richard E. Day, *The Shadow of the Broad Brim* (Valley Forge, Pa.: The Judson Press, 1934), 175.

9. Helmut Thielicke and John W. Doberstein, trans., *Encounter with Spurgeon* (Grand Rapids: Baker, 1975), 214.

10. C. H. Spurgeon, *The Metropolitan Tabernacle Pulpit* 10 (1864): 21.

11. C. H. Spurgeon, *The Metropolitan Tabernacle Pulpit* 14 (1868): 374–75.

12. Ibid., 376–77.

13. C. H. Spurgeon, *The Metropolitan Tabernacle Pulpit* 48 (1902): 109.

14. Ibid., 110–11.

15. C. H. Spurgeon, *The New Park Street Pulpit* 5 (1859): 169.

16. Ibid.

17. Ibid., 169.

18. Ibid., 170–71.

19. C. H. Spurgeon, *The Metropolitan Tabernacle Pulpit* 35 (1889): 522.

20. C. H. Spurgeon, *The Metropolitan Tabernacle Pulpit* 19: 409.

21. C. H. Spurgeon, *The Metropolitan Tabernacle Pulpit* 16 (1870): 268–69.

22. Ibid., 269.

23. C. H. Spurgeon, *The Metropolitan Tabernacle Pulpit* 57 (1911): 268.

24. C. H. Spurgeon, *The Metropolitan Tabernacle Pulpit* 16: 269.

25. C. H. Spurgeon, *The Metropolitan Tabernacle Pulpit* 57: 265.

26. C. H. Spurgeon, *The Metropolitan Tabernacle Pulpit* 19: 8.

27. Ibid., 8–9.

28. C. H. Spurgeon, *The Metropolitan Tabernacle Pulpit* 48: 604.

29. Ibid., 605.

30. Ibid.

31. C. H. Spurgeon, *The Metropolitan Tabernacle Pulpit* 57: 269.

32. C. H. Spurgeon, *The Metropolitan Tabernacle Pulpit* 18 (1872): 350–51.
33. C. H. Spurgeon, *The Metropolitan Tabernacle Pulpit* 57: 269–70.
34. C. H. Spurgeon, *The Metropolitan Tabernacle Pulpit* 54 (1908): 305.
35. C. H. Spurgeon, *The Metropolitan Tabernacle Pulpit* 16: 273.
36. Ibid.
37. Ibid., 274.
38. Ibid., 274–75.
39. C. H. Spurgeon, *The Metropolitan Tabernacle Pulpit* 54: 301–2.
40. Ibid., 306.
41. C. H. Spurgeon, *The Metropolitan Tabernacle Pulpit* 57: 270.
42. C. H. Spurgeon, *The Metropolitan Tabernacle Pulpit* 48: 496.
43. Ibid., 497–98.
44. C. H. Spurgeon, *The Metropolitan Tabernacle Pulpit* 36 (1890): 338.
45. C. H. Spurgeon, *The Metropolitan Tabernacle Pulpit* 25 (1879): 278–79.
46. C. H. Spurgeon, *The Metropolitan Tabernacle Pulpit* 30 (1884): 657.
47. C. H. Spurgeon, *The Metropolitan Tabernacle Pulpit* 32 (1886): 47.
48. Ibid., 44–45.
49. C. H. Spurgeon, *The Metropolitan Tabernacle Pulpit* 19: 404–5.
50. C. H. Spurgeon, *The Metropolitan Tabernacle Pulpit* 11 (1865): 488–89.
51. Ibid., 566.
52. Ibid., 567.
53. C. H. Spurgeon, *The New Park Street Pulpit* 3 (1857): 394–95.
54. C. H. Spurgeon, *The Metropolitan Tabernacle Pulpit* 8 (1862): 161.
55. Ibid., 161–62.
56. C. H. Spurgeon, "Be of Good Cheer."
57. Ibid.
58. Ibid.
59. Ibid.
60. Ibid.
61. Ibid.
62. Ibid.
63. Ibid.
64. Ibid.

Chapter 5: *Loneliness*

1. C. H. Spurgeon, *The Sword and the Trowel* 3 (1871, 1872, 1873): 40.
2. Colin M. Turnbull, *The Mountain People* (New York: Simon and Schuster, 1972), 286.
3. Ibid., 263–64.
4. Ibid., 290.
5. Ibid., 291.
6. C. H. Spurgeon, *The Metropolitan Tabernacle Pulpit* 32 (1886): 450.
7. C. H. Spurgeon, *The New Park Street Pulpit* 2 (1856): 254–55.
8. Matthew Arnold, "Dover Beach," in George Benjamin Woods and Jerome Hamilton Buckley, *Poetry of the Victorian Period* (Chicago: Scott, Foresman & Company, 1955), 483.
9. C. H. Spurgeon, *The Metropolitan Tabernacle Pulpit* 32: 46–47.
10. C. H. Spurgeon, *The Metropolitan Tabernacle Pulpit* 36 (1890): 514.
11. C. H. Spurgeon, *The Metropolitan Tabernacle Pulpit* 21 (1875): 400–401.
12. Ibid., 401.
13. C. H. Spurgeon, *The Metropolitan Tabernacle Pulpit* 38 (1892): 412.
14. Ibid., 412–13.
15. Ibid., 413.
16. Ibid.
17. Ibid., 436.
18. C. H. Spurgeon, *The Metropolitan Tabernacle Pulpit* 48 (1902): 112.

19. Ibid., 113.

20. C. H. Spurgeon, *The Metropolitan Tabernacle Pulpit* 21: 626.

21. C. H. Spurgeon, *The Metropolitan Tabernacle Pulpit* 12 (1866): 435.

22. C. H. Spurgeon, *Lectures to My Students*, vol. 1 (Pasadena, Tex.: Pilgrim Publishing, 1990), 170–71.

23. C. H. Spurgeon, *The New Park Street Pulpit* 2: 255.

24. Spurgeon, *Lectures*, vol. 1:175.

25. Ernest W. Bacon, *Spurgeon: Heir of the Puritans* (Grand Rapids: William B. Eerdmans, 1968), 135.

26. Ibid., 138.

27. Ibid., 145.

28. Lewis A. Drummond, *Spurgeon: Prince of Preachers* (Grand Rapids: Kregel, 1992), 785.

29. C. H. Spurgeon, *The Metropolitan Tabernacle Pulpit* 35 (1889): 266.

30. Ibid., 267.

31. Ibid., 276.

32. C. H. Spurgeon, *The Metropolitan Tabernacle Pulpit* 10 (1864): 397–98.

33. C. H. Spurgeon, *The Metropolitan Tabernacle Pulpit* 21: 678–79.

34. C. H. Spurgeon, *The Metropolitan Tabernacle Pulpit* 52 (1906): 20.

35. Ibid., 20–23.

36. C. H. Spurgeon, *The Metropolitan Tabernacle Pulpit* 48: 113–17.

37. C. H. Spurgeon, *The Metropolitan Tabernacle Pulpit* 21: 674–75.

38. C. H. Spurgeon, *The Metropolitan Tabernacle Pulpit* 48: 232.

39. Ibid., 232–33.

40. Ibid., 233.

Chapter 6: *Change*

1. C. H. Spurgeon, *The Metropolitan Tabernacle Pulpit* 38 (1892): 566.

2. C. H. Spurgeon, *The Metropolitan Tabernacle Pulpit* 12 (1866): 274–76.

3. C. H. Spurgeon, *The Metropolitan Tabernacle Pulpit* 10 (1864): 194–95.

4. C. H. Spurgeon, *The Metropolitan Tabernacle Pulpit* 18 (1872): 349.

5. Ibid., 355.

6. Ibid., 354.

7. C. H. Spurgeon, *The Metropolitan Tabernacle Pulpit* 21 (1875): 56.

8. Ibid., 57.

9. C. H. Spurgeon, *The Metropolitan Tabernacle Pulpit* 36 (1890): 80–81.

10. C. H. Spurgeon, *The Metropolitan Tabernacle Pulpit* 10: 469.

11. Ibid., 68.

12. C. H. Spurgeon, *The Metropolitan Tabernacle Pulpit* 18: 515.

13. C. H. Spurgeon, *The Metropolitan Tabernacle Pulpit* 36: 80.

14. C. H. Spurgeon, *The Metropolitan Tabernacle Pulpit* 21: 48.

15. Ibid., 622.

16. C. H. Spurgeon, *The Metropolitan Tabernacle Pulpit* 36: 320.

17. C. H. Spurgeon, *The Metropolitan Tabernacle Pulpit* 11 (1865): 664.

18. Ibid., 664–65.

19. C. H. Spurgeon, *The Metropolitan Tabernacle Pulpit* 36: 321.

20. Ibid.

21. C. H. Spurgeon, *The Metropolitan Tabernacle Pulpit* 19 (1873): 385.

22. C. H. Spurgeon, *The Metropolitan Tabernacle Pulpit* 50 (1904): 469.

23. C. H. Spurgeon, *The Metropolitan Tabernacle Pulpit* 36: 200.

24. C. H. Spurgeon, preface, "Be of Good Cheer," apparently unpublished ms. (1880).

25. C. H. Spurgeon, *The Metropolitan Tabernacle Pulpit* 30 (1884): 214.

26. C. H. Spurgeon, *The Metropolitan Tabernacle Pulpit* 11: 145.

27. C. H. Spurgeon, *The Metropolitan Tabernacle Pulpit* 26 (1880): 47.

28. Ibid., 21.

29. Ibid., 21–22.
30. Ibid., 22–23.
31. Ibid., 30–31.
32. C. H. Spurgeon, *The Metropolitan Tabernacle Pulpit* 30: 187.
33. C. H. Spurgeon, *The Metropolitan Tabernacle Pulpit* 43 (1897): 578.
34. C. H. Spurgeon, *The Metropolitan Tabernacle Pulpit* 19: 401.

Chapter 7: *Transition*

1. C. H. Spurgeon, *The Metropolitan Tabernacle Pulpit* 55 (1909): 340.
2. Personal papers of Elizabeth R. Skoglund.
3. Ibid.
4. Ibid.
5. C. H. Spurgeon, *The New Park Street Pulpit* 2 (1857): 220.
6. Ibid., 221.
7. Ibid., 221–23.
8. Ibid., 225–26.
9. Ibid., 227–28.
10. C. H. Spurgeon, *The Metropolitan Tabernacle Pulpit* 36 (1890): 505.
11. C. H. Spurgeon, *The New Park Street Pulpit* 1 (1856): 48.
12. C. H. Spurgeon, *The Metropolitan Tabernacle Pulpit* 55. 340.
13. Ibid.
14. C. H. Spurgeon, *The Metropolitan Tabernacle Pulpit* 10 (1864): 20.
15. C. H. Spurgeon, *The Metropolitan Tabernacle Pulpit* 20 (1874): 349.
16. Ibid., 355.
17. C. H. Spurgeon, *The New Park Street Pulpit* 6 (1860): 458.
18. C. H. Spurgeon, *The New Park Street Pulpit* 5 (1859): 231–32.
19. C. H. Spurgeon, *The Metropolitan Tabernacle Pulpit* 21 (1875): 592–93.
20. C. H. Spurgeon, *The Metropolitan Tabernacle Pulpit* 32 (1886): 531.
21. Ibid., 538.
22. C. H. Spurgeon, *The Metropolitan Tabernacle Pulpit* 38 (1892): 584.
23. C. H. Spurgeon, *The Metropolitan Tabernacle Pulpit* 21: 568.
24. C. H. Spurgeon, *The Metropolitan Tabernacle Pulpit* 32: 534.
25. C. H. Spurgeon, *The New Park Street Pulpit* 6: 143.
26. C. H. Spurgeon, *The New Park Street Pulpit* 1: 328.
27. C. H. Spurgeon, *The Metropolitan Tabernacle Pulpit* 40 (1894): 164–65.
28. C. H. Spurgeon, *The Metropolitan Tabernacle Pulpit* 17 (1871): 64–65.
29. C. H. Spurgeon, *The Metropolitan Tabernacle Pulpit* 10: 2–3.
30. C. H. Spurgeon, *The Metropolitan Tabernacle Pulpit* 19 (1873): 473.
31. C. H. Spurgeon, *The Metropolitan Tabernacle Pulpit* 15 (1869): 128–29.
32. C. H. Spurgeon, *The Metropolitan Tabernacle Pulpit* 26 (1880): 24.
33. C. H. Spurgeon, *The New Park Street and Metropolitan Tabernacle Pulpit* 7 (1861): 86.
34. C. H. Spurgeon, *The Metropolitan Tabernacle Pulpit* 32: 535.
35. C. H. Spurgeon, *The Metropolitan Tabernacle Pulpit* 18 (1872): 469.
36. Ibid., 470.
37. Ibid., 471.
38. C. H. Spurgeon, *The New Park Street Pulpit* 6: 158.
39. Ibid.
40. Ibid., 161–62.
41. Ibid., 163.
42. C. H. Spurgeon, *The Metropolitan Tabernacle Pulpit* 36: 658–59.
43. C. H. Spurgeon, *The Metropolitan Tabernacle Pulpit* 9 (1863): 203.
44. C. H. Spurgeon, *The New Park Street Pulpit* 5: 13.
45. C. H. Spurgeon, *The New Park Street Pulpit* 1: 327.
46. C. H. Spurgeon, *The Metropolitan Tabernacle Pulpit* 19: 119.

47. C. H. Spurgeon, *The Metropolitan Tabernacle Pulpit* 8 (1862): 220.
48. Ibid., 221.
49. C. H. Spurgeon, *The Metropolitan Tabernacle Pulpit* 9: 18–19.
50. *From the Pulpit to the Palm-Branch: A Memorial of C. H. Spurgeon* (London: Passmore and Alabaster, 1892), 69–70.
51. C. H. Spurgeon, *The Metropolitan Tabernacle Pulpit* 8: 525.
52. C. H. Spurgeon, *The Metropolitan Tabernacle Pulpit* 38: 10–11.
53. C. H. Spurgeon, *The Metropolitan Tabernacle Pulpit* 7: 629.
54. Ibid., 63–64.
55. Ibid., 65.
56. Lewis A. Drummond, *Spurgeon: Prince of Preachers* (Grand Rapids: Kregel, 1992), 751.
57. C. H. Spurgeon, *The Metropolitan Tabernacle Pulpit* 34 (1888): 433–34.

Elizabeth Ruth Skoglund is the author of more than twenty-five books. She has a private counseling practice in Burbank, California.